BANK NOTES AND SHINPLASTERS

AMERICAN BUSINESS, POLITICS, AND SOCIETY

SERIES EDITORS
Andrew Wender Cohen, Shane Hamilton,
Kimberly Phillips-Fein, and Elizabeth Tandy Shermer

Books in the series American Business, Politics, and Society explore the relationships over time between politics, society, and the creation and performance of markets, firms, and industries large and small. The central theme of this series is that culture, law, and public policy have been fundamental to the evolution of American business from the colonial era to the present. The series aims to explore, in particular, developments that have enduring consequences.

A complete list of books in the series
is available from the publisher.

BANK NOTES AND SHINPLASTERS

THE RAGE FOR PAPER MONEY
IN THE EARLY REPUBLIC

JOSHUA R. GREENBERG

PENN

UNIVERSITY OF PENNSYLVANIA PRESS

PHILADELPHIA

Published by
University of Pennsylvania Press
Philadelphia, Pennsylvania 19104-4112
www.upenn.edu/pennpress

Printed in the United States of America
on acid-free paper

1 3 5 7 9 10 8 6 4 2

Library of Congress Cataloging-in-Publication Data

Names: Greenberg, Joshua R., author.
Title: Bank notes and shinplasters : the rage for paper money in the early republic / Joshua R. Greenberg.
Description: Philadelphia : University of Pennsylvania Press, [2020] | Series: American business, politics, and society | Includes bibliographical references and index.
Identifiers: LCCN 2019045000 | ISBN 9780812252248 (hardcover)
Subjects: LCSH: Paper money—United States—History—18th century. | Paper money—United States—History—19th century. | United States—Economic conditions—To 1865. | United States—History—1783–1865.
Classification: LCC HG591 .G74 2020 | DDC 332.4/044097309034—dc23
LC record available at https://lccn.loc.gov/2019045000

CONTENTS

INTRODUCTION

From Madison to Monroe

In his 1815 satire *The History of a Little Frenchman and His Bank Notes: "Rags! Rags! Rags!,"* James Kirke Paulding told the story of a newly arrived and thoroughly confused French visitor as he navigated the unique American paper money system. The Frenchman landed in Savannah from Cuba and deposited $8,000 in gold in a local bank. However, they offered only bank notes when he tried to withdraw the funds. He assumed that, like Banque de France notes, the bills were a convenient stand-in for gold or silver and circulated at face value. So, "ignorant of the depreciation of paper money, arising from the refusal to pay specie [coined gold or silver], and from the erection of such an infinite number of petty banks in every obscure village without capital or character, he took the worthless rags" and set out for Boston.[1]

Each of the Frenchman's subsequent transactions exposed the foreigner's inexperience with bank notes and shinplasters—paper money issued by nonbank entities like merchants or municipal corporations—because he could not discern which notes were good and which were worthless. In one typical episode, he offered to pay for a drink in a Bristol, Pennsylvania, tavern with a bill issued by the landlord of a Philadelphia hotel where he had previously stayed. His traveling companion explained that the hotelier, "in order to be in fashion, had also commenced Banker among the rest." Yet the Bristol landlord refused outright to accept the bill. The rejection upset the Frenchman; how was he to understand the difference between a note issued by a hotel operator or local postmaster and one from the Planters Bank of the State of Georgia?[2]

The problem for the Frenchman was that he did not have enough monetary knowledge to understand how bank notes and shinplasters actually worked, so he blindly received all of them equally. American paper money was more complicated than that. Though at first glance different bills might appear similar, some circulated at face value, others passed only with a discount, and a final group were accepted as currency only by their issuer. When someone finally explained the difference between a tavernkeeper's shinplaster and a depreciated bank note, the bewildered Frenchman asked, "Does the legislature of your country permit this system of swindling, this inhospitable custom, which falls so heavily on the traveler and stranger, to pass without censure or punishment?" If banks or merchants issued notes that only circulated with large discounts or failed to pass at all, how did anyone know which paper money was good and which was bad?

The Frenchman's companion offered a tongue-in-cheek response about the way Americans approached bank note transactions. He explained that "it is supposed that every body knows the value of every species of bank paper as well as the credit of every individual who issues notes, and to be ignorant of such things, is only to suffer those consequences which naturally spring from ignorance in every circumstance." The bank note and shinplaster system persisted, but only because everyone supposedly maintained a comprehensive knowledge of all bills and their producers. This was too much for the Frenchman to accept. He threw up his hands and exclaimed, "Le diable est aux vaches!" (There is the devil to pay!). More than just a satire of perilous market transactions, Paulding's story astutely identified several key aspects of early republic currency: the diversity of circulating paper money, the advantage bankers possessed when they issued notes, the ineffective role of government regulation, and especially the amount of monetary knowledge needed to keep up in the paper money market.[3]

In this book, I investigate the state bank note system that thrived over the nation's first seventy-five years as well as the legal tender monetary culture that replaced it during the Civil War era. Early republic paper currency needs to be unpacked because it bears so little resemblance to the modern circulation of Federal Reserve notes—sometimes called greenbacks—that are printed by the United States government and legal tender for all transactions, public and private. Previous attempts to describe early republic paper currency usually devolve into institutional narratives of banking where the public's daily experiences play little part; cultural histories of capitalism often sidestep the minutiae of monetary policy. This study instead examines how professional bankers, brokers, and carpetbaggers constructed the bank note system to maximize personal gain and how all Americans materially, culturally, and politically utilized that system to navigate the market. The cash economy was not merely imposed on the population, it was negotiated by everyone who used early republic paper money.[4]

Early republic Americans' lived experience with paper money forms the narrative and conceptual core of this book. We see how the general public accumulated and wielded the monetary information needed to navigate interpersonal bank note transactions that were influenced by both the quality of their money and their demographic standing in society. Essential to this experience was the material culture of paper money, including the seemingly endless collection of vignettes and symbols on the notes themselves. Noteholders did not, however, just accept bills as they were produced; they manipulated their cash by ripping it, burning it, and scribbling all over it.

While Part I and Part II provide a social and cultural history of paper money to detail Americans' daily encounters with bank notes, Part III of the book shows how such lived experiences affected the nation's politics and illuminates the process that created the federal legal tender system that we have today. It was a process that not only altered the nation's political economy but also profoundly changed the public's relationship with their currency and their need for financial knowledge. The book concludes with a brief epilogue that reflects on modern Americans' loss of this monetary intelligence and what that meant in the wake of the banking crisis of 2008 and the rise of cryptocurrencies like Bitcoin.

Paper money first appeared in British North America in 1690 when Puritan officials, including Cotton Mather, tried to prop up the Massachusetts economy and pay soldiers who had just returned from a failed invasion of Quebec. Over the next seventy-five years, this proved to be no isolated event. Supposedly curtailed by Parliament in the Currency Acts of 1751 and 1764, a lack of specie prevented paper money from disappearing entirely. Paper money became the dominant currency in the 1770s as Americans used unprecedented amounts to pay for their revolution and finance their new nation.[5]

Residents of the new United States probably had more familiarity with paper money than anyone else in the Atlantic world, but their experiences were not necessarily positive. Under the Articles of Confederation, Congress's incapacity to collect direct taxes severely limited its ability to redeem past or future notes, diminishing public confidence in its paper promises.

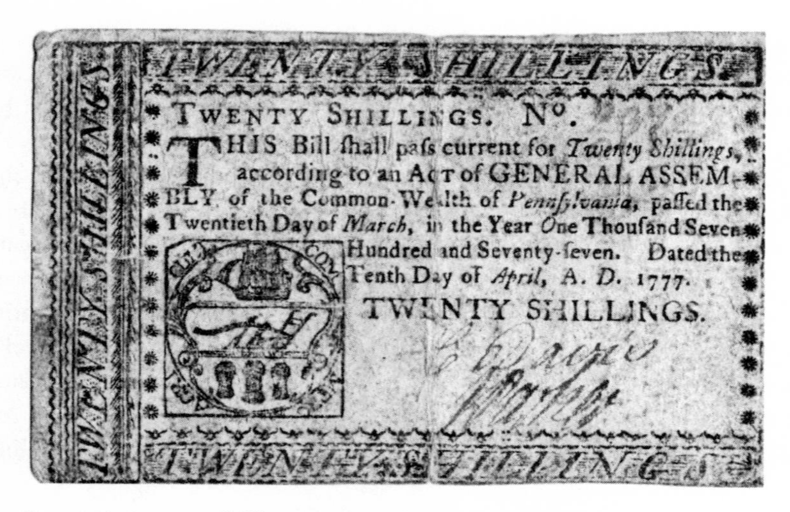

FIGURE 1. A twenty-shilling note from the Revolutionary War. It was part of £200,000 in bills issued by the Commonwealth of Pennsylvania in 1777 that quickly lost value and became invalid by 1791. Author's collection.

By April 1781, Continental notes had declined in value to near zero and were no longer in wide circulation. Even before the Revolutionary War ended, the phrase "not worth a continental" signified the delicate relationship between the aspiring nation's political fortunes and the reputation of its paper currency. Peacetime meant that state governments could use their tax authority to back their own currencies and better protect their face value, but state legislators confronted direct pressure from voters who demanded debt relief through an increased money supply. Creditors opposed such moves and argued that too much paper currency led to dangerous inflation that robbed them of their fair investment. In an era of combustible politics between debtors and creditors, a focal point of the disagreement became how to stabilize the value of paper money.[6]

The problem was acute across New England. A newly elected pro–paper currency administration in Rhode Island issued huge quantities of state notes in 1786 that fell in value to eight cents on the dollar not long after they were printed. Moral questions arose about debts paid off with the bad money and even led Baptists to discipline members who tried to repay their creditors with paper bills rather than specie. The state government's response was to hold creditors liable if they did not accept paper money as legal tender and remove trial by jury or appeal for those violating the law. However, none of this propped up the bills. The state court finally overturned the regulations as an attack on due process in the landmark *Trevett v. Weeden* case.[7]

The situation became even more heated when state governments chose not to print paper currency. Just days after the *Trevett v. Weeden* decision, hundreds of armed New Hampshire farmers confronted the state legislature to demand a new issue of paper notes. Governor John Patterson called out the militia to round up the farmers and the protest subsided. Neighboring Massachusetts badly miscalculated when it simultaneously raised taxes, pushed through tax collecting reform, and opted not to print any paper money of their own. An increased tax burden was hard enough for farmers in the western part of the commonwealth, but the defaults quickly piled up without a ready supply of currency to make payments. The lack of paper money was not the only cause of the uprising that followed, but regional monetary policies certainly helped inspire Shays' Rebellion.[8]

It was in this context that representatives met at the Constitutional Convention in 1787. The proliferation of poor-quality state-issued bills and the public's demand for paper money preoccupied the framers. On the first day of the convention, Edmund Randolph noted that when the Articles of Confederation were drafted, "the havoc of paper money" had not been foreseen. Others expressed their alarm at democratically elected officials' willingness to satisfy constituents' currency demands even if it upset local credit markets. Noah Webster was worried that "a rage for paper money, bordering on madness" had occurred when the Maryland House of Delegates gave in to popular pressure on monetary policy. James Madison summed up these fears when he warned in the conclusion of Federalist #10 that "a rage for paper money" would likely infect factions within the society. Such concerns informed constitutional debate on a federally issued national currency, but what resulted in the final draft was silence on federal paper in lieu of the explicit power to "coin Money" and a formal declaration that "No State shall . . . coin Money; emit Bills of Credit; make any Thing but gold and silver Coin a tender in Payment of Debts." Article 1, Section 10 removed the problem of state-issued notes to the applause of Federalists who deemed it one of the most vital parts of the Constitution, but the lack of direction on other types of paper money left a gaping hole in the new nation's currency supply.[9]

Following the lead of Alexander Hamilton, the government chartered the First (1791–1811) and later Second (1816–1836) Bank of the United

States (BUS) to print bank notes and oversee money markets, but it provided only a fraction of the nation's currency supply before the Civil War. At the height of its issues in the mid-1830s, the BUS only had $17 million in circulation at a time when the American economy was utilizing over $100 million in paper bills. So, where did the rest of the money come from? Between the 1790s and 1860s, the nation's paper currency derived largely from bank notes circulated by state-chartered or state-regulated institutions. When the Constitution was ratified only three banks existed in the United States, but the number rose swiftly: 24 by 1800, 181 by 1815, 320 by 1830, and 596 by 1845. More than 2,000 banks opened between 1782 and 1860 and on the eve of the Civil War almost 1,400 banks remained in operation across twenty-nine states, one territory, and the District of Columbia. This meant that before the National Currency Act of 1863 and National Bank Act of 1864 enforced uniform paper currency, Americans endured a chaotic monetary landscape made up of nearly ten thousand unique bank notes issued by hundreds of banks under numerous competing and sometimes contradictory state regulations. These legal bills did not even include the countless quasi-legal shinplasters issued by merchants, corporations, or municipal governments.[10]

What complicated the early republic paper money system was that bank notes could be traded at par (face value) near the institution that issued them or at varied discounted rates based on their perceived market worth as they physically traveled away from their point of origin. Discounts also occurred if the public lost faith in the bank's ability to redeem them for specie. Legally, each institution was responsible for redeeming its bills when they were presented at the counter, but notes often traveled great distances away from home as they circulated. This meant that each bank note transaction ultimately hinged on an interpersonal discussion over the note's value, an often manipulative process separate from any haggling over the price of goods or services for sale. So Americans (or visitors like the little Frenchman) required financial information to properly use bank notes, but monetary knowledge was not equally distributed throughout the population. Some individuals possessed more than others. With so many moving parts in the circulation of antebellum currency, ample opportunity existed to honestly or dishonestly use such negotiations for one's own benefit.

Anyone who bought or sold in the market encountered bank notes and developed strategies for their complicated use, but for many people this process occurred exclusively during commercial transactions and not within the lobbies of financial institutions. Only a small percentage of antebellum Americans had savings accounts or took out commercial bank loans, so if an individual needed to obtain or exchange bank notes, every town had brokers or an informal money market where local and out-of-town bills could be bought and sold based on fluctuating rates. In order to best traverse these markets, the public attained and maintained monetary knowledge and tracked which banks and notes should be offered confidence and how they should be valued. Many early nineteenth-century Americans learned to recognize subtle differences in bank note vignettes, identify which banking institutions printed trustworthy bills, and conduct sophisticated paper money transactions even if they had never entered a bank.

Without legal tender bills or a guarantee that paper money would circulate at face value, each transaction required the employment of financial and monetary knowledge on a microlevel. Participation in the market economy created a need to understand how to buy and sell goods and services and how to wield the tools of the trade. The mechanics of the paper money system were not easy to master and whether someone was a middle-class clerk, poor white farmer, enslaved African American woman, or a government official, everyone had to learn the difference between a solid bank note that could trade at par, an uncurrent bill that could only be traded at a discount, and a questionably legal shinplaster issued by a local business. Individuals of all sorts engaged the early republic paper money system, accumulated the monetary knowledge necessary for bank note transactions, and exercised that information in market and political settings. Vigilance was necessary because money market inefficiencies and state banking-regulation inconsistencies meant that bank note quality varied widely. Using almost any out-of-town or out-of-state bank note meant the need to negotiate its purchasing power, rather than just assuming it would be granted face value.[11]

Observers might assume that an economy with so much bad currency could not function, especially if they have heard of Gresham's Law. This economic principle, named after the sixteenth-century English financier Thomas Gresham, insists that bad money causes market participants to consciously pull good money out of the economy. So it might be expected that merchants hoarded specie and notes issued by stronger banks and left a marketplace filled exclusively with bills issued by defunct banks, shinplasters, and even counterfeit currency. But that is not what happened.[12]

Authoritative economics scholarship on how honesty and information influenced used-car sales suggests how this jumble of good and bad money actually functioned on the ground, arguing that a used-car dealer has ample opportunity and incentive to misrepresent the quality of their product. In such transactions, the seller has more knowledge about the car's quality than the buyer, which creates an asymmetry of information. Without equal access to information, Gresham's Law does not hold, either for cars or for early republic bank notes. Moreover, in paper money transactions, neither buyer nor seller could always discern quality. So, even though both good (face value) and bad (uncurrent) bank notes flowed throughout the economy, one type did not necessarily replace the other. Even an uncurrent bill could be considered valuable if someone obtained it cheaply and passed it at a higher rate. Instead, persistent questions about the quality of the bills ensured that they could only transfer from party to party if buyers and sellers agreed to the same terms. Unfortunately, such bank note negotiations commonly employed asymmetrical information where confidence was earned through dishonesty or manipulation; money market engagement was a precarious endeavor.[13]

Perhaps the easiest way to understand how this system worked in practice is to examine the experience of one small community and the various kinds of paper money that circulated locally. During the 1830s, Monroe, Michigan, was a frontier boomtown with a lack of good cash and ineffective banking regulations where residents clamored for whatever currency they could get into their hands. Monroe's persistent cash shortage meant that as residents chose how much value and confidence to grant each unique bill in front of them, they also attempted to forge a workable paper money system with enough overall purchasing power to fund their rapidly growing economy. They tried notes backed by gold, backed by land, or backed purely by faith that someone would take whatever they were handed, but the overall result was years of currency instability.[14]

The experiences of Nathaniel (Nat) Saltonstall Howe and Richard Varnum—cousins from an influential family of politicians, bankers, and merchants who had moved to Monroe from Haverhill, Massachusetts—highlight the difficulty that Monroe residents faced as they sought to conduct business as part of a national marketplace. When they lived back east, they had enjoyed as much monetary stability as was possible in the bank note era under the guidance of the Suffolk Bank system. The Suffolk was a private arrangement, begun in 1824, which ensured that most bills from

Boston-area banks circulated locally at face value. However, once they entered the chaotic world of Monroe, the boys had to contend with paper currency issued by questionable institutions which fluctuated wildly in value.[15]

Nat and Richard concocted a scheme to invest family funds in Michigan, but the plan did not work out well. Their uncle Nathaniel Saltonstall back in Salem was "decidedly against" the idea because any money they would draw from Massachusetts would be converted into poor-quality local paper money. He explained to them that the "premium of 10 per cent for Eastern funds (Specie) should be no inducement, unless you had some ulterior plans to dispose of the Michigan Money immediately—such as the purchase of land." At all costs, he reiterated, avoid "any dealings in Michigan Bank paper, or Notes, payable in that currency" or "you will stand a good chance of loosing your Money." The advice was clear: if you want to keep your money, do not deal in Michigan bank notes. Saltonstall reasoned that even with a 10 percent premium granted eastern money as it moved west, the quality of Monroe bank notes was so poor that it was impossible to retain their value in local currency. Nat heard the advice and planned instead "to shave small Notes," but Uncle Nathaniel objected that it was a "very hazardous and troublesome business." Great profit could be made by those who shaved, or traded on the rapidly fluctuating exchange rates of questionable paper money, but it was risky and required a lot of local and national monetary knowledge.[16]

Why did Nathaniel Saltonstall have such a low opinion of Monroe bank notes? At different points in the 1830s, Monroe had two chartered banks, the Bank of Monroe and the Bank of River Raisin, as well as the Merchants & Mechanics Bank, which operated without a formal charter and under a loose set of regulations passed as part of Michigan's 1837 free banking laws. Collectively, these banks issued hundreds of thousands of dollars in paper, but they struggled to convince anyone outside of town that the notes should be received at face value. It was not from a lack of effort. The artwork on village bank notes projected the image of a prosperous western boomtown with ample economic opportunities. Bank of Monroe five-dollar bills featured a majestic view of the town designed by famed engraver Peter Maverick, and its two-dollar notes included a vignette of Lewis Cass, the territorial governor of Michigan, as he negotiated the Treaty of Fort Meigs. The bank specifically chose the image because Cass personally embodied expansion in the upper Midwest and the treaty symbolized the seemingly orderly process by which native land was freed up for white settlement. Other Bank of Monroe bills linked the community to a more national sense of growth and unity; they juxtaposed local commercial imagery with a portrait of the town's namesake, former president James Monroe.[17]

Such visual gestures obscured the fundamental inability of these banks to convince the public that their paper money was as good as gold; crusty New Englanders like Uncle Nathaniel suspected that the banks did not hold enough specie in reserve to meet their obligations. Monroe bank notes traded back east between 2 and 10 percent below par for much of the 1830s, but particular circumstances resulted in higher discounts or listings as "broken," "uncurrent," "stopped," or "no sale." The newspaper listings with these designations revealed something important about how such paper notes circulated even apart from their price fluctuations. The overall dearth of cash in the 1830s American economy meant that whether it had a discount of 10 percent or came from a broken institution, there was still a market for poor-quality paper money. Discerning customers might try to avoid notes from Michigan, but there was always someone willing to obtain a ready supply of bills for the right price. A public desperate for any cash to pay for goods and services continued to circulate bank notes even when there was general agreement that they were worth anything but face value.[18]

Take, for example, the Bank of Monroe. Originally chartered in 1827, it closed in 1830 after a series of bad investments only to reemerge in 1835 to capitalize on a new land boom in town. However, bank note reporters—newspapers that publicized and helped set currency exchange rates—continued to list Monroe notes as "uncurrent" or 'broken" between 1830 and 1834. The fact that bills stayed on the bank note table for years after the institution ceased operations highlights something vital about how people actually used this money. Once they entered circulation, bank notes took on a life of their own apart from the banks that issued them. Even if newspaper price lists told readers that a bill was uncurrent, the cash-poor public might still infuse notes with some small value on their own terms and separate from the health or even the operational nature of the issuing institution.[19]

The circulation of repurposed, uncurrent notes did not mean that public confidence in financial institutions was meaningless. The reopened Bank of Monroe came under fire in 1836 from the eastern press as part of a campaign against fraudulent western banks, which these newspapers labeled "wild cat" institutions. The term referred to banks that flooded the market with bad paper money and prevented note redemption by being located in areas so remote that only wildcats lived nearby. The *New York Herald* warned readers not to accept any notes from Michigan banks and celebrated what it saw as the imminent demise of the Bank of Monroe as a representative of the "insolent" wildcat banks, "which flood this city with paper rags [and] have reached the end of their reign." It also remarked that money brokers in Philadelphia no longer accepted any notes from the Bank of Monroe, even at a steep discount. Bank officials understood the need to retain public confidence, so they protested that they had more than enough specie to cover their bills in circulation and Monroe residents issued statements about the bank's solvency. The local outcry kept the bank afloat, but in early 1837 its board members sought outside investors. That is when the Mormon Church came knocking.[20]

Joseph Smith and the Mormon Church had just heard that the Ohio assembly had turned down the charter application for their Kirtland Safety Society Bank and they scrambled to legalize bank notes they had already printed. They simultaneously reorganized the institution as a joint stock company, added a stamp over the word "BANK" on their notes to transform it into an "ANTI-BANKING Co.," and began to look for a legitimate partner. Smith, just ahead of an indictment for illegal banking, traveled with church leaders to Michigan to negotiate a formal relationship between the Kirtland and Monroe institutions. While this was seemingly a slapdash plan to cover up the fraught Ohio banking scheme, Joseph Smith indicated that the financial project had a providential design. Warren Parrish, a Kirtland Safety Society officer before he left the Mormon Church, explained that Smith "declared that the audible voice of God, instructed him to establish a Banking Anti-Banking institution, which like Aaron's rod should swallow up all other Banks (the Bank of Monroe excepted,) and grow and flourish and spread from the rivers to the ends of the earth." In this statement, the Bank of Monroe stood alongside the Mormon's Kirtland bank as a righteous institution singled out for triumph as all others failed. In reality, the Mormons probably selected their partner based on church leader N. K. Whitney's close ties with Henry Smith, the president of the Bank of Monroe, with whom he had served during the War of 1812. By the end of February 1837, the Mormon Church owned a controlling interest in the Bank of Monroe; a church member, Oliver Cowdery, was a bank director and vice president who personally pledged his reputation by signing their bank notes. No other church members served as bank officers, but Cowdery, who was Joseph Smith's scribe during the translation of the Book of Mormon, represented an important link.[21]

How was this convoluted story of money and Mormons relevant to Monroe residents like Nat Saltonstall Howe and Richard Varnum? Participation in the bank note economy required constant vigilance about the quality of bills in circulation, so any development that might affect the standing of a local institution needed to be watched carefully. If the Bank of Monroe hoped to solve its public confidence problems through a deal with the Mormon Church, it did not pick the right partner. Kirtland banking anti-banking notes traded at 12.5 percent off face value and even the benign pastoral images on their one-dollar bills served as fodder for anti-Mormon jokes. One newspaper mocked that "Joe Smith's Kirtland Bank Notes have the appropriate vignette of a sheperd [*sic*] *shearing his flock.*" When the Bank of Monroe president Henry Smith resigned a month after the merger, the anti-Mormon *Cleveland Daily Gazette* launched a new wave of doubt about the stability of the institution and claimed that it had $122,000 in circulation with only $1,200 in specie in its vaults.[22]

The decision by the bank to partner with the Mormon Church also raised red flags for banking regulators. The Michigan Bank Commission officially questioned "the character of the Bank of Monroe" and inquired about repealing its charter. Under public pressure, the bank suspended redemption and temporarily closed its doors. The *Painesville Telegraph* gleefully announced that the "Monroe Mormon Bank closed its doors against all demands for specie, after having for its presiding officer about three weeks the wonderful and noted Oliver Cowdery, one of the fathers and translators of the Golden Bible." Even these religious, financial, and regulatory controversies did not end the circulation of Bank of Monroe notes. The thirst for cash of any quality in the frontier community meant that the same *Monroe Times* issue that disclosed the bank's temporary suspension of payment also included an announcement from a local businessman, Jefferson S. Bond, that he would accept their bills at par. Such actions allowed the Bank of Monroe to limp along into 1838 before it fully suspended operations and lost its charter in 1842.[23]

Since aspiring Monroe merchants like Richard Varnum could not place their confidence in poorly capitalized local banks, they sought other means to create stable currency. Richard planned to set up his own trading firm and reached out to relatives for advice. His uncle, Representative Leverett

Saltonstall of Massachusetts, was wary of the plan for a new store in Monroe given the "wretched currency as Michigan is suited with." Fisher Howe, a New York merchant in the family, also suggested that Varnum postpone his plans because of the "miserable conditions of your monied institutions in Michigan" which "had the influence to destroy all confidence in western merchants." Just as in Uncle Nathaniel's letter quoted above, Fisher suggested that Richard invest in land instead of goods because "if you get Michigan funds, they are likely to be very much under par for a long time to come." Even as more conservative eastern relatives warned of the quality of Michigan bank notes, they seemed open to dealing in Michigan's ample real estate.[24]

Local, state, and federal officials agreed with this analysis and made numerous attempts to transform Monroe's land sales into a strong paper currency. The second federal land office in Michigan opened in Monroe in 1823 and, by 1835, it had sold more land and collected more money than any office in the Northwest. Attempts to convert this land into paper value took two forms in these years: town-issued paper shinplasters and military land scrip. After 1827, the village of Monroe printed municipal bills in denominations that represented money received by the town for lots of land "in the new Plat of Village Lots & Farms which is to be called the City of Monroe." Notes circulated as worth one lot, or $5, and a third of a lot, or $1.67. Intended to physically resemble bank notes, the shinplasters featured vignettes by the New York engravers Capewell & Kimmel of white women sitting in chariots and on haystacks as well as a Native American woman, evoking the tamed beauty of the West. Supposedly issued by the village as receipts for land sales, the bills represented a conscious attempt to produce bank note–like paper that functioned as a locally circulating currency. In a community with little specie and only one questionable bank in the late 1820s and early 1830s, town officials responded by using the value of recently sold land to create a usable and familiar paper medium. Monroe's land bills served as a local currency until around 1835, when more banks opened in town in response to a land boom that prompted a wide variety of settlers and speculators to visit the federal land office.[25]

Land-starved new arrivals to Monroe made use of a wide variety of currency during the height of the boom; in addition to specie, bank notes, and municipal shinplasters, another type of paper money floating around Monroe was military land scrip. Issued by the federal government and the Commonwealth of Virginia to veterans of conflicts from the Revolutionary

War to the War of 1812, military land scrip enabled the purchase of specific tracts of land reserved for certificate holders. Initially limited to use in parts of Ohio, Indiana, and Illinois, an 1832 federal law made military scrip receivable at any land office in the nation. Land sales rose quickly in the years that followed before they slowed to a trickle in the aftermath of the Panic of 1837. Military land scrip never accounted for a majority of payments received in Monroe, but tens of thousands of dollars in scrip moved through the town's federal land office in a few short years.[26]

Military land scrip became more important in Monroe in July 1836 after the Treasury Department's announcement of the Specie Circular (or Specie Clause), which declared that, with few exceptions, federal lands could only be purchased with specie. Though this action seemed drastic, the effect of the circular was supposedly tempered by the Distribution Act, passed just weeks earlier, which moved surplus government specie into state-chartered banks around the nation. While the deposit institutions, like the Bank of River Raisin in Monroe, were supposed to hold the federal funds until the government needed them, they acted as if their own capital holdings had radically expanded and used them for long-term loans or other projects that expanded the region's credit. Both the Specie Circular and the Distribution Act played significant roles in Monroe, with a federal land office that took in over $850,000 in the mid-1830s and the Bank of River Raisin which received $80,000 in federal deposits. The circular called for new land purchases solely in specie, with two exceptions: military land scrip and, until December 15, 1836, bank notes that could be used by "bona fide" settlers who purchased under 320 acres.[27]

A separate act preventing the federal government from collecting any paper money that originated from banks which issued small-denomination notes under five dollars complicated this rule. Given that both Monroe banks in 1836 issued denominations between one and five dollars and Michigan did not allow out-of-state notes under five dollars at all, this act drastically limited the ability of settlers to use any bank notes in the fall of 1836. With these laws in effect, all that remained for purchasing federal land was specie and military land scrip. The cascading set of regulations that governed the currency supply in 1830s Monroe was endlessly complicated. However, just as residents engaged in the bank note economy needed to monitor banking activities to keep abreast of changes to the money market, they also had to be aware of legal changes that governed what types of paper money would and would not circulate.[28]

Like most paper currency, land scrip was not tied to its initial recipient, so if the veteran holder had no desire to move west or speculate, he could sell his bills at discounted rates in the nation's money markets. Newspapers like *Thompson's Bank Note Reporter* listed the purchase rates for land scrip alongside bank note values, so potential customers could monitor price changes and make educated decisions about their bills. Discount rates for land scrip, like bank notes, varied greatly based on national monetary and land policies. Land scrip sometimes traded at par or alternatively at 30 or 40 percent off current land prices. When the Specie Circular curtailed demand for other types of paper money in Monroe, the market for military land scrip heated up. Brokers and speculators placed ads to purchase scrip for the highest cash price. However, the mid-1830s boom did not last and, in the wake of the financial Panic of 1837, property values tumbled.[29]

The collapse of property values was particularly troubling for residents of Monroe because, earlier that year, state officials had passed the controversial Michigan free banking law of 1837. This first-in-the-nation legislation allowed anyone to establish a bank without a charter provided they had raised $50,000 (including 30 percent in specie) and followed certain guidelines. Almost overnight, nine state banks became forty, and their new bank notes flooded the nation. Monroe's free bank, the short-lived Merchants & Mechanics Bank, raised most of its supposed $150,000 in capital from mortgage values. It was yet another attempt to turn land into a viable currency and even their bank notes included the text: "Real Estate Security."

One editorial stated that the "confidence of the community in banking issues" was undercut by the new system because banks drew their capital from "artificial contrivances" rather than solid funds. Worse yet, were stories about scams perpetrated to trick state specie audits, such as when barrels of nails with a layer of silver on top were presented to auditors as a large quantity of hard money or when a handful of institutions shared a chest of coins and ferried them from bank to bank just in time for an inspection. The Mechanics & Merchants Bank closed soon after opening, just like more than forty other free banks, and the public was stuck with over $9,000 in worthless bills. Like other poorly capitalized Monroe banks, their tiny specie reserves could not convince anyone inside or outside of Michigan to trust their notes at face value.[30]

During the heady days of the 1830s, Monroe's residents were caught between their need to run a local economy consistently short of cash and

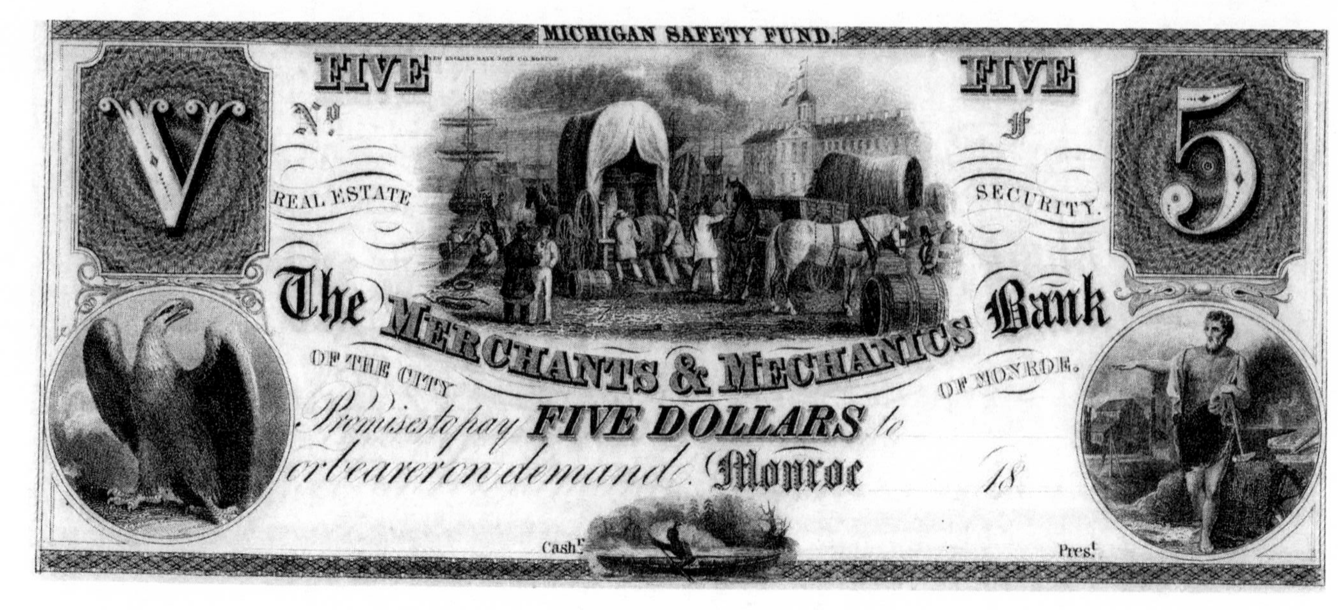

FIGURE 2. The Merchants & Mechanics Bank of Monroe opened under Michigan's 1837 free banking legislation. Backed largely by real estate securities, it failed in 1839. Author's collection.

their failure to build banks that supplied a viable currency. Land-backed and small-scale specie-backed paper money did not always satisfy the demand, so sometimes business owners printed their own shinplasters, backed merely by the community's confidence that they should circulate. The experience of William Wells Brown, who arrived in Monroe in 1835 a year after he had escaped from slavery in Kentucky, is telling. In his 1852 European travel narrative, *Three Years in Europe; or, Places I Have Seen and People I Have Met*, Brown, against the backdrop of a visit to the majestic Bank of England in London, described his elaborate scheme to issue shinplasters and manipulate discounts on wildcat bills from his little barbershop in Monroe. In other words, he simultaneously shaved faces as he shaved bank notes. Through his insightful portrait of antebellum economics, Brown explained that, within the context of the dysfunctional Monroe money market, even an African American barber could find customers to instill value into his shinplasters with their confidence. Literary scholars and historians have debated how well Brown's real life matched up to his narrative; most have characterized his Monroe story as a tale that crossed the line between what was real and what was counterfeit, or as one study described it, "shinplaster fiction." Brown may have embellished his writing, but his specific knowledge of Michigan's monetary system grounded the anecdote.[31]

William Wells Brown wrote that when he arrived in Monroe in the autumn of 1835, the lack of small change was particularly acute, providing him with an opportunity to boldly create paper money from nothing but the confidence of the community. Michigan prohibited bank notes under one dollar and the specie cash infusion from the Distribution Act and Specie Clause was over a year away. So Brown's story took place during a discrete moment when the specific regulatory regime had produced a crisis in the quantity, not just the quality, of money. Even his definition of shinplasters as notes that could be issued in any amount "from 6 to 75 cents in value" situated the small-denomination bills within Michigan's actual currency laws. This precise explanation clarified why members of the Monroe community would feel comfortable, or even eager, to take notes from a newly arrived, formerly enslaved man and why local authorities and bankers would not have been interested in preventing Brown's activities. Shinplasters capped at seventy-five cents did not compete with paper money legally in circulation and buttressed the supply of small change in the town. Brown even referenced the lack of specie when he concluded his narrative and brought the reader back to the clerks at the Bank of England "shoveling out the yellow coin upon the counters." William Wells Brown's final observation served to clearly contrast his shinplaster operation in Monroe, backed by nothing tangible, and the grand institution in London built on solid gold.[32]

The experiences of Nathaniel Saltonstall Howe, Richard Varnum, and William Wells Brown show that monetary instability was the norm rather than the exception in 1830s Monroe. By 1840 the paper money shortage was worse than ever as fallout from the Panic of 1837 left the controversial River Raisin & Lake Erie Rail Road Company as the only institution in town that still printed notes. The common council responded with a new round of municipal shinplasters issued in small denominations by the "Treasurer of the City of Monroe" that were "Receivable for Taxes & all city dues." Ostensibly a temporary move by the town to help with the currency shortage, the bills perfectly encapsulated the problem of paper money in Monroe. The town printed the notes on the back of sheets of useless one-dollar bills from the defunct Merchants & Mechanics Bank. In the end, the value in these bank notes turned out to be from their paper, not their money.[33]

Monroe's paper money market may have been a little more chaotic than other small towns, but the same variety of bank notes and shinplasters that confounded its residents on a daily basis circulated across the country. Importantly, the chaos did not alienate residents from monetary matters as much as it forced them to actively engage the currency available to them. This did not mean an equality of outcomes; it meant that merchants, religious prophets, and the formerly enslaved all had to accumulate financial knowledge and literally come to terms with their paper options to navigate the economic landscape. Not every early republic paper money transaction required an encyclopedic knowledge of bank note quality and regulatory guidelines, but the public had to be prepared because any transaction might.

While it was a necessity for all Americans to navigate complicated paper money transactions in the early republic, most had little control over the broader contours of the system. The public clamored for a substantial and stable currency, but unless they took William Wells Brown's initiative to issue their own bills, they relied on professional bankers to generate the notes that accounted for most of the nation's money supply. This was a risky practice. Bank officials conducted business along a spectrum of behavior from those who tried to prudently grow their deposits without too much risk to those who exploited the vagaries of the paper money system to turn a quick profit. Chapter 1 picks up on these themes to fully explore how banks produced notes and utilized a network of money brokers and carpetbaggers to circulate them profitably and efficiently throughout the nation.

PART I

Circulation

CHAPTER 1

Passing the Buck

IN THE MIDST of the Panic of 1857, the Georgia Supreme Court ruled on *Hutchings & Co. vs. the Western and Atlantic Railroad*. The case concerned whether an individual who carried large amounts of cash in his luggage was responsible for a freight charge separate from his passenger ticket. The issue came up when Louisville exchange broker Eusebius Hutchings traveled through Georgia in possession of a large carpet bag filled with $87,000 in bank notes and specie. When train officials charged him a forty-dollar freight fee even though he held his bag during the entire trip, he protested. The ruling ultimately hinged on a passenger's obligation to pay published rates, but the case provided a rare glimpse into a money broker's activities and how professional paper money handlers expedited the movement of currency around the country. Eusebius left his thriving Kentucky business to make stops in Dalton, Atlanta, and other Tennessee and Georgia bank towns before he returned home. His trip served two functions: to push new bills into circulation at a noticeable distance from their banks of issue and to redeem notes for specie at their home institutions.[1]

This chapter examines how professional paper money men like Eusebius Hutchings facilitated the circulation of bank notes in the early republic economy. Such individuals acted as conduits for the nation's paper money to ensure that bills moved from one place to another in ways that benefited banks' and their own bottom lines. The work of bankers, brokers, and carpetbaggers demonstrates that early republic institutions did not just print up bills and release them into the wild, but rather calculated how best to manipulate bank notes to create profit. Banks employed several methods to push notes into circulation: they issued short-term business or personal loans; they issued loans to professional brokers; they purchased assets for the bank; or they came to an arrangement to swap bills with a distant institution. The corporate quest to maximize profit—not the state's interest to create a stable economy—determined the nation's currency supply and its circulation patterns. While it was paramount to the government to monitor inflation and ensure that enough cash existed to meet both mercantile investment and personal spending demands, individual banks' interest in circulating whatever amount of paper money would generate the best returns controlled the money supply. Moreover, an American economy with a persistent cash shortage gave paper money men powerful leverage when they chose to push bank notes only where and when it suited them.[2]

The phrase "paper money men" is not just lyrical; it is demographic, based on the fact that it was overwhelmingly white, male individuals who organized and engineered the early republic bank note system. Women used paper money in daily commercial and personal transactions, actively participated in credit markets, and occasionally issued loans, but bankers, brokers, and the legal system of coverture denied them access to the formal positions that produced and arranged the monetary system. So, even though institutions such as R. K. Swift's banking house in Chicago offered special afternoon hours "for the benefit of Ladies" to conduct their business, there were few official opportunities for women to organize the wider currency regime. This was not new in the nineteenth century. Scholars have shown that years before the Revolutionary War, urban women's familiarity with both currency and credit transactions highlighted their central place within commercial settings even as they generally remained outside key parts of the financial sector.[3]

Likewise, although both free and enslaved African Americans utilized paper money in their market activities, they had few opportunities for formal relationships with banking institutions and no African American men managed chartered banks before the Civil War. A small group—like Philadelphia barber Joseph Cassey, master sailmaker James Forten, and lumber and coal merchant Stephen Smith—operated as private money brokers, provided loans, and exchanged bank notes for individuals who often could not obtain credit or favorable rates from white-run institutions. Madame Eulalie "CeCee" d'Mandeville Macary similarly challenged numerous categorizations when, in addition to her other New Orleans merchant activities, she used her considerable wealth to discount notes. However, legal barriers such as an 1853 Maryland statute that prevented savings banks from being run by African Americans circumscribed most finance opportunities and led the National Negro Conference to organize a Banks and Banking Institutions Committee to advocate for a black-run bank. That would not happen until more than a decade later.[4]

Whether inside or outside formal monetary networks, all parts of the population depended on financial institutions for their supply of cash because it was the banks, rather than the government, that produced most of the legal paper money used in the United States between the 1790s and 1860. Government officials certainly hoped that when this system functioned properly, enough capital and currency would be available to grow the economy, but without adequate controls on the money market the potential for abuse and collapse was ever present. One 1814 pamphlet stated that banks worked together to "keep up a kind of perpetual motion of bills, which amounts to an important circulation. But the motion is like that of a drunken man. It must be kept up, or serious consequences may follow to the institutions." The country's currency supply was therefore not tied to any predetermined amount that was meant to produce stability; the process that capitalized the nation rested in the hands of bankers who sought benefits for themselves and their institutions and not the general welfare of the nation.[5]

A shortage of ready cash did not exist in every area of the country, but at certain times could be acute and provided bankers with a population eager for investment money or just an acceptable currency to buy daily necessities. There was no widespread resistance to the adoption of a paper money economy. There just wasn't always enough cash to make it work. Barter systems even persisted in some locations because currency shortages prevented the nation as a whole from making a quick transition to a cash market system. Such conditions affected all potential consumers, not just merchants and businessmen. As late as the 1830s, Roxanna Stowell of St. Johnsbury, Vermont, wrote that sometimes "money is so very scarce and we must have some." The growing nation never seemed to have enough paper money to meet the demand.[6]

Just the prospect of a new bank in a small town offered a community hope of access to credit and a cash infusion. In his diary in 1804, Dr. Nathaniel Ames of Dedham, Massachusetts, noted a "Rage for Banks triumphant" among the population south of Boston as different villages competed for new charters. The promise of a new source of paper money gave immense power to bankers who found recipients for their notes regardless of quality. One Panic of 1837 pamphlet explained that "no kind of money is too bad to suit a needy borrower." Not all banks reacted equally to this leverage. Some exploited the money market more than others to benefit themselves and their institutions, but all sought advantages by using their ability to make money by making money.[7]

Simply put, an early republic bank note was a piece of paper that promised its face value in coin when returned to the issuing institution; how banks produced and distributed these bills was not so simple. Each bank note represented a liability for its home institution, but banks understood that the "doctrine of chances" said that their paper money could not all be redeemed at the same time. Conservative institutions limited this liability by only issuing notes at two or three times the amount of specie they held in their vaults, while more reckless ones might have tens of thousands of bills in circulation and a bare cupboard at home. Regardless of how many notes they released, every bank had an interest in keeping their bills in circulation as long as possible before they returned for redemption. Separate from properly managed note-to-specie ratios, fraudulent wildcat institutions with no intention or ability to redeem their notes actively engaged in misdirection to trick bank regulators and the public into thinking that they could redeem bills just like any other bank.[8]

Banking institutions that operated to maximize profits primarily used business and personal loans to release their bank notes. Early republican bank loans did not function like modern loans. They were paid out with paper money issued by the institution itself, a fact that dramatically affected bank decisions about how much currency to circulate. Banks took interest on loans in advance, so a ninety-day loan of $1,000 at 6 percent would yield $985 in paper money to the borrower. The full $1,000 had to be repaid by the end of ninety days, at which point the loan could be reissued for another $985 in cash. Given the number of satirical pieces that mocked merchants for last-minute "shinning"—a term for running around and borrowing money to make a payment—few loans seem to have been repaid in advance and most were paid off just in time for renewal. So, as soon as the borrower obtained his bank notes, a race began to see what would happen first: the repayment of the loan or the redemption of the bills. Since only the interest was prepaid, any bank notes that came back for redemption before the loan's principle was repaid represented a loss for the bank. The longer the bills circulated the more the bank earned from the interest. If a bank got really lucky some of the notes might be lost or destroyed and never come back home.[9]

It should be no surprise to learn that bankers who controlled the production of paper money often used institutional loans to improve their own fortunes and not necessarily to do what was best for the nation's monetary needs. The satirical "Diary of a Bank Director," cheekily stated that banks were "not established by people who want to lend money, but by people who want to make money." This sentiment buttresses the argument that New England industrialists and businessmen used their position as bank officials to steer loans to themselves and their corporate allies through what one scholar terms "insider lending." Among better-capitalized banks in the Middle Atlantic, credit was still not distributed equally around the community; even white, male artisans found it extremely difficult to obtain loans in the early republic.[10]

When banks and borrowers entered into negotiations over loan terms, each side looked to use whatever advantage they could obtain. Borrowers learned from guidebooks like *The Young Merchant* that they had some leverage because "the bank is under a great temptation to give large credit, for the sake of the greater circulation of these profitable notes." So borrowers understood that promises they made to banks about a slow redemption of notes could yield tangible results like a reduced interest rate on a loan from 6 percent to $5\frac{3}{4}$ percent. Banks conversely understood that customers needed capital to conduct business and that anything they arranged to ensure extended circulation would make the loan more profitable. Bankers hedged their bets with an investigation into where their notes would travel geographically, how long it might take before they returned, and what terms might be reached about the quality of the cash involved in the loan payoff. Aside from loans structured with short repayment terms (sixty or ninety days were common), banks developed a variety of schemes to complicate or dissuade the return of their bank notes. These impediments extended circulation times but created a more complicated currency landscape for the rest of the population.[11]

Bank officials and customers understood that not all bank notes circulated with equal confidence, so the quality and type of bills being loaned and those subsequently used for the payoff could be negotiated. One Cleveland borrower told a Michigan bank that if he were given low-denomination notes, the bills would enjoy a long circulation because the city severely lacked small change. Current law held that federal deposit institutions could not issue notes worth under five dollars and every bank in Cleveland held federal funds. The result was a city without small bills and a merchant who hoped to use that monetary information to obtain increased credit. Questionable banks in the old Northwest often asked borrowers to pay back loans of wildcat bills with higher quality paper money. For example, the Western Reserve Bank agreed to a four-month loan to Samuel Rhoads provided the money was repaid in "Eastern Paper." However, there were limits to how questions of value could officially enter a loan agreement. Banks with poor-quality notes could not legally profit from a loan of bad money with the hope that the bills would appreciate by the time of repayment. *Nashville Bank v. Hays & Grundy* ruled that a loan made in bills with a 25 percent discount and repaid at par constituted usury as it altered the terms of the original loan and gave the bank a significant extra profit.[12]

Bank officers tried to plot the journey their notes would travel because they understood that distance equaled time for note redemption. Promises to move bills to other states met with approbation. James B. Ralston asked the Concord Bank in New Hampshire for good terms on his loan since he had the ability to "scatter [bills] in the north and west" of Vermont where he resided. John Norton, the cashier of the Michigan State Bank, likewise approved one applicant who promised to "go south for the purpose of purchasing produce this month and the money will have the best of circulation being paid only to farmers for wheat." Better yet, the Bank of Wisconsin dealt with one Cleveland customer who pledged to "give your bills as extensive a circulation in Ohio as we possibly can and in such manner that they will not be returned until [the loan is repaid]." Such individual guarantees could track the circulation of small quantities of bank notes, but institutions sought more intricate plans to frustrate mass redemption.[13]

Banks sometimes used redemption terms written on a bill itself to control its circulation. Most bank notes were payable to the bearer on demand, but others altered that language to prevent a payout before the completion of the loan or to track which borrower was responsible for redemption. The easiest way to do this was with a post note redeemable only after a specific date, stated on the bill itself, from ten days to over a year after being issued. Connecticut banks used several variations of post notes during the War of 1812, such as a Hartford Bank two-dollar note "payable two years after the war." After the conflict, Providence newspapers complained that Rhode Island was overrun by the bills and that "many an honest man has been *hoaxed* with the 'two years' notes as they are precisely similar to the old notes, and the difference cannot be discovered without a perusal of the promissory clause." Luckily, few institutions circulated post notes because their charters or state regulations required notes to be paid immediately on demand; moreover, post notes raised serious red flags for a public constantly trying to determine which banks deserved their confidence.[14]

Another option for banks was to circumscribe who could redeem the note right on its face. This was usually accomplished by spelling out the borrower's name, such as when the Bank of Pennsylvania issued a bill bearing the words "Promises to pay DeWitt Clinton or bearer on demand Ten Dollars." While nothing stopped Governor Clinton of New York from passing along the bill to someone else who could redeem it, the bank could use the note marked with his name to hold him responsible if it was redeemed too soon. In *The Nature and Uses of Money and Mixed Currency*, political economist Amasa Walker explained that if a customer received $10,000 worth of marked notes under the condition that they would circulate for six months, the institution would quickly know if any returned prematurely. Then, "as fast as these bills are returned to the bank, [the customer] is obliged to redeem them at once with other money." Banks were guaranteed not to lose any money with this method. It was rare, but one last way a bank could alter a note was to tie it exclusively to one person by changing the words "or bearer" to "or order." Such bank notes did not circulate widely because they functioned more like checks, which did not become common until later in the century.[15]

Rather than tracking individual bills, financial institutions often fashioned agreements with remote partners to help them design more predictable circulation patterns. In the endlessly malleable world of early republic banking, formal or casual relationships between distant institutions could either help or hinder the movement of their notes. Dumping a bunch of bills with a collaborator could generate a circulation far enough away that redemption was unlikely. When a bank wanted to create efficiencies and give customers more flexibility to use their capital, it might forge an alliance with a bank in New York City that ensured easy and predicable redemption in the nation's financial center. The most significant attempt to establish an advantageous regional system of paper money circulation was through the Suffolk Bank system.[16]

In reaction to a series of New England bank failures early in the century, the Suffolk Bank became the leader of six Boston institutions that, in 1824, hatched a plan to streamline bank note circulation and redemption in the region. Country banks that joined the association could have their notes received throughout Boston at face value as long as they permanently deposited in the Suffolk Bank's vaults a minimum of $2,000 in specie, interest free, plus an extra deposit to redeem their notes. The Suffolk Bank acted as a central bank for member banks that received all the system's deposited notes and returned them without further redemption of specie. To convince country banks to join, the Suffolk Bank threatened to collect and redeem large numbers of their bank notes en masse. The small, rural banks had a choice: deposit thousands of dollars in specie at the Suffolk Bank in Boston or face the possibility of tens of thousands of their own bank notes coming back all at once for redemption in specie. The coercion worked and most New England banks eventually joined the Suffolk system.[17]

For decades, the Suffolk Bank seemed to keep New England bank notes at par. Once the system became fully operational, most paper money circulated easily and discounts on country bank notes fell to less than .25 percent in Boston. Even in the face of the calamitous Panic of 1837, the Suffolk system survived by using the institutional relationships that gave it a national reputation for good banking and market stabilization. As long as member institutions played by the Suffolk Bank's rules, it continued to advance them credit even during the worst of the economic conditions between 1837 and 1843. However, New England banks that chose to weather the panic by opting out of the Suffolk system faced retribution. Even though the Bank of St. Albans in Vermont continued to redeem their notes in specie, their decision to end their account at the Suffolk Bank landed them on a list of "Bills Uncurrent in Boston" along with banks that stopped their payments.[18]

The rarefied status achieved by the Suffolk Bank as a stable force within the usual disorder of the American market economy is evidenced by the way authors used it as a convenient plot device in antebellum fiction. A character in Sarah Josepha Hale's *Northwood; or Life North and South* tracked down some missing bills then traveled to Boston and went "directly to the Suffolk Bank, and describing the notes, inquired if they had been presented." There was no other explanation of banking in the novel. Hale did not need to rationalize why this query was made at the Suffolk Bank. This was assumed knowledge for American readers in the 1850s. In darker stories by George Thompson, such as *Brazen Star* or *Life and Exploits of the Noted Criminal, Bristol Bill*, counterfeiters targeted the institution to demonstrate their skill. Given the reputation and position of the Suffolk

Bank, a criminal's claim that he could "deceive the bank officers themselves," was the greatest boast he could make.[19]

While the Suffolk Bank system guaranteed the efficient movement of bills around parts of New England, banks that hoped to prevent the redemption of their own notes sought partners to ensure a remote circulation. The long-time banker Alexander Bryan Johnson explained that partnerships between banks were instrumental to the operation of a money-issuing institution. He wrote that "a bank at Buffalo may receive one per cent. for collecting a note payable at Utica, while a bank at Utica may receive one per cent. for collecting a note payable at Buffalo" and if the "two banks can exchange this paper with each other" through the mail for less than one percent in postage, they would make an easy profit. Bankers saw this as simple arithmetic, not deception, but the exchange was not always benign. When the Stillwater Canal Bank of Orono cemented a deal with the Washington Bank of New York, it already had a questionable reputation. The relationship cost the Maine bank a $3,000 deposit in New York, but it allowed their bills to be redeemed in the nation's financial capital. Newspaper bank note tables captured a swift increase in the public's confidence in Stillwater Canal Bank bills. They previously traded at a 10 percent discount, but after the Washington Bank deal they sold at only 1.5 percent off face value. Bank officials in Orono maximized the partnership and dumped tens of thousands of bills into the market that they knew would never come back for redemption. The bills cycled through the New York metropolitan area at a small discount while, back in Maine, Stillwater Canal Bank's specie reserves topped out at a lofty $5.41. The plan lasted only as long as the Washington Bank kept afloat; its failure brought down both institutions late in 1841.[20]

Rather than forming relationships with other institutions, banks with multiple branches used geographic misdirection to create cash that seemingly belonged in two places at once. The State Bank of Illinois operated nine branches beginning in 1835 that promised to stabilize currency values, but instead infuriated the public because it functioned like an elaborate shell game. Branch locations covered the state from Chicago in the north to Danville in the south, but the markings on individual bank notes designated them as payable only at specific locations. The bank complicated the distribution of its notes when it based their point of inception on the maximum distance from the branch where they were ultimately payable. For example, ten-dollar bills redeemable in Mt. Carmel were only distributed to the branch in Quincy more than 275 miles away. Using State Bank of Illinois notes forced individuals to appreciate the relationship between branches and also to master the specific textual instructions on the bank notes in question.[21]

Instead of elaborate schemes to move notes to distant locations, some bills confounded consumers with text that masked their redemption terms. The fraudulent Bank of Constantine in Michigan included the stamped or handwritten phrase, "Payable in Ohio or Indiana Bank Notes" on some of their bills; others read "Payable at Buffalo, in Ohio Funds, at the Office of L. F. Tiffany." These later notes skirted several regulations when they offered redemption only at an out-of-state location in a third state's paper money and, even then, only at the office of a broker named Lucius Fernando Tiffany. That Tiffany was also one of the directors of the Bank of Buffalo did not make the arrangement any more confidence inspiring. A notorious post note, boldly headed "North River Banking Company, State of New York," offered textual misdirection based on time and space. Ostensibly from New York, the fine print on the bill said it could only be "redeemed at the German Bank of Wooster in the State of Ohio" twelve months after the date on the front. Massachusetts legislators tried to discourage such geographic trickery when they outlawed the practice as "hazardous to the public," but wildcat banks usually outflanked regulations. Such bank note manipulations created extra profit for bankers by stalling redemption and generated confusion for customers who expected a certain relationship between time, distance, and value in their currency. Confronted by bills that did not conform to these rules, Americans learned an alternative geography of bank notes that reconfigured how they understood distance and the relationship between different parts of the country.[22]

Wildcat bank operators might use geographic misdirection to make redemption more difficult, but other bank officials created notes that featured clues to their location. Whether this encouraged note redemption is questionable, but maps or directions to a bank on the face of a bill both advertised and inspired confidence for institutions located outside major urban centers. A 12½ cent note from the Farmers' Bank of New Jersey spelled out its location in rural Mount Holly with the phrase "17 Miles from Philadelphia," while the Jefferson County Bank's ten-dollar bill literally put its home on the map with a large vignette of the counties and towns of Upstate New York, Upper Canada, and Lake Ontario, with the bank's location in Watertown at the center. Such images served more to reassure potential holders of the bank's trustworthiness than to speed redemption. The Jefferson County Bank was a twenty-year-old, reputable institution by the time they issued these notes in the 1830s, but the 300-mile trip from New York City to upstate Watertown was still arduous.[23]

It became particularly difficult to decipher these geographic clues when the personal or institutional relationships that undergirded how and where certain notes could best be redeemed remained shielded from the general public. Stamps on the back of Bank of Commerce bills in the late 1850s, for example, alerted holders that in addition to their home in Savannah they could be "REDEEMED BY BANK REPUBLIC NEW-YORK AT 3/4 P. CT. DISCOUNT." This message mapped out an alternative geographic path for Bank of Commerce notes. They did not just have one official point of redemption; they had two—eight hundred miles apart and at slightly different exchange rates.

The outbreak of the Civil War complicated the partnership of the Bank of Commerce and the Bank of the Republic. Gazaway Bugg Lamar, from Georgia, resigned as president of the Bank of the Republic in the spring of 1861 and left New York after he had simultaneously nursed his terminally ill wife and stealthily helped Confederate secretary of the Treasury Christopher Memminger arrange a contract with the National Bank Note Company to print over $1 million dollars in Treasury notes for the new Southern government. After he arrived in his native Savannah, Gazaway became president of the Bank of Commerce and canceled its agreement with the Bank of the Republic. Most individuals on the street did not follow Lamar's career, but they belatedly received an update on the back of Bank of Commerce notes. In the summer of 1861, bank clerks scratched out the stamps on the back of the bills with ink to indicate that they were no longer accepted at the Bank of the Republic at the prearranged discount. Every one of these bank note stamps and marks mattered as consumers tried to make sense of a bill's value even though professional money men always seemed a step ahead as they crafted the circulation of paper according to their geographic or calendar preferences.[24]

Separate from bankers, money brokers, referred to as shavers, colluded with and competed against banks to buy and sell notes. As early as 1786, New York broker Jacob Reed Jr. advertised that he traded in out-of-town "bank notes at a moderate discount." What began with individuals like Reed—who tried to shave some profit off the circulation of bills as they

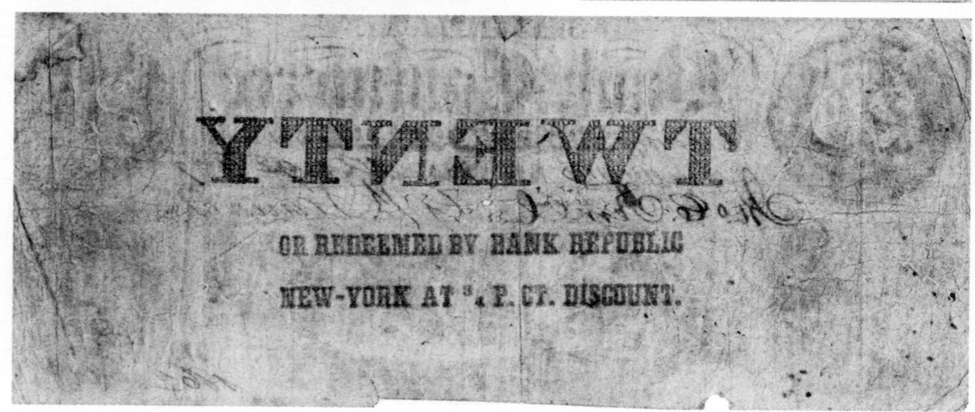

FIGURE 3. The obverse and reverse of a twenty-dollar note from the Bank of Commerce. This 1857 bill was also redeemable at the Bank of the Republic in New York. After the outbreak of the Civil War, clerks used ink to scratch out the stamp on the back. Author's collection.

moved through the economy—spread so that by the antebellum period almost every town had an exchange market where out-of-town or uncurrent notes were bought and sold at varied discounts. Brokers' profits increased the more they used asymmetrical monetary information to shave bills as they moved through the system; brokers also enticed business with multiple products that created full-service money markets. When the narrator in Asa Greene's *The Perils of Pearl Street* tried to exchange a "western bill" for ten dollars, a broker asked if he would like to purchase a lottery ticket. To sweeten the deal, the broker promised to "take uncurrent money" for the ticket and exchange the western bank note without the going rate of 5 percent.[25]

Sometimes shavers worked with banks to push bills into circulation. The Boston brokers Bridge & Renouf explained to Samuel Sparhawk at the Concord Bank in New Hampshire that their contacts could move several thousand dollars across Connecticut and Rhode Island. They promised that "not more than one third of them would reach the Bank in one year from the time they were distributed." They had previously moved $3,000 for another institution and claimed that "not more than 10% of these bills have found their way to the Bank." Not all these arrangements worked out in the bank's best interests. Dunbar & Grannis promised to circulate $4,000 in Concord Bank notes "in the usual friendly way," but the bills found their way back too quickly for the bank to recognize the expected profit.[26]

Brokers and bankers sometimes forged relationships where the fuzzy lines between their agendas enabled them to use insider information to create personal financial gains at the expense of a confused public. When Henry Grew purchased a bundle of Nahant Bank notes from broker Matthew Bolles, he believed he had paid a good price for the Lynn, Massachusetts, bills. Grew promised Bolles that "the bills should not be put into circulation for six months, or if they were so put into circulation and went into the bank within that time, he would redeem them." However, the bank soon folded, and when Grew sued to recover the value of the notes, he claimed that the circulation deal with Bolles led him to believe that the broker was "acting as agent for the bank." The court disagreed and argued that a broker who shaved notes at various discounts might have an interest in the long circulation of particular notes separate from those of the issuing institution. Even though it didn't help his case, Grew was correct that two Nahant Bank officials had hired Matthew Bolles to push the notes into the economy, albeit with a six-month delay. Alternatively, warning bells went off when J. S. Lake, the cashier of the Bank of Wooster, advertised to shave notes from his own bank at a 1 to 1.5 percent discount. Lake attempted to make a short-term profit at his bank's expense and raised the alarm across the money market. Ohio newspapers called for an investigation of the institution and it collapsed less than two years later.[27]

When brokers issued their own notes in the form of small-denomination shinplasters, it blurred the line between their activity and that of an unchartered or private bank. During the Panic of 1837, the owner of "a shaving shop" in New York circulated notes worth less than one dollar and promised to redeem them in "good current bank notes." Butchers from the Fulton market rounded up four dollars in bills and sent a young boy over for redemption. The broker promptly turned him away and explained that New York State law did not allow him to pass bank notes of less than five dollars. The move angered the butchers, who lured the shaver to their market where they attacked him with pumpkin pies, rotten eggs, and a "bloody beef's liver" while they papered him over with one hundred dollars of his own shinplasters.[28]

Whether they worked for banks or independently for themselves, brokers did not just respond to financial information; they helped create it. With so much to gain as they manipulated local money markets based on the notes they wanted to buy or sell, there was a strong motivation to shape the public's confidence in individual banks. In this way, a subtle (or not so subtle) dance was played out between bankers and brokers who both tried to use the paper currency supply for their own benefit. With the public caught in the middle, professional paper money men caused bank runs, sell-offs, and panics in the money market. A "broker in the interior" of Michigan told a *Detroit Tribune* reporter to "give the irresponsible issues of Tecumseh a wide berth" as he hoped to drive down the price of some notes that he wished to unload. He was not alone. Another critic publicly accused the bank of "thimble-rigging" when it issued large quantities of bank notes without enough corresponding specie. The poor press took its toll and the Bank of Tecumseh collapsed shortly thereafter.[29]

If loan officers pushed bank notes into existence and money brokers helped move them along in their circulation, a third group—alternatively called express agents, carpetbaggers, or carpet bag men—specialized in physically moving paper money around the nation at the ideal velocity. Men with carpet bags full of bank notes started their travels as general messengers or express agents, not dedicated movers of paper money. Advertisements for Dearborn & Company's express delivery between Boston and Newmarket, New Hampshire, highlighted their "safe and speedy conveyance of Packages, Bundles, Specie, Bank Notes" to any towns along the route. Eventually, bankers realized that the movement of paper money was not just another line on a crowded ledger sheet; it was a potentially valuable logistical system that required agents who specialized in moving currency. Once supplied with a carpet bag full of notes, these agents dispersed paper money in a variety of ways. That might mean a trip to a

FIGURE 4. Brokers sometimes manipulated public confidence in poor-quality notes from institutions like the Bank of Tecumseh to profit from local money markets. Author's collection.

distant state to push the bills into circulation or a deal struck with a remote institution that sought a distant partner. The fraudulent Bank of Sandstone in Michigan even employed a carpet bag man to convert their unbacked notes into as much livestock as possible before the public caught on and the notes became worthless. Most of their activity was more routine as carpetbaggers speedily returned bank notes to their home institutions and redeemed them for specie.[30]

Although the word "carpetbagger" scarcely appeared in antebellum print sources, stories about these men proliferated. A typical report from a month before the attack on Fort Sumter noted that Illinois country banks kept a "sharp look-out for these carpet-bag men" to guard the "specie in their vaults." After the Civil War, Albion Tourgée explained the origin of the "carpetbagger" in *A Fool's Errand, by One of the Fools.* He wrote that the antebellum term related to a scheme devised by issuers of "wild cat money . . . for preventing the solvency of the State banks from being too readily tested." To ensure that the notes circulated far and wide without returning, they were put into "circulation by means of agents, who carried the bills about the county in *carpet-bags*, and were hence denominated, 'Carpetbaggers.'" By whatever name, carpet bag men did seem to be familiar cogs within the bank note system.[31]

Some states pushed back against these money market manipulations. Vermont passed legislation as early as 1807 to prevent out-of-state currency, or "foreign bank bills," from local circulation, but the law was hard to enforce as persistent currency shortages meant that even questionable bills from Rhode Island remained in demand. Decades later, New York tried to stop carpetbaggers who dumped poor-quality, small-denomination notes from western and southern states. An 1844 law fined "every person who becomes an agent for banks in other States, and attempts to circulate their paper here, or redeems it for the purpose of circulation." Little came of the law as the paper money market was so large that the fifty-dollar fine was well worth the cost to dispatch an agent who earned thousands.[32]

Even with these minor hurdles, it was easy to push bank notes into circulation, but it proved more difficult to navigate the tangled web of wildcat institutions specifically designed to prevent bank note redemption. Sometimes carpetbaggers were more than messengers from point A to point B; they had to be detectives just to find point B. Charles Woodward, an agent for Adams & Co.'s Express, set out for northwest Indiana to find the Bank of America in Newton County so he could redeem $1,000 in notes for specie. Woodward could not find anyone who knew of the bank or its hometown of Morocco until he came upon a blacksmith. The man walked him next door to his house—the only other building around—and announced that he had arrived at the bank and found the cashier. Woodward learned that the bank was closed for the day, so he had to stay overnight to conduct business. The blacksmith/cashier offered to hold the $1,000 and proceeded to place the bank notes in a barrel that he covered with potatoes. The next morning Woodward was surprised when the blacksmith counted out $1,000 in gold coins from a bag labeled $5,000 housed at the bottom of the potato barrel and then refused to accept any payment for the supper and breakfast that he had eaten. The blacksmith claimed it was a reward for being the first one to find the bank and the promise not to tell anyone else its location. Reportedly capitalized at $500,000, the Bank of America shortly closed its barrel after less than a year with nearly $50,000 circulating at a 30 percent discount.[33]

Charles Woodward got lucky on his trip to Indiana, but for those who carried tens of thousands of dollars in cash through the night or traveled blindly to remote areas of the frontier, a carpet bag man's precarious life did not always go as planned. Henry Witter was robbed in a waiting room at the Norwich, Connecticut, train station while he was transporting bank notes. He was sleeping on a couch at one o'clock in the morning when he was knocked out with a billy club and "robbed of his carpet bag, containing about $40,000." Witter quickly recovered, but his haul of bank notes never made it to their destination in Boston. Attacks and robbery were not the only liabilities for carpet bag men who journeyed back to small towns to return bank notes to their home institutions.[34]

Bank officials monitored their note circulation carefully and took steps to ensure that their bills stayed in the market for prolonged periods of time. When the activities of carpetbaggers altered or disrupted those plans, bankers noticed and responded. On a visit to Detroit early in 1838, Henry Stringham, the cashier of the Bank of Wisconsin, wrote back to his organization's president about a carpetbagger named Mr. Fretus, "who has given the banks here so much trouble" and was reportedly "trying to collect a quantity of our paper" so that he could visit their bank in Green Bay. While he did not argue that they should withhold specie (it would have been a violation of their charter), Stringham suggested that they should delay any payments to Fretus to "give him a great deal of trouble for his pains." In the end, the scheme did not matter much as the bank soon failed.[35]

Bankers usually did not have to thwart carpetbaggers on their own. Especially in small towns with few financial institutions, specie deposits might represent a significant amount of the saved monetary wealth of the community and wary residents did not want to see that taken away in a carpet bag by a stranger. It was common for townspeople to monitor gold reserves and the cashier's behavior to ensure the bank's solvency and the health of the local economy. In the mid-1850s, a Lexington carpet bag man named Barclay made numerous trips to a branch of the Commercial Bank of Kentucky in Versailles. Like in Illinois, individual notes from the bank could only be redeemed at one of its seven branches, so it took some effort to obtain only those bills that hailed from Versailles. Barclay's skill for manipulation within the Kentucky money market seemed to outpace the bank's as his "constant and heavy drafts" severely cut into their specie supply. Townspeople from Versailles reacted to the loss of coin and "passed resolutions denouncing the conduct of Barclay, and then proceeded to hang him in effigy. The indignant people also promised to make summary work with Barclay, or his clerk, if either ever again molested the vault of the bank."[36]

Confrontations between carpetbaggers and crowds that hoped to protect local resources erupted during the financial tension associated with the financial Panic of 1857. In Frankfort, Kentucky, the townspeople took great pleasure in their standoff with agents "from Cincinnati with carpet-bags and bank notes." They described the event in heroic terms and claimed that the "best citizens" confronted the "knights of the carpet-bag" and scared them off with a motion toward a barrel of eggs ready to be thrown before the agents could claim "the golden buds of our country." Victorious, they boasted that "our citizens will not submit to the depletion of our commercial interests by these Cincinnati blood suckers, and the sooner these blood suckers realize this fact, the better it will be for their necks." A Louisville newspaper that reprinted the story warned its readers that the "people in the interior have determined to show no mercy to the 'carpet-bag men' in the future."[37]

This was not an isolated event in Kentucky. The same week as the events in Frankfort, the Cincinnati banking house of Kinney, Espy & Co. sent an agent to the Commercial Bank of Kentucky in Paducah "to exchange a carpet bag of rags for one of gold." He was met with an unusually hostile reception. A mob accosted him at the bank and demanded that he not redeem the notes. Another mob greeted his approach to the Paducah branch of the Bank of Louisville. Bank officers refused his inquiry for specie and even turned down his request to exchange their notes for New York or Ohio bills. Egged on by the bankers, the crowd forced the agent out of town while they shouted insults at him. In an interesting foreshadowing of the evolution of the term "carpetbagger," someone in the crowd cried, "Move him, the damned Ohio Abolitionist." The quick escalation from anti-banking sentiment to anti-abolitionism reflected the particular way that small-town communities identified carpetbaggers as external, existential threats to their economic well-being. The fact that everyone understood that banking rules required notes to be redeemed on demand did not matter to the mob in that moment, nor did the carpet bag man's unstated views on slavery or race. What did matter was that he came from out of state (a free state three hundred miles to the northwest) and that he came to remove resources that were vital to the town.[38]

Bank officials who appealed to the public to help them protect deposits for the sake of the community risked being held to the same standard. As shown in the case of Versailles, Kentucky, residents took action against Barclay, the Louisville carpetbagger, for his frequent trips to remove specie from the small bank, but they did not stop there. Convinced that the Commercial Bank in town had too readily redeemed notes for specie and that the bank's reserves had decreased too quickly, the crowd burned the cashier in effigy. They also threatened to harm the bank president and his clerk if they went to the bank vault again.[39]

Community allegiances could change quickly if the locals believed that a bank did not satisfy the people's financial needs. In early 1842, Cincinnati's money market exploded after the Miami Bank refused to redeem its fraudulent notes. This was not a random decision by the cashier; the institution's vault only held $1,261 in specie and had over $200,000 out for circulation. The Miami Bank was not the only culprit in the neighborhood. *Brother Jonathan* reported that "there appear to have been something like a dozen of these shaving shops in Cincinnati" which issued poor-quality, small-denomination notes that they never intended to redeem. When the Bank of Cincinnati responded to the Miami Bank run with a posted "notice upon its doors announcing a suspension for thirty days," a mob attacked it as well as two more institutions on the same block. They "forced open the vaults, and stole some specie and bank notes, as well as notes of those companies that had been redeemed [and] destroyed every thing they could get hold of, throwing the remains into the streets." Such radical mood swings about banks—a riot to protect one and alternatively a riot to punish another—stemmed from the intensely personal way that Americans engaged in paper money transactions in the early republic. Bankers who tried to prevent redemption walked a fine line when they tried to gain enough of the public's trust to keep their notes in circulation and protect the institution's specie reserves. Once that trust was completely lost, the public felt entitled to take whatever they could from the bank's vault to avoid getting stuck with nothing.[40]

The work of carpetbaggers exposed how paper money men organized the bank note system to extract the maximum advantage. It was only profitable to pay a carpet bag man to redeem bills for specie if a large amount of cash was involved and it was just not feasible or cost effective for most Americans to redeem distant bank notes at their source. Even if an artisan was lucky enough to obtain one hundred dollars in out-of-state bills, he could not benefit as much as a professional with connections and resources. An appeal to workers explained that "a dealer in these bills may exchange them for *one per cent.*, which is one dollar only; whereas if the mechanic [should] undertake to effect the same exchange himself, he must leave work, he must pay his traveling expenses, he must lose the interest of the money till it is exchanged, and he must incur the risk of losing it on the way." So if he had to "pay this money into the Bank, his best and only course is to pay the difference of exchange." It was not economical for most Americans to travel to redeem their bank notes, especially when brokers or local money markets offered only a small discount on the exchange. The broker could choose to send the money back to its source with a carpetbagger, but it was usually more profitable for them to shave the notes locally where they earned a commission on each exchange. Bank officials who constructed this national monetary system understood how each of these groups would act and continued to reap the profit.[41]

Even when ordinary Americans did travel around the country for unrelated reasons and tried to use the opportunity to redeem bills, this did not always work in their favor. A trip west from New York by R. H. Harding was marred by disappointment when he tried to deal in Michigan bank notes. He wrote in his diary:

> My business with the Detroit Banks . . . was attended with much trouble in consequence of the bad repute of their money and the money of other banks in this state commonly called Wild Cat and Red Dog money the latter of which could not be disposed of out of the state and hardly in it, as they had no specie of any account to redeem their bills. . . . [After] stopping a few hours at Jacksonburgh for the purpose of negotiating with the Bank for exchange of the bills which they of course refused my next remedy was to demand specie. . . . [They eventually reached] a compromise but not without insulting me with language little becoming gentlemen.

Even under the lax regulation of Michigan's free banking law of 1837, banks legally had to redeem their notes for specie. However, on the ground, men like Harding found out that things were not so easy, especially without institutional connections that might lubricate the deal.[42]

As Harding's experience shows, professional paper money men worked together to create a system that was simultaneously efficient and profitable to those who had set it up and complex and chaotic for everyone else. An 1873 speech by Congressman William D. Kelley of Pennsylvania included an extended and insightful description of how the antebellum bank note system worked in two fictional towns. He explained:

> I am giving you a historic fact when I tell you that I first became acquainted with that term [carpetbagger] in designating those fellows who were traveling from one out-of-the-way place to another with a carpet-bag full of notes to exchange, so that the notes put in circulation in Skunktown couldn't find their way back to Frogtown, because the people in Skunktown didn't know where Frogtown was, and the people in Frogtown didn't know where Skunktown was—and if they did they couldn't get there; the people in one place couldn't get to the other to get the specie on which the notes were based. Then after the bank at Frogtown had paid out the Skunktown notes, the bank at Frogtown would refuse to receive the Skunktown notes, but it would send the holder, who was a debtor, around the corner to a broker, who would buy them at seven or nine per cent. discount, and then the broker and the bank would divide the proceeds of this gold basis transaction.

The towns in the anecdote were not real, but the glimpse inside how bank notes moved around the economy would have been eerily familiar to most Americans of the time.[43]

William Kelley's description of Frogtown and Skunktown provided a holistic view of how bankers, brokers, and carpetbaggers worked together to manipulate currency markets and squeeze profit from the paper money system, while most townspeople lacked the knowledge or economic resources to bend currency markets to their advantage. It would not have shocked anyone to discover that banks did not exist to equally share their resources, but at a time when federal oversight of the money market was practically nonexistent and the currency supply was outsourced to state-regulated institutions, there seemed to be few safeguards. The collusion by these paper money men was all the more unfortunate because it privileged personal and corporate profits over what was best for the nation as a whole.

Not all professional paper money men profited from the bank note system, but their organization of the market left other participants to try to accumulate as much information as possible just to keep up. This was an exceedingly difficult proposition as banking institutions and regulations multiplied across the nation and added to the database of available financial intelligence. Other factors, such as educational opportunities and demographic realities, erected roadblocks for many individuals as they sought to employ their knowledge and personal experience during paper money negotiations conducted on a playing field that was far from even.

Chapter 2 examines how Americans of all sorts attempted to accumulate enough monetary information to engage in the complicated and often unjust early republic bank note economy.

CHAPTER 2

Face-to-Face Value

PROFESSIONAL PAPER MONEY men maximized profits through the quick movement of bank notes and their redemption for specie, but, for most Americans, bank notes were an unwanted headache that served primarily to obtain goods or services. A Panic of 1837–era pamphlet called *Exposition of the Effects of Paper Credit on the Prosperity of the Town of Bubbleton* noted that for the general public there was no actual relationship between the circulation of a bank's paper money and the expectation of redemption. The narrator explained that "A takes a note in payment, not because he knows or cares whether the issuer can redeem it, but because B, C, D, &c. will take it from him in payment." Americans required bank notes for participation in market exchanges and their value derived from their ability to move from person to person, not just travel back to their home institution. However, every time someone used a bank note in a transaction, they risked a loss in its value. It was problematic to jeopardize purchasing power with every purchase, but this process mirrored other contemporary risky economic behavior, such as early republic horse racing and spectator gambling, that developed in the context of new business and partisan networks. Money might be lost, but it was spent in ways that ensured the construction of certain economic and political hierarchies. The creation and maintenance of the bank note system paralleled this story as paper money men forged currency networks that benefited themselves and made everyone else scramble just to keep up. The choice to accept bank notes with unstable value represented the opportunity cost of participation in the early republic market.[1]

Since bank note values were highly variable, a whole series of factors affected their circulation. The literary critic John Neal explained that, as a young store clerk in Portland, he had dealt with good, bad, and questionable bills while he followed the maxim: "If you buy the devil, the sooner you sell him, the better." When he received poor-quality or counterfeit money, he was taught to accept it and then quickly work on "passing it to another person." The task fell to him, he said, because he was the "youngest, and by far the most innocent-looking with my blue eyes, golden hair, and Quaker bob-coat." While any customer would do to pass along questionable bank notes, he wrote that because of his looks, he "found it easier and safer to cheat women than men." Neal's anecdote highlights two critical aspects of early republic bank note circulation: billholders needed to assess the quality of the money in front of them through whatever information they could accumulate, and demography affected the interpersonal transactions needed to move paper from one person to the next.[2]

The uncertain quality of much of the paper money in circulation meant that noteholders required a negotiation to fashion confidence in the person on the other side of the transaction and the value of their money. This step was necessary because early nineteenth-century paper money lacked a legal tender designation, so Americans did not have to accept bank notes to participate in the economy. A Senate report on the nation's currency simply noted that "citizens are at liberty to receive bank paper in payment of their debts, if they think it safe to do so." In urban settings like New York City, transactions were particularly fraught because it was not small-town acquaintances who haggled over potentially questionable bills but rather strangers who were engaged in an "anonymous exchange." Especially when they dealt with an unfamiliar trading partner, early republicans who operated in a system without uniform currency could not afford to treat bank notes or shinplasters as indistinguishable scraps of paper. They needed to make an emotional and intimate connection to each and every bill, even if it were fleeting.[3]

This process was complicated because each transaction contained an asymmetrical negotiation about the quality of the paper currency being used that turned on how much monetary knowledge each person possessed and how they wielded this information. Americans tried to accumulate as much knowledge as possible about banks and bank notes to aid in these exchanges, but financial information was not the only variable. Paper money negotiations involved actual human beings with varied social standings and backgrounds who brought different amounts of power or leverage to each currency exchange. How much financial information individuals possessed and their social position—based on racial, gender, and class identity—meant that the experience of using paper money varied widely. If a person used a bank note, it mattered if they were a middling white farmer, a newly arrived European immigrant, the daughter of a banker, or a member of a Native American tribe, just as it mattered whether they handed the bill to a wealthy white merchant, an enslaved woman in an outdoor market, or a representative of the federal government. Based on who was involved and what bills they held in their hand, no two of these transactions looked the same. The early republic paper money economy was endlessly complicated. This chapter examines how the American public navigated the bank note system and how demographic realities like wealth, race, gender, and access to monetary information affected that experience.

Americans had the legal right not to accept unwanted bills, but they could not rely exclusively on specie and book debt. The ubiquity of paper money meant that it was not really an option to shield oneself from bank notes. Even in James Fenimore Cooper's *The Pioneers*, set in 1793, the avoidance of paper money seemed quaint and dated. When Elizabeth and Oliver said goodbye to Natty Bumppo at the end of the book, they handed "a parcel of bank-notes to the hunter" to take on his travels west. After he "examined them with a curious eye," Bumppo exclaimed: "[This] is some of the new-fashioned money that they've been making at Albany, out of paper! It can't be worth much to they that hasn't larning!" He handed it back and explained that it wouldn't do him any good. Cooper's iteration of Natty Bumppo in *The Pioneers* was a relic of an earlier age. Published in 1823, but set thirty years earlier, his lack of familiarity with paper money is a marker of his inability to fit in even in a small frontier town. However, Bumppo's reaction to the bills shows that some learning was necessary for individuals who accepted bank notes. The story also locates monetary knowledge within a wider "diffusion of information" that occurred in these years as early republic men and women attempted to acquire the knowledge needed to satisfy their social responsibility. The new nation required and expected its citizens to learn new things.[4]

Forced to accumulate knowledge about how to use paper currency, Americans turned to a variety of sources from formal educational texts to economic stories in newspapers and especially the daily trial and error of market encounters. To use bank notes, a person not only needed to learn enough math to add and subtract but also to understand the federal monetary structure of dollars and cents. Sources that taught quick, mental arithmetic proliferated in the early republic and dispersed a vision of rational, democratic mathematics to children. Paper currency grounded arithmetic lessons for those boys and girls lucky enough to attend school. Textbooks featured a "Federal Money" section with problems that calculated dollars and cents. For example, in Littleton, Massachusetts, Charles Bulkeley's 1820s arithmetic workbook included the question: "If I am indebted 59 dollars 112 dollars 98 cents 113 dollars 19 cents 15 dollars 21 dollars 50 cents 200 dollars 73 dollars 35 dollars 17 cents 75 dollars 20 dollars 40 dollars 33 cents and 16 dollars What is the sum which I owe?" An identical problem appeared in thirteen-year-old Harriet Upham's arithmetic study book just a few years later. Popular texts like *The Child's Arithmetic* by Samuel Goodrich (who wrote as Peter Parley) and *Arithmetic Designed for Academies and Schools, (With Answers)* by Charles Davies also included Federal Money sections, but only described face-value paper money. Mathematics could explain what something should cost; it could not explain how many bank notes it would actually take to pay for it.[5]

Basic arithmetic and currency recognition were enough to participate in the paper money system, but to utilize bank notes without consistently losing money required specialized information. However, there was not one body of knowledge, but hundreds. Every transaction hinged on a new set of variables based on what bills were involved and their location. Monetary literacy first meant keeping track of the ever-changing state regulations that governed how bank notes could and could not be used across the nation. Dr. Nathaniel Ames of Dedham took notice when Massachusetts passed a law ending the issuance of private notes and bills under five dollars after April 10, 1805, under penalty of a fifty-dollar fine. That April morning, he wrote in his daybook that he had sent four dollar bills to "Boston to get changed this being the last day of their legal currency as money." Ames, a self-righteous justice of the peace and former court clerk, was a keen observer of legal minutiae, but not everyone had the time or ability to keep such a close watch on bank note rule changes.[6]

The most pressing issue for the public was determining whether a strange bank note presented to them was legitimate. Judging by the alarm expressed in periodicals, the fear of fake money permeated every transaction. Early in the century, Abel Brewster had asked, "Who can determine from a bill, which has not become familiar, whether it was lawfully or fraudulently issued, or of two bills nominally the same, but particularly different, which is genuine, or which is spurious?" It was impossible to have comprehensive knowledge of the vast numbers of bills in circulation, but there were publications that aided the community. *Hodges' New Bank Note Safe-Guard* provided "fac-simile descriptions of upwards of ten thousand bank notes embracing every genuine note issued in the United States & Canada." The guide contained a list of every note by bank and denomination, along with mini-diagrams of each bill, and a short description of each vignette. A quick glance shows that a five-dollar bill from the Northern Bank in Providence, Rhode Island, would have an image of a "Milkmaid, cow and calf" on the right and a depiction of "Dr. Kane and party in the Arctic Regions" on the left. This was not a fun read, but served as a reference, like a chart that shows the official design of driver's licenses from different states made for bartenders who want to spot a fake ID. *Sylvester's Bank Note and Exchange Manual* specialized in monetary information including a state-by-state list of "Insolvent Banks and Fraudulent Institutions" and a "Complete List of Counterfeit and Altered Notes." Such counterfeit detectors were not cure-alls. They contained visual cues that helped identify fakes, but professional counterfeiters used them as guides to subtly change their products and stay ahead of detection.[7]

Even if a counterfeit detector helped identify that a bill was from a lawful institution, it didn't guarantee that it was bankable. In 1842, one publication counted over 1,200 banks in the nation but listed more than 300 as "broken" so their notes could not be redeemed, 64 that were fraudulent, over 40 in the process of closing, 55 whose notes circulated at a 35 to 90 percent discount, and another 62 where the discount ranged between 2 and 20 percent. In total, only 52 (less than 5 percent) of the banks in the country had notes that traded at par in New York City. Bank note discounts varied widely based on numerous factors, but unless it came from the Bank of the United States (BUS), paper money did not circulate nationally at face value. So it was useful to determine that you held a legal five-dollar note from the Bank of River Raisin in Monroe, Michigan, but it was imperative to know that in November of 1839 in New York City that specific bill could only purchase $4.25 worth of dry goods. This was the central problem of a bank note system with numerous variables that determined value. Every time an American confronted a new bill they had to learn whether it was legal and its current discount off face value in their present location before they could move forward with any transaction of goods or services. This labor-intensive process required the accumulation and application of monetary information and ideally needed to be replicated for each and every bank note.[8]

The most common place to find current paper money prices was a bank note table. Bank note tables ran in nearly every major newspaper in the early republic and broadcast local discount rates on bills from across the country. The creation of simple tables was a necessity in a system with widely circulating, negotiable currency, but also had a colonial precedent. The *American Negotiator* provided merchants, grocers, and artisans exchange rates for a variety of British currencies; it was so popular that the 1765 subscriber list went on for over fifty pages. Along with coverage in major outlets, small newspapers and rural publications included bank note tables so that most Americans could access at least some monetary data before they used their bills or traveled to a nearby market. Seen as essential sources of information, even niche religious or antislavery periodicals like the *Christian Advocate* or *Signal of Liberty* regularly included bank note tables.[9]

Publications that specialized in monetary intelligence provided a valuable service, but also raised questions about the quality of their information and their impartiality. Robert Bicknell's *Counterfeit Detector and Bank Note List*, for example, began with an advertisement from Bicknell that directed country merchants who visited Philadelphia with uncurrent bills to stop by his office where he shaved notes. His promise that "his rates of discount, and his terms for transacting . . . are as low, and in many cases lower than those of any other Broker in the city" did not reassure readers about the prices on his list. Bank officials also worked the referees as they influenced editors of publications that printed exchange rates or other paper money intelligence. John Thompson, an exchange broker and the publisher of the *Bank Note Reporter*, recounted a conversation with a Captain Morgan who pleaded with him to list his previously broken Jacksonville Bank when he tried to revive it. Thompson's public refusal supposedly displayed his independence and honesty, but also highlighted the behind-the-scenes conversations related to the formulation of bank note tables. Overall, Americans found immense value in the tables even though not all bank note data was current and paper money men moved quickly to manipulate markets before the press and public could catch up. The difference between a little knowledge and no knowledge of bank note prices often provided the confidence needed to engage in market activities.[10]

Lists of current money market rates provided a momentary snapshot of trading value, but they did not guarantee the future value of a particular bill. Sometimes it was worth the risk to pocket a questionable bill in the hopes of better terms in the days to come. Likewise, notes from shuttered institutions might take on a life of their own and retain some value. Should an individual hang on to these zombie notes and wait for a bank revival or dump them as soon as possible to get some value for the bill? Such decisions occurred within a market where shavers continued to manipulate note values even after the death of a bank. *The Experiment*, a Norwalk, Ohio, newspaper, listed Bank of Michigan notes at an 80 percent discount on March 6, 1844. This was a poor offer, but given the fact that the Bank of Michigan had closed in 1842, the ability to get 20 percent of face value might have been a good option for someone who was stuck with the bills. Should Bank of Michigan holders have sold their notes at this price? Maybe not. A month later, the Chicago-based *Prairie Farmer* advertised that they would pay twenty-five cents on the dollar for "notes of the old Bank of Michigan." The editors even promised their readers that they would return them to the defunct bank immediately and not speculate on the bills. If holders missed the *Prairie Farmer* offer and lamented their chance to get rid of their Bank of Michigan notes, they were not out of luck. Three years after the bank closed, there were brokers in Ohio who still offered twenty cents on the dollar for the bills in the summer of 1845. These rock-bottom rates should have cleared the remaining Bank of Michigan notes out of circulation, but some lived on in other forms. The *Louisville Daily Courier* warned that counterfeiters altered Bank of Michigan bills to resemble those from the Bank of Xenia in Ohio and passed them in local markets. The dogged persistence of bank notes to circulate indefinitely was owed largely to the consistent shortage of currency in the economy, but it also forced the public to routinely update their monetary knowledge by whatever means available.[11]

Textbooks, counterfeit detectors, and bank note tables provided certain types of currency information, but nothing could replace the personal experience of life in the paper money world. When teenager Lucy Ann Ward traveled from her home in New England to Baltimore in 1815, she reported back to her parents that instead of silver dollars, she was "obliged to take little paper bills from one cent to an hundred." Seven-year-old Frederick W. Seward received his paper money education during the Panic of 1837 when specie circulation was limited. Instead of the usual change he collected for his "money-box," he received little pieces of paper that read "'Good for 5 cents,' or Good for sixpence,' or 'Good for 1 shilling,' and they bore the name of some merchant or tavern-keeper." The notes "seemed to pass from hand to hand as easily as other money," so he put one in his box for safekeeping. However, he learned from his grandfather that these were "shinplasters" that "might prove worthless any day," and the "only thing to do was to get rid of [them] as speedily as possible." He didn't fully appreciate the difference between the unregulated shinplasters and formal bank notes at the time, but Seward learned that a dollar was not always a dollar and that he should inspect his bills carefully and carry a healthy dose of skepticism into his paper money transactions.[12]

Did this monetary education work? It is difficult to quantify how much the general public knew about the quality of the bank notes in circulation, but one clue may come from how little context or explanation early republic writers employed when they satirized fraud and instability in the American economy. The humorist Mortimer Thomson offered such a moment when his titular character Doesticks visited Barnum's Museum in New York. When the doorman asked for a quarter to enter, Doesticks explained that he "necessitated to get a bill broke; offered him Washtenaw, but that was too effectually *broke* to suit his purpose." When he later sold patent medicine, Doesticks provided a testimonial of the time he applied his tonic "to the Washtenaw Bank after its failure, and while the Balsam lasted the Bank redeemed its notes with specie." The success of Thomson's jokes depended on his quick wit and a widespread understanding of the amazingly poor quality of Bank of Washtenaw notes. Founded in Michigan in 1835, the bank failed in 1839 only to be revived and fail for a second time in 1855. Within days of Thomson's publication of *Doesticks*, Washtenaw bills traded at a 60 percent discount in New York. The *New York Daily Times* explained that a Michigan judge enjoined the bank from corporate activities and the institution would finally close, "the sooner the better, as the victimized bill holders are anxiously waiting to learn how much they must pay to get rid of the notes in their possession." Readers did not need all these details to understand Thomson's Washtenaw jokes, but the satire only worked because the public possessed enough monetary information to make the bills universally suspect. While even small amounts of financial literacy would have alerted someone to guard against the notorious Bank of Washtenaw, the sheer volume of information needed to navigate the paper money economy meant a wide disparity in what the public knew and did not know. Professional paper money men wielded the most monetary knowledge, while other Americans tried to accumulate just enough data to not lose too much during paper currency negotiations. Not everyone succeeded.[13]

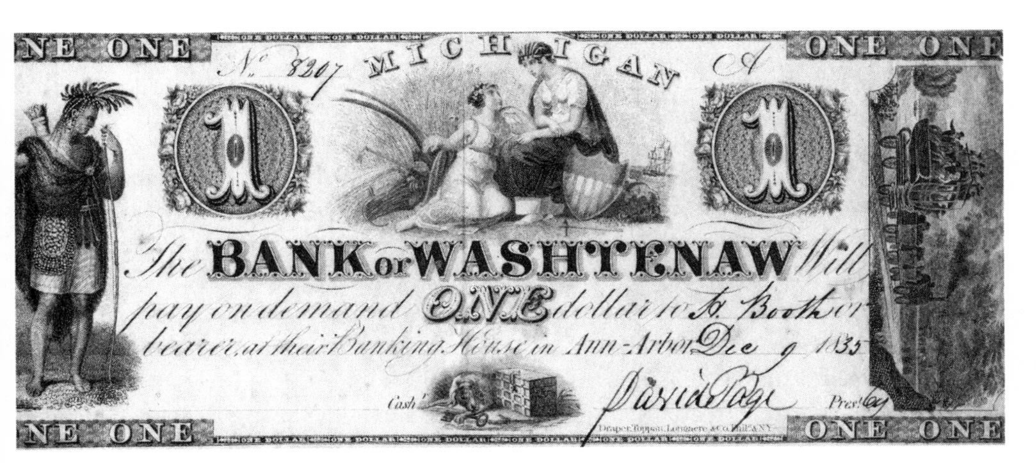

FIGURE 5. A note from the wildcat Bank of Washtenaw. It issued thousands of dollars in bills, but failed to redeem them. Author's collection.

Confidence men, who were quick to exploit gaps in the public's ability to judge what was authentic, utilized humbugs, mock auctions, or counterfeit goods to separate early republic Americans from good notes and pass them worthless scraps of paper. Robert Montgomery Bird's semi-autobiographical 1839 novel, *The Adventures of Robin Day*, details a standard bank note scam. Robin arrived in Philadelphia as a wide-eyed young man and quickly bumped a porter with a wheelbarrow into some pottery as the man whistled "Yankee Doodle." The pottery merchant demanded a dollar in payment for the broken bowls, so Robin handed over a five-dollar bill from a New Jersey bank to pay for the damage. The merchant declared that "New Jersey banks" only circulated in the city at a discount and "refused to receive it, unless I allowed him an additional half-dollar by way of premium." Robin was seemingly rescued when a Good Samaritan stepped in to explain that New Jersey notes actually circulated at par in Philadelphia and paid the merchant with a "dollar bill of some Philadelphia bank, and handing me four others as change." His momentary relief was shattered "about five minutes afterwards" when Robin learned that the "four bills given me by the good-natured stranger were counterfeit." The event was painful, but it was an important introduction to big-city life where trust could no more extend to a stranger than a strange note.[14]

Even if they were not targeted like Robin Day because of their inexperience with the system, foreign travelers quickly observed firsthand that a bank note's value was contingent on time, location, and confidence. One German visitor to a Broadway shop in 1833 didn't want to master the system; she just wanted to understand it. She explained that the "first thing I bought I was asked one dollar and fifty cents. I laid a bank note of two dollars on the counter. The shopkeeper immediately put it in his till, and went to attend [to] something else." The traveler eventually got back some change with the help of another customer, but it was not for the correct amount. Perplexed and disgusted, she left the store and only later came to understand that when she used a bank note, she needed to agree on the terms of the transaction (and preferably have a witness) before she handed over any cash. Perhaps she should have consulted James Kirke Paulding's 1828 guide for New York visitors entitled *The New Mirror for Travellers.* He suggested that new arrivals carry a "pocket book, well filled with bank notes," but explained that the quality of the notes did not matter. "Any money is good enough for travelling," he wrote, "if one wont take it another will, Dont be discouraged at one refusal—try it again." Eventually, someone would accept any bank note, especially "if you are well dressed." Frazzled foreign customers might not have gotten Paulding's sarcastic tone, but his analysis about the bank notes was insightful.[15]

Paulding, a collaborator of Washington Irving and later secretary of the navy, was not a foreign visitor, but often used travel writing to probe American culture. His previously mentioned *History of a Little Frenchman and His Bank Notes: "Rags! Rags! Rags!"* explained how geographic mobility offered both a crisis and an opportunity for travelers who tried to navigate the paper money system. As the Frenchman headed to Boston from Savannah, he entered one ill-fated currency transaction after another as he learned which bills would pass and which would not. At one point he paid a carriage turnpike toll with a twenty-five-cent note he had obtained from a steamship captain only to be rebuffed by the driver who "pointed his whip to a little brook about three hundred yards behind, and mentioned they did not pass beyond that, northward." The traveler's lack of financial knowledge consistently put him on the wrong side of asymmetric negotiations. The problem was that he received all notes equally "not understanding the distinction made by a discerning publick." The Frenchman did not bring the same experience to paper money transactions as the domestic population, so he lacked the skill to judge a note's worth and negotiate a

FIGURE 6. Shinplasters from turnpike companies or hotels with geographically limited circulations confounded foreign and domestic travelers alike. Author's collection.

good deal. However, all was not lost for the little Frenchman; he learned from a friend in Boston that he could make back his lost money if he used his seemingly worthless rags and his new pecuniary knowledge to go "shaving his way back to Savannah." Mobility and a little experience offered him redemption and a chance to reset the value of his currency.[16]

Access to specific monetary knowledge could be used to one's advantage, but financial resources and opportunity did not always help in paper money dealings. The physician Nathaniel Saltonstall and his attorney/politician son Leverett came from one of Massachusetts's leading families and while they were not bankers, they occupied positions where they could leverage their social connections to negotiate preferential bank rates. However, when a crisis hit the New England money market after the collapse of Andrew Dexter Jr.'s banking empire in 1809, even the Saltonstalls scrambled. Nathaniel owned property in Boston and gave Leverett precise instructions for how to collect the rent. He wrote that tenants should "pay in Boston Money. They must, as the fluctuating State of Country Banks is a sufficient reason for refusing them for rent. In the last payment for rent in Country Bills, I lost several Dollrs. by counterfeits. . . . I must have Boston Money."[17]

This was not a one-time problem. When William Minot later collected rent for Nathaniel, he reported that a Mr. Joseph Bright "offered me foreign [out-of-state] money which I refused, and says he can pay Boston money next week. There is some excuse for Bright, this time, money is very scarce and Boston money bears a premium of 2½ per Cent. Next week I presume I shall be able to collect his rent." Leverett had paper money problems of his own. He wrote to Minot that "we have great alarm here on account of the reported depreciation of Berkshire Bank bills this morning. Every body is counting his money with terror." There was a difference between the ability to obtain sophisticated knowledge of the money market and the opportunity to wield that information to profit. The Saltonstalls' access to monetary intelligence and resources outpaced most in the economy, but even they did not escape the complex reality of the bank note system.[18]

For people without personal financial resources, the uncertain paper money market was even more difficult to navigate. A series of articles by muckraking journalist George Lippard explored how a succession of Philadelphia bank runs in 1842 affected the city's journeymen artisans. Outside a shuttered institution, a "hard working mechanic stood silent and alone, fingering the valueless notes which he held in his hand." Lippard later suggested that the crowd should oppose their worthless, "greasy notes" and look to the Cincinnati bank riots as a model. Notes were still circulating on the second day of crowd activity, so when a "big Irishman" showed up to redeem ten dollars in "d—d rotten money which I got last night," he was distraught because he could not make them bankable, especially with his "children at home without food to eat or fire to warm 'em." Lippard wrote about another journeyman who accused his boss of collusion with corrupt bankers. The journeyman exclaimed, "Here is all that's left of the money I got from my employer last night, He gave me three dollars in Moyamensing notes, and I had to go and trade 'em off for two in specie." His boss was not a bank director, but he "used to git fat discounts in this neighborhood of Second and Chestnut. Howsomever, they made out to diddle me out of a dollar d—n 'em." The problem for these artisans was that their monetary information did not necessarily result in advantageous negotiations because they did not have the leverage in their personal transactions to avoid uncurrent notes.[19]

Journeymen often confronted the problem of bad money in the workplace. One cabinetmaker explained that his employer obtained cheap, uncurrent bank notes from a broker and then boasted that his weekly savings of three to six dollars on the workers' wages was enough for his "pocket money during the ensuing week." When his boss heard that there were massive discounts on Washington and Warren Bank notes, he bought up $200 worth of them and paid his employees the following Saturday night. The artisans soon learned that no one in town would accept the bills; however, they could not "take any legal measures to compel him to make good their loss . . . lest he might discharge them from his employ." Given what their bosses' actions demonstrated about their lack of power in the workplace, it was no surprise that labor activists cited paper money as one of the main sources of hardship for artisans. In the *Mechanics Free Press*, "Justice" championed Philadelphia's trade unions because he believed that collective organization gave workers "the power of refusing to take bank notes for labour." A compatriot called for laborers to "refuse bank notes . . . when our employers cheat us." Workers who received bad bills as pay had to decide whether to protest against the quality (not just the quantity) of their wages or keep their jobs.[20]

Independent craftsmen did not have employers, but they faced the hassle and imposition of daily negotiations with customers over whether and how fees would be paid in bank notes. A shoemaker with "some doubt as to the goodness of the note" he was offered in payment immediately traveled to a broker who verified that the note was good, albeit at a 12.5 percent discount. He then went back to the customer to get the note, only to return to the broker who gave him $4.37½ in silver for the five-dollar bill. If even a few sales a day required such steps, it certainly put a damper on business transactions. Butchers who operated in high-volume public markets had to stay vigilant for problem notes. During the Panic of 1819, a New York butchers' group met to discuss the poor value of certain bills in circulation around the city. They resolved to "receive no country bank notes that are below par in New-York" and implored others for the "prosperity of the city and the protection of the poor" not to accept the discounted notes. This was not a new issue for the butchers. At a meeting two years earlier, they had cited "depreciated bank paper" as one of the "principal causes" of "the extreme injury of the butchers and citizens, and more especially the poorer and uninformed, who are constantly suffering by the receiving of bank notes, without means of information with respect to their current value." Rather than advice to avoid paper money entirely, the butchers' prescription contained specific geographical insight. They asked the public "to reject all the Banks north of Newburgh whose paper is not at par at the Banks in New-York." Reliant on good paper money for their shops to survive, the butchers' shared monetary knowledge with the public in hopes that the information would circulate to their customers and that the local money market would improve for everyone.[21]

No matter how much monetary information they possessed, farmers located away from banking centers routinely complained about not having access to paper money other than uncurrent bank notes. An ongoing discussion in the *Prairie Farmer* focused on farmers' unique difficulties when only "depreciated currency" was available and they had to deal with distant merchants. The newspaper called for farmers to form associations and sign a pledge to "*take nothing in payment for their produce but specie, the notes of a specie paying bank, or U.S. Treasury notes.*" Such pledges did not produce lasting results because farmers needed to sell their produce in a timely manner and could not wait out buyers with more flexibility to come around to their currency demands.[22]

Poor-quality notes did not just cause trouble for farmers in their role as sellers; bad bills rippled through the economy as they moved from consumers to suppliers to producers and back again. Farming communities without good paper money hampered the efforts of peddlers like backcountry book traders early in the century. Ministers who worked with publisher William Woodward to sell religious books on the frontier had to decide whether to accept uncurrent bank notes that would not circulate at par back in Woodward's home in Philadelphia or not make a sale at all. If they sold to farm families for currency at too great a discount, the traveling-sales ministers would not be able to pay off the expense of the books and would end up in debt to the publisher.[23]

The longer the supply lines between customers, resellers, and producers, the more complicated was the role of bank notes in facilitating trade. A Kentucky merchant, Christian Shultz, ordered copper and tin from the Philadelphia firm of Nathan Trotter & Co. for resale to his farming customers, but the weak buying power of Kentucky bank notes between 1818 and 1821 meant that he could not easily pay for the shipments. Schultz explained that what little cash he had was under par and that he "could not now Purchase Eastern funds for Less than 55 or 60 per Ct Advance." Even when he got his hands on $800 specifically to pay his bills, he sat on the money because it was Kentucky "common wealth Paper" that would not pass in Philadelphia. Since bank notes lost value as they moved around the country, anyone who bought or sold for paper money over long distances had to figure the cost of fluctuating currency values as an integral part of their estimation of what was a profitable deal.[24]

Businesses that conducted operations across state lines, rather than in face-to-face negotiations with customers, adopted strategies to successfully navigate a paper money system where distance equaled a discount in value. This was a persistent problem for newspaper and magazine publishers who sought new readers from across the country. Orville Taylor, the editor of the Albany-based *Common School Assistant*, informed subscribers that while current bank notes would be accepted for the paper, "'Shin-plasters' have been sent from Tennessee, Maryland, Pennsylvania, &c. They are entirely useless to us." He explained that even posted fifty-cent pieces were "preferable to bank notes from the extreme south and west." Religious periodicals like the Utica-based *Evangelical Magazine and Gospel Advocate* also took the time to describe their payment terms for subscribers. The editor, Dolphus Skinner, suggested that readers who did not live near an agent should join with a neighbor and send in a "$3 bill—it will pay in advance for two copies." He added that if readers "live in a State where bank notes do not circulate of a less denomination than $5. let them send us by mail, securely enclosed a five-dollar bank note, and it will pay for the present and two next volumes." Such advice made good economic sense for the newspaper and provided a way to morally conduct business within the complicated hodgepodge of national currency regulations.[25]

It was not just religious publications that encountered bad money; charitable groups that relied on paper money donations spent precious time and resources to reconcile the effect of discounted bank notes on their operating budgets. Annual financial reports by Herman Lincoln, the Baptists' General Missionary Convention treasurer, explained that the organization lost 3 percent of one $150 donation because it was made in out-of-state bills and needed to be exchanged into New York funds. Lincoln's records showed other losses for "exchanging uncurrent money," "uncurrent money, 2 per cent," a "counterfeit bill received in New York," "a two dollar bill bad money," "Four per cent. discount on 50 dollars Georgia money," and a variety of other transactions to make the organization's money bankable in New York. Such problems were nondenominational. When the Princeton Theological Seminary hired an agent to travel around the country to raise funds in March 1824, they paid him $20, but also accounted for a "discount on Southern notes" that reduced his received pledges by $5.74. None of this was unique to these institutions. Any person or organization that engaged in the market economy and used bank notes had to reconcile the difference between how a system of face-value currency was supposed to function and how the paper money system comprised of bills with rapidly fluctuating prices actually worked in real time.[26]

These examples of predominantly white, male craftsmen, merchants, farmers, and religious leaders who navigated bank note transactions demonstrate that wavering paper currency values and the asymmetry of monetary information made each business deal a potentially fraught moment. However, financial knowledge and geographical location were not the only factors that determined a bill's purchasing power. Who handed over a bank note could be just as important as what was in their hand. Bank note negotiations took place between human beings, and the positions they occupied in society inherently affected the outcome of their conversations over value. The political, social, and cultural power of individuals who participated in bank note transactions mattered.

Perhaps the greatest political imbalance for most Americans came when they dealt with the government; bank note transactions with the state required a different set of strategies than a negotiation with other producers or consumers in the economy. Early republic Americans' primary interactions with the federal government came through their daily dealings with the mail. Bank notes flowed in and out of post offices, so when northern Illinois mail clerks began to dispense notes from the Bank of the City of Washington as change and wages for mail contractors in the fall of 1833, the community suddenly had to deal with a glut of out-of-state notes. Local merchants had "not only no knowledge, but [were] utterly ignorant even of the existence of this favored institution," so they refused to accept the bills and forced noteholders to send the cash to St. Louis and pay a 4 or 5 percent discount to convert them to local money.[27]

At other times, post office regulations determined what notes could be accepted as payment. When the Washington correspondent of the *Commercial Advertiser* picked up his mail on January 23, 1834, he discovered that he could only pay with his "U.S. Bank fives" because of a new rule that refused all "New York city Bank notes, pets and all." There was some irony that during the height of the Bank War, an order from Andrew Jackson's postmaster general, William Barry, restricted state bank note usage and forced the reporter to use Bank of the United States (BUS) notes. The ban even prevented customers from using notes from the pet banks specifically chosen by the Jackson administration as the destination of government deposits when it turned against the central bank.[28]

Andrew Jackson's attempts to overhaul the use of paper money in government transactions raised similar complications for government workers' wages. New regulations in the summer of 1834 required that "no payments shall be made in bank notes that are not at par value at the places where payment is made," but that was not the case when the crew of the USS *Lexington* docked in Portsmouth, New Hampshire. *Niles' Weekly Register* reported that the sailors received "bills of banks in the extreme parts of N. York, and of the bank of Michigan, which they were compelled to make sale of, at 2 or 3 per cent. dis. before they could buy 'even a glass of grog.' " The public relations problem of sailors being prevented from buying liquor led Isaac Waldron, the president of the Commercial Bank of Portsmouth, to protest that the crew was actually paid in current paper. Soldiers and sailors routinely faced such complications with their wages. The crew of the USS *Peacock* unfortunately returned from their three-year cruise during the Panic of 1837 and could only receive their back pay in Virginia bank notes. Given that the notes did not "pass at par in Philadelphia or New York," the sailors asked for a portion in gold or silver, but they were "told that the government had provided no commodity to pay with." Under the title "The People's Currency," the press recounted the story of the honorable man who stuffed "his shinplasters into his fob, and sallied forth to find some accommodating Shylock to convert them into specie, upon his own terms." The sailors' treatment was due to macroeconomic conditions rather than anything personal, but the men could not help but feel disrespected at their loss of pay.[29]

Geography also disrupted government attempts to streamline and rationalize its bank note operations. In 1840, Secretary of the Treasury Levi Woodbury asked every federal disbursing agent across the country to report on how they received and made their payments. Aside from the obvious notice to guard against counterfeits, he warned against "the notes of banks not at par, or not convertible into specie on the spot, or not issued by institutions of high credit." Likewise, he issued a reminder that, as required by an 1836 law, federal agents were "not to pay out any bank note under twenty dollars, and which is not redeemable in specie, and equivalent to it at the place where offered in payment." And if they did accept bank notes they should make those notes the first to be paid out.[30]

The reports filed by the agents highlight how local monetary conditions and personal whim dictated transactions between early republic citizens and their government. Thomas Forster, the Office of Public Works agent in

Cattaraugus Creek, New York, conducted business though the Silver Creek Bank and explained that "the bank is considered as safe and solvent as any in western New York, and always pays specie for its notes on presentation." Likewise, Lieutenant D. H. McPhail, the acting assistant quartermaster at Cantonment Atkinson in Lake Charles, declared that his only paper money payments were five twenty-dollar bills from the Bank of the State of Missouri when he could not find change. It is hard to determine exactly how much purchasing power the notes had in rural southwestern Louisiana in 1840, but even locally in Missouri they circulated at between 3 and 3.5 percent off face value. The situation was considerably worse in Detroit where customs collector John McDonell had no better option than to make payments in notes on the "Bank of Michigan, and Farmers and Mechanics' Bank of Michigan, and the banks of Upper Canada." However, the first two had suspended specie redemption and their notes traded at an 8 to 10 percent discount, while the notes from Canada were discounted at 4 to 5 percent.[31]

Even if the agents who paid them out only did so once or twice, transactions using uncurrent bank notes came at great expense to Americans who conducted business with the federal government, as well as to the Treasury Department's bottom line. A separate report by Secretary Woodbury figured government losses prior to 1837 due to depreciated bank notes at $5.5 million. He estimated that the public lost $66.5 million from bank note discounts during the financial downturn that began with the Panic of 1837 and ended as the economy recovered in 1841. The accuracy of Woodbury's report is debatable—he calculated the figures based on the total face value of bills in circulation and the estimated effect when banks stopped redemption without any consideration for the profit made by members of the community on these paper money value fluctuations—but his larger point was important. The American people and their government lost a considerable amount of wealth merely because they conducted business in paper money that did not always retain its face value.[32]

It was difficult enough for citizens to deal with the government, but the process became more complicated and unjust when mediated through Native American treaties. The Cherokee Nation might have been promised almost $10,000 in yearly annuities, but treaties left the form of payment up to local Indian agents. During the Panic of 1819, agent Return J. Meigs paid the annuity in Tennessee, Georgia, and Alabama bank notes. Since the Cherokee Nation bordered four states across the Southeast, it was imperative for them to utilize currency that moved seamlessly across vast distances without losing purchasing power. The Cherokee national treasurer Charles Hicks immediately realized that if he accepted the notes, it would mean a compromise of the annuity's value. Hicks protested to Meigs that he could not believe that the federal government would "wish the Nation should be paid in bad money," so subsequent annuities must be paid in specie or universally accepted bills from the BUS. But the state bank notes kept coming. Thomas C. Hindman took over as sub-agent in 1821 and pocketed $2,800 when he converted nearly $19,000 in federal drafts into uncurrent bank notes which he used to pay the Cherokee and run his office. Broken promises and government turnover led to the assignment of a new agent, Hugh Montgomery, who offered to pay the annuity in North Carolina notes from the Bank of Newbern and Bank of Cape Fear which circulated in Georgia at a 5 percent discount. The problem remained unresolved despite Charles Hicks's yearly protests when the annuity arrived in subpar notes. As late as 1830, the *Cherokee Phoenix* eagerly reported that North Carolina bank notes finally traded "on a par with the United States' Bank notes" after a long circulation at a discount. Currency issues were not the primary complaint lodged by the Cherokee, but they were a persistent reminder of how the United States government used its power in the 1820s and 1830s.[33]

Conflicts over bank notes and annuity payments also plagued the Sac and Fox. It is unclear which specific bank notes agent Marmaduke S. Davenport dispersed in August 1834, but within months both nations made formal protests about their $20,000 annuities to the federal government. In memorials sent to Congress, "about four hundred and fifty Sac and Fox Indians" objected that their chiefs traveled to "Saint Louis, which is about 250 miles from our villages, and 200 from the nearest part of our country" and "were there required by our great father's agent to sign a receipt for the same, which was *all* paid in *bank notes* (a thing unheard of before in the payment of our annuities)." There were multiple layers to this criticism. Tribal members understood that bank notes from distant institutions would not retain their face value after the chiefs brought the bills home from hundreds of miles to the south. No chartered banks existed in Missouri in 1834, so the bills most likely did not even circulate at par in St. Louis. The memorials also charged that the annuities had been paid entirely to Sac chief Keokuk, who quickly handed them over to the American Fur Company. Such criticism coincided with Keokuk's reputation among some tribal members for being too cooperative with government interests. Congressional debate overlooked this nuance as Representative John Reynolds of Illinois, a veteran of Black Hawk's War, used the memorials to claim that the Sac and Fox complaints about the annuity structure revealed hidden demands for individual payments made outside of the tribal system.[34]

The tension over annuity payments did not disappear among the Sac and Fox and their understanding of the relationship between distance, timing, and circumstance in paper money transactions altered the debate just a few years later. When a delegation led by Keokuk arrived in St. Louis to receive the annuity during the height of the Panic of 1837, its members volunteered to be more flexible with government payments. Keokuk reportedly "expressed a willingness to receive *bank notes*, or any thing else which could be paid to their creditors, in the discharge, of their debts." Even though the Sac and Fox resided on the northwestern frontier, they brought to their annuity discussions a sophisticated knowledge of financial relations with the government and a familiarity with the current money market dislocation. This mattered because it reinforced the notion that negotiations between Native Americans and the government hinged on power and authority dynamics rather than a lack of economic understanding.[35]

As Keokuk's actions suggested, financial information and demographic and cultural realities collided during early republic paper money transactions. When African Americans utilized bank notes, they needed to delicately decide when to employ monetary knowledge for advancement or liberation and when to cautiously guard against charges of fraud and imposture. Currency transactions between African Americans and whites were particularly fraught when they involved unfree men and women. Whether as buyers or sellers of their own goods and services or on behalf of slaveholders, enslaved individuals routinely used bank notes during the antebellum period. These exchanges could be sanctioned or illicit given local regulations, which created another complication for any currency negotiations that occurred as part of the deal. Such market interactions in South Carolina grew after the Panic of 1837, when slaveholders' dedication to cotton production led them to significantly shift subsistence activities onto enslaved people. In 1858 alone, James Sparkman purchased crops, hogs, and sugar molasses worth hundreds of dollars from unfree men and women on his own planation. Such scenarios became widespread in these years as an increase in enslaved individuals' market activity meant both a growing familiarity with cash and an inability to engage in certain slave-quarter activities without it.[36]

When they dealt with slaveholders, illicit traders, or professional shopkeepers in bank note negotiations, enslaved African Americans simultaneously utilized their monetary knowledge to achieve beneficial terms and guarded against attempts to have their paper money's quality questioned because of their status. Charles Ball, who escaped from a plantation in Maryland, explained that he preferred to spend his hard-earned paper money in country stores. He could get good rates because "storekeepers are always ready to accommodate the slaves, who pay cash, whilst the white people require credit." When exchanges occurred in less formal settings, increased opportunity existed for race and power to influence currency negotiations. Extensive, albeit sometimes illicit, trade between enslaved men and women and poor whites occurred in the Carolinas, but whether in goods or money, poor whites held an advantage during negotiations. This meant ten cents' worth of molasses might be obtained for twenty-five cents' worth of corn or produce paid for with an out-of-state, uncurrent bank note at face value. Questions about confidence always came up when someone passed an out-of-state bill, but the tension heightened when racial superiority and currency exchanges came together. In March 1838, slaveholder John Blackford sold a stick of timber to a Mr. Brinn for his forge in Washington County, Maryland, but it was paid for by "Negroe Peter," who Brinn had sent to pay the $4.50 bill. Blackford's statement that Peter "gave me a very suspicious looking note of the Lancaster Bank of Ohio" raised immediate questions about how much his reaction depended on the quality of the bill and how much it was a reaction to Peter.[37]

Even possession of a questionable bank note was more dangerous for enslaved men and women than for southern whites. When Jim from Camden, South Carolina, paid Mary Cunningham for a night of boarding with a two-dollar bill from the Bank of Cape Fear, she questioned him about how he had obtained the note. It is uncertain how much of this scrutiny was owed to Jim's race and how much to the poor reputation that Cape Fear Bank notes carried in 1822. There had been a rash of counterfeits on the bank up and down the Eastern Seaboard and even legitimate bills from the bank carried a discount outside of North Carolina. Ultimately, Cunningham was comfortable enough with Jim's answers to use the bill herself at a local butcher shop. The Bank of Cape Fear note circulated through town until it arrived at John B. Merges's store. Merges and his clerk, Samuel Saul, claimed to recognize the bank note from its markings as one that had been stolen from them. Jim was arrested, tried, and eventually executed, but Mary Cunningham was not charged for her part in passing the note. Whether Jim had stolen the paper money or was used as an example to the local enslaved population to police their economic activity in the immediate aftermath of the Denmark Vesey conspiracy was unclear, but the trial and excessive punishment did not follow usual practice. Evidently, the mere possession of a questionable note could be enough to prove guilt for an enslaved man.[38]

Paper money became instrumental for enslaved individuals' daily exchanges, but also played a complicated role in wider questions of slavery and freedom. The growth of southern banks and their creation of credit through bank notes and other paper financial devices enabled more investment in slavery. Much of the $4 million in bank notes circulated by the Bank of Louisiana, for example, was spent on plantation real estate and enslaved men and women. Antebellum slave traders likewise maximized their profits when they collected financial information on cotton markets and consumer confidence and adjusted their market activities accordingly. These men combined northern and southern banking information to develop travel routes that allowed them to profit from the differences in regional money market rates. At certain times, this meant the indiscriminate purchase of as many individuals as possible at auction in order to dispose of uncurrent bank notes.[39]

In the face of slaveholders and traders who maximized paper credit to expand the institution of slavery, individual men and women found ways to utilize bank notes as tools of liberation. Using paper money to purchase freedom meant both the deployment of saved cash and the employment of knowledge about the bank note system. Newly emancipated Solomon Bayley arranged the "purchase of my wife" in 1799 while he reconciled the currency vagaries on the Delmarva Peninsula. From his home in Delaware, he negotiated a payment of "one hundred and three dollars and a third, which is thirty one pounds Virginia money." Five decades later, Albert Coleman obtained the "permission to buy my freedom" from John Mitchel of Mason County, Kentucky, for $900, but could not easily save the cash in the days before the Civil War. He later remembered that he "had some shinplasters, but not enough, so after the war broke out I sked[da]dled and enlisted." Paper money proved vital for runaways like Coleman.[40]

The ability to properly utilize paper money was an important component for some individuals as they escaped north. Escapees obtained bank notes to pay travel expenses or sought them as part of the performance of freedom while on the move. Henry Bibb escaped during the winter of 1837 when currency conditions on the ground complicated his movements. He traveled from Trimble County, Kentucky, to Ohio, but only carried a small amount of change to pay for food and lodging on his way to Canada. An attempt to stay in a tavern backfired because this was "about the time that the 'wild-cat banks' were in a flourishing state, and 'shin plasters' in abundance" and he did not have any locally circulating paper money. Some quick thinking exhibited his comprehension of the money market and got him through the night. Bibb's ability to demonstrate his familiarity with bank notes and remark on the convoluted currency system is an example of how he fashioned his identity through the manipulation of his possessions. Along with clothing, jewelry, and other material goods, bank notes served as conspicuous tools to display one's identity as a free, rather than enslaved, individual during an escape.[41]

However, items used for self-fashioning could subsequently be targeted in runaway slave advertisements that tied material objects to the identification of escapees. Unlike ads that described a runaway's clothing, mentions of paper money usually doubled as accusations that labeled escapees as thieves. In 1794, one announcement that sought "a mulatto fellow named Ben" stressed that "he stole a pocket book containing 180 dollars in the paper of the bank of the United States at Philadelphia." This identified Ben not only by his appearance but also by the amount and type of bank notes in his possession. An advertisement with even more detail described John Allen, who was accused of "having stolen immediately before his departure between three and four hundred dollars in five- and ten-dollar notes of the Bank of Alexandria, Farmer's Bank of Alexandria, and United States Branch Bank at Washington." A notice entitled "STOP THE THIEF" listed few specifics about Ben, an escaped barber from Cape Fear, but offered precise details about the money he carried: "one ten dollar bill, bank not recollected; two five dollar bills, W. B. State Bank . . . two dollar bill, Cape-Fear, torn from one end almost to the other, and two single dollar bills, in all twenty-four dollars." Such advertisements highlighted the contradictory nature of bank note usage among African American escapees; confident participation in the cash market both demonstrated freedom and simultaneously made some whites more suspicious of one's behavior.[42]

Liberation from bondage did not ease the difficulties of currency negotiations. Even among free northern populations, African Americans constantly fought against expectations that they did not understand the bank note economy or their place in it. The community's response was to promote its monetary knowledge. *Freedom's Journal*, the first African American newspaper, alerted its readers in October 1828 to a case of "gross villany" that occurred when a New York "sharper" bought a dollar bag of chestnuts from a country vendor. The seller accepted a five-dollar bill for the nuts "without examining it minutely" and returned four dollars in paper money as change. The text of the note, reprinted in the article, read: "The Derby Bank promises to pay at the FULTON BANK in the city of NEW YORK five dollars." Given the size and boldness of the print, the bill was easily mistaken as hailing from the Fulton Bank and not from the Derby Bank in Connecticut which went bankrupt in 1825. The anecdote reminded *Freedom's Journal* readers to examine their bank notes closely, be wary of paper currency transactions, and recognize that bills from shuttered institutions still circulated years later. The warning about the Derby Bank note was useful, but it did not address the unique challenges of African Americans who tried to navigate the city's paper money economy.[43]

Whenever African American proprietors or customers entered into bank note negotiations with white individuals, racialized expectations further charged already tense moments when questions about trust and confidence determined value. Numerous cases in New York City's indictment papers reveal how simple exchanges devolved into dispute or even violence due to a mixture of racist animus and contested currency negotiation. The paper money was not necessarily the cause of these disagreements, but the combination of racial and monetary tension made each transaction potentially combustible. In one case, William Dunbar paid Aaron Jacobs for a meal with a suspect three-dollar bill. Jacobs claimed it was from a broken bank and refused to accept it or return the note to Dunbar, who attempted, unsuccessfully, to shoot Jacobs with a pistol. Was the attempted murder based on the fact that Aaron Jacobs was African American or was Dunbar's reaction largely a drunken response to being caught passing an illegal note? Conversely, was African American Phillip Boon singled out when he tried to pass a three-dollar bill from the Stillwater Canal Bank of Orono, Maine, because the bank had failed the previous year or was his arrest part of a regular crackdown on potential counterfeiters?[44]

While they were no more likely to pass counterfeit notes than other demographic groups, African Americans often encountered questions about their knowledge of the paper money in their possession. Some confidence men played on the racial stereotype to develop a method of "burning" others when they used bank note system complexity and some audacious risk taking to manipulate changing a bill into an opportunity for theft. The scheme generally featured African Americans who offered to change bank notes and then made a quick getaway once they had obtained the mark's funds. Different versions of the con existed. In one tragic example, four African American men in Saint Louis accidentally killed a young man during a robbery attempt. They had entered a paper money counting house after hours to ask if the clerk could check the "validity of a Bank note." While he was preoccupied with the bill, one robber struck the clerk in the head with an iron bar and beat him until he died. Whatever the specifics, each manifestation of burning played on racial stereotypes and hinged on confounding white expectations of African Americans' monetary knowledge. Burners deployed their insight about paper money transactions and upended social roles when they surprised their targets, quickly stole their money, and disrupted their notion of African Americans.[45]

Paper money confidence schemes worked because bank note negotiations both reinforced power dynamics and provided an opportunity to alter social relationships between the parties involved. This was especially the case for gender relations. There were not too many public forums in the early republic where men and women who might be complete strangers entered into intimate face-to-face discussions. Single-sex monetary transactions might have involved the same bank notes as those between men and women, but such exchanges were not the same. Just as in other aspects of the economy, sex and gender mattered as participants engaged in currency trades. This was not a new phenomenon in the early republic. Even as colonial models of currency and political economy gave way to new institutions, gender and race helped order how money was used and understood. The types of paper money in circulation changed with the adoption of state banking, but women who bought or sold goods for cash remained integral to market relations while they constantly fought to ensure that their monetary knowledge was not disregarded.[46]

Women's use of paper money permeated American culture; historical and sentimental novels reinforced the centrality of bank notes to women's economic activities. In a pivotal moment in Catherine Maria Sedgwick's religious Cinderella fable, *A New-England Tale*, Mrs. Wilson, the wicked aunt, enters a shop in her rural town to pay a small debt. After she intently inspects one of the bank notes she is given as change, the shop owner explains that he believes "that it is a good bill" even though he "was a little suspicious of it too at first." The note had come to the store from Mrs. Wilson's son David, who had stolen it from his mother and used it to pay off a debt earlier that day. Mrs. Wilson's consternation came from the fact that she "recognized this bill the moment she saw it, as one of the parcel she had received the day before, and which she had marked, at the time, for she was eagle-eyed in the detection of a spurious bill." The scene highlights two characters: a male shopkeeper and a housewife who both have intimate knowledge and discrete opinions about a particular bank note that is circulating in their small town. While their relationship to the note is quite different—the shopkeeper doesn't really care about it even as it reveals important plot points to Mrs. Wilson—Sedgwick's story places a housewife in the middle of a bank note transaction as an expected and natural part of her daily activities without any further explanation or exposition about the finer points of monetary policy.[47]

Caroline Kirkland's *A New Home—Who'll Follow?* provides a more direct economic analysis through her firsthand explanation of wildcat banking on the Michigan frontier. She referred to these institutions as a "fungous growth" and argued that the term "Wild Cat" was "justified fully by the course of these cunning and stealthy bloodsuckers; more fatal in their treacherous spring than ever was their forest prototype." She provided the example of the "beautifully engraved bills" of the "Merchants' and Manufacturers' Bank of Tinkerville" that were supposedly "better than gold or silver, because they were lighter in the pocket" and backed by a row of heavy boxes in their vault. In reality, the bank officers deceived the Michigan Bank Commissioners and townspeople alike; the boxes in the vault only "contained a heavy charge of broken glass and tenpenny nails, covered above and below with half-dollars." The community was ruined. Kirkland's deft economic critique reminded readers that familiarity with and integration into the bank note economy in no way shielded women from the pitfalls of paper currency transactions.[48]

Some female noteholders learned that having a little bit of erroneous financial knowledge could be just as dangerous as having none. George Lippard reported on an elderly widow who became distraught when she learned that a bank run on the Manufacturers' and Mechanics' Bank in Philadelphia had made her twenty-dollar bill worthless. A few weeks earlier, she had converted all her money into notes from that bank because, she said, "[I had] heard a good deal about the banks being bad, but I thought this bank couldn't but be good, for Mr. Hunt, the President, belongs to our church, and sings and prays with us each Sunday." In this case, the widow had accumulated monetary information and taken a proactive step to protect her vital funds. Unfortunately, it turned out to be the wrong decision based on her trust in a banker's morality.[49]

Female employees paid with paper money should have earned some economic independence, but for live-in domestic servants, the nature of their work compromised their market leverage. The servants not only received little cash because they boarded with their employers; they also faced longer pay cycles that subjected their discounted paper money to the whims of expedited monetary velocity. If they wanted to save up for a large purchase, it meant holding on to individual bank notes for extended periods of time, which posed a danger when their bills did not maintain their value. One "hard working woman" from Baltimore complained that she had saved nine dollars in shinplasters, "every cent of which now proves to be worth nothing!" Such travails eventually pushed Irish domestic servants to utilize savings banks at significantly high rates even though those institutions tightly limited access to one's own funds. By one measure, female Irish domestic servants accounted for one-third of all depositors in New York City's Emigrant Industrial Savings Bank.[50]

As producers and consumers, women navigated an often unjust market while they deployed accumulated monetary knowledge. When Mary Marshall sold thirty dollars' worth of "tongues, ham, &c." to Charles Tozer at her shop in New York's Fulton Market, he paid with notes from the nonexistent "Jefferson Banking Company of Vermont." When Tozer returned to Marshall's shop, he promised to replace the fake notes with "good money," but after she handed back the Jefferson notes, he "immediately tore the bills into pieces and threw them into the stove of the store." Marshall picked up the shreds from the unlit stove and enlisted the police to arrest Tozer. Tozer was a serial swindler, but his overconfidence in returning to the scene of the crime at Marshall's shop and his brazen attempt to destroy the bills right in front of her stemmed from his expectation that she would not offer resistance.[51]

What about when the roles were reversed? The controversial relationship between female shoppers and male salesmen in antebellum dry goods stores ranged from sensual to antagonistic as youthful "counter jumpers" enticed middle-class women to part with their money. Bank notes sometimes became a source of friction during the transactions. The sporting newspaper *The Rake* sarcastically called out one clerk "who told a lady, in the most courteous manner, to go to H-ll, because she refused to take [as change] a five dollar bill worth some sixty cents on a dollar." Dry goods stores catered to female customers; they also created a new contested space where men and women came together in intimate exchanges that tested their financial acumen. The anecdote showed that it did not always go smoothly.[52]

The urban landscape offered endless occasions to use paper money and a corresponding number of possible outcomes based on the quality of the bills and the attitude of the person on the other side of the transaction. One final example of how gender roles and monetary knowledge came together during a bank note exchange involved a female Brooklynite who ran into trouble with the toll taker on a ferry trip to Manhattan. She did not have any change, so she offered a one-dollar bill to pay for the one-cent fare, but was informed that she could not "pass unless she consented to have three cents deducted from her dollar!" When her husband retold the story, he explained that his wife, "not happening to be a woman's-rights woman, and having no taste for haggling and stopping up the passage way, . . . accepted the latter alternative, and this chivalric gentleman accordingly cheated this timid, retiring lady out of her two cents." It was debatable whether the unnamed woman agreed with her husband's characterization, but the anecdote highlights the difficulty women experienced when they tried to use paper money. Bank note exchanges required contemplation and a negotiation that set their value separate from the good or service for sale. Individuals who feared confrontation or worried that they did not enter negotiations from a position of equality and strength immediately became targets for characters like this ferry officer who sought to cheat or manipulate the transaction for gain. The variability of paper money meant that who brought money to an exchange mattered as much as what money they brought with them.[53]

Whether it was the noteholder's demographic background, the intended recipient's social standing, or merely questions about the proper discount to apply to the bill's face value, every early republic exchange that included paper currency held the potential for complication. With so many variables involved in each bank note transaction it is almost a surprise that anything was bought or sold. Even the simple purchase of some fruit from a street vendor was not easy. In October 1841, Goodman Poor of Charlestown sold a bushel of apples to George Stone in Boston for fifty cents. Stone paid with a five-dollar bill from the Franklin Bank of Greenfield after he promised that it was good and current note. Poor delivered the apples to a false address given to him by Stone, then "suspected that the bill was bad, and upon inquiry found that it was the bill of a broken bank, whose bills had ceased to pass and were of no value." At his trial for "obtaining money by false pretenses," George Stone's attorney argued that "persons, who take the bills of broken banks, are bound to look out for themselves, and take such bills at their own risk." However, Massachusetts chief justice Lemuel Shaw declared that such risk could only be assumed if "both parties know that the note is the note of a broken bank," not when one side misrepresents a bill as being sound when it is not. Shaw continued, "The modes in which a pretense or representation may be made, so as to induce belief in the mind of another, may be greatly diversified." He concluded, "Such representations need not be by words. It may result from signs and tokens, from false personation, or from the relation in which a person stands." This explanation of the nuances of negotiation makes clear that there was not one specific way to manipulate a bank note transaction; every time paper money traded hands, a variety of verbal and nonverbal cues facilitated its movement.[54]

The most important aspect of a bank note transaction was the actual note in question. Separate from the individuals who attempted to buy or sell in the marketplace, paper money was a participant at the center of any negotiation. With so much riding on whether and how bank notes could pass at face value, the physical characteristics of any bill affected how Americans utilized it. The appearance of a bank note mattered in how much confidence it inspired. Chapter 3 delves deeper into the material culture of paper money with an examination of the imagery and text on the notes themselves.

PART II

Material Culture

CHAPTER 3

Dollars and Senses

When the Canal Bank in New Orleans issued a specimen for a forthcoming ten-dollar bill in the autumn of 1854, the *Daily Picayune* published a detailed analysis of the new note's layout. There was nothing unique about the release of new Canal Bank bills. They had printed dozens of different designs and had even issued three separate ten-dollar bills since their founding as the New Orleans Canal and Banking Company in 1831. No one worried that the bills were fraudulent; the bank's reputation was so solid that locals treated their ten-dollar bills no differently than gold coins. The bank received a positive review from the Louisiana Board of Currency during the 1853–1854 legislative session, which cited its circulation at about $2 million and its total assets as over $6 million.[1]

Even though the new bill was ordinary and there were no questions about the bank's solvency, the city's leading newspaper printed an extended description of the bank note.

> [It was] of very chaste design and clever mechanical execution. On the left side, at the top are figures denoting the value of the note engraven on a wavy elliptical lozenge, surmounted by a garland; in the centre beneath is the spread eagle, surmounted with the national motto, and with one claw supporting a shield against a bale of cotton and one cornucopia, to the left, while the other grasps another cornucopia, and at the bottom is the word denoting the value of the note on a prettily variegated ground in a regular ellipse. At the top of the body of the note are an excellent representation of the City Hall, and the figures of the note's value on a fancy ornate lozenge.

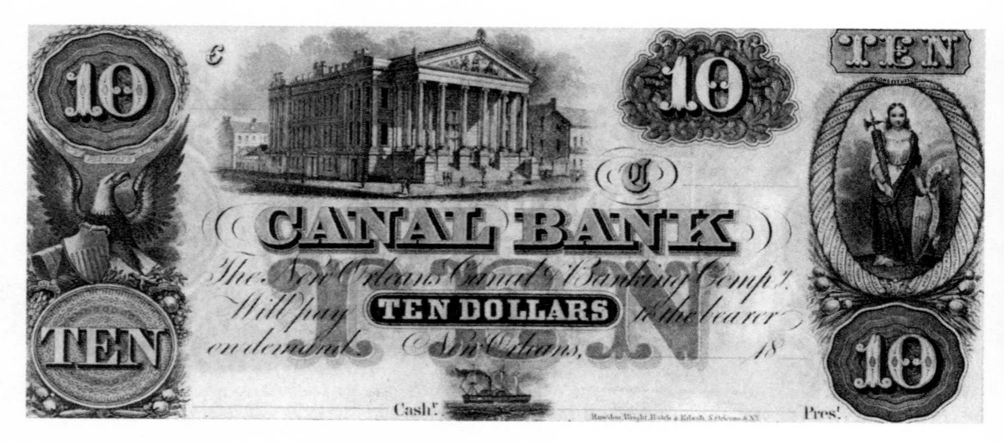

Figure 7. Uncirculated $10 Canal Bank note described in the New Orleans *Daily Picayune*. Author's collection.

> At the bottom, a miniature steamship, *en route*, is represented. On the right hand side, at the top, are the words denoting the value of the note in a parallelogram. In the centre stands the goddess of liberty, supporting national symbols, and surrounded by an oval scroll, bearing the names of the thirty-six States and Territories, minutely engraved, surmounted by the word "constitution," and at the bottom are again the figures as in the left hand corner at the top.

The simple design highlighted the relationship between national symbols (the eagle and Constitution) and local civic (City Hall) and economic (cotton and steamship) ones, but whatever its content, the *Picayune* considered the design of a bill a relevant subject of interest for how the public assessed a bank and its prospects. Most consumers identified with even the most iconic institutions through their paper money, so any alterations to their public face was important news. Americans accepted that bank note vignettes both reflected and shaped a bank's identity and therefore needed to be digested as part of how people accumulated banking information and navigated the chaotic world of early nineteenth-century currency.[2]

Paper money negotiations required both parties' confidence in the quality of the bill based on their personal financial knowledge. There was no more important database of bank note information than the money itself.

Many Americans' interactions with banks occurred primarily through their dealings with an institution's notes, so the physical characteristics of a bank's currency were one of the most important factors in how they gained public confidence. Therefore, bank officials, engravers, and printers fashioned recognizable brands for financial institutions after a process of experimentation; bank notes and shinplasters did not just appear by happenstance. Paper money producers arranged bank note vignettes and textual components in an aesthetic project to manufacture trust and create notes that elicited consumers' feelings of loyalty, security, stability, and even excitement. How notes looked, felt, or even smelled were not accidental byproducts of the market; they were vital reference points in the production and consumption of monetary data.

Consumers' firsthand experience with physical currency forged an emotional connection between them and the bank note through a sensory interaction. The individual vignettes might not have been meant only for them, but engravers and designers produced notes that attempted to convey a particular sentiment. If the public placed confidence in a note, then banks judged it a success. The process was far from impersonal and indifferent. Americans engaged with paper money as discrete physical objects, not mere promiscuous scraps. In this chapter, we will take a quick look at currency engravers and the production of paper money, then turn to the bills themselves to examine how their look and feel affected noteholders. We will specifically scrutinize bank note vignettes to argue that visual representations of work and labor fashioned and reinforced regional economic stereotypes, while depictions of maps, historical events, and personalities situated individual financial institutions within a wider geographic and political landscape.

Any discussion about the production of paper money must begin with the regulations and anti-counterfeiting laws that controlled which designs or language appeared on bank notes. The 1809 Massachusetts Banking Act, for example, mandated that all notes under five dollars use Jacob Perkins's process of stereotype steel plate printing. Perkins's method supposedly allowed the "finest and most delicate vignette" to be "transferred from a flat piece of steel to a steel cylinder, which being hardened by chemical action" retained all the detail of the original while it produced significantly more prints than copper plates. The law did not create a uniform design for all notes, but the regulation did award a huge monopoly to Perkins, who promised the most technologically superior anti-counterfeiting

FIGURE 8. Bank notes produced by Jacob Perkins offered sophisticated designs and lathe work rather than the elaborate vignettes common on later bills. Author's collection.

production at the time. Perkins published his *Bank Bill Test* to explain different facets of the law, offer the public samples of what the new, official bills looked like, and provide "directions for gauging and comparing suspected bills." The publication taught Massachusetts residents how to properly view their money within the context of state regulations on its visual appearance. Perkins's bank notes did not contain the evocative images that dominated bills by the 1830s, but they still produced beautiful, elaborate designs. On a trip to the Baltimore Museum in 1815, eighteen-year-old Lucy Ann Ward observed that one of the "curiosities" on display was a "New England Bank Bill that was put there because one dollar was repeated on it 365 times." The New England Bank of Boston note in question featured only text, but included a pattern made out of the words "one dollar," printed 365 times on the bill's face. The institution used the popular and elegant design for almost thirty years.[3]

Perkins was not alone in his push for bank note standardization. In 1810, Abel Brewster, a silversmith and inventor from Hartford, Connecticut, published *A Plan for Producing an Uniformity in the Ornamental Part of Bank or Other Bills Where There Is Danger of Forgery* that included a sample of his note design along with a standard for visually deciphering bills.

Intriguingly, Brewster marketed his plan based on security and public interest, not artistic merit. He explicitly declared that his bills were not "more *beautiful* than usual, although they might be considered handsome."

This was acceptable for Brewster because "*beauty* is not an infallible criterion of worth—even in a *Bank Bill*." However, bank administrators overwhelmingly rejected Brewster's vision of paper money and instead opted to circulate unique, visually enticing bills that provided an emotional connection with their consumers.[4]

The bank note firms enlisted by bankers to realize their artistic vision were not just hired craftsmen; many engravers and printers designed paper money as part of a larger aesthetic project. Pastoral landscape artists like Asher B. Durand and John W. Casilear led the evolution of paper money vignettes from simple designs to extravagant panoramas, workplace depictions, and classical scenes. The experience of Asher Durand is particularly illustrative. In 1824, Durand partnered with his brother Cyrus, who invented a lathe for engraving intricate designs on paper money. They produced memorable bank notes with elaborate designs that featured Asher's combination of "classical allegorical figures" and American landscape settings. Most of his engravings and intricate geometrical designs remained anonymous, but he did sign a particularly beautiful portrait of Benjamin Franklin sitting at a stone podium that graced several notes including the Franklin Silk Company's two-dollar bill.[5]

Work as a bank note engraver did not offer many opportunities for an open discussion of artistic theory, but Asher Durand's later career as a Hudson River School artist and frequent public commentator on aesthetics provide some context for his paper money contributions. In the mid-1850s, Durand explained his method and goals in a series of "Letters on Landscape Painting" printed in *The Crayon*, one of the nation's foremost artistic journals. He wrote that to "paint with intelligence and sincerity," one must look to nature and its "influence on the mind and heart." It was in contact with nature that Hudson River artists like Durand hoped to find truth. But what did these lofty artistic goals have to do with bank notes?[6]

Certainly not all bank directors ascribed to such visual theories, but Nicholas Biddle did. Biddle's position as president of the Second Bank of the United States in the 1820s and 1830s placed him at the center of American banking just as paper money began to feature more elaborate designs. Through his appreciation of art, architecture, and literature, Biddle attempted to forge a bond between classicism and high finance. He specifically hoped to use Greek design to inspire national unity and confidence in his bank and its currency, while being keenly aware that imagery and symbols played a vital role in civic engagement. Even bankers less aesthetically minded than Nicholas Biddle eventually bought into the artists' material vision. Whatever motivated them to pick such images, every time they used one of Durand's or his colleague's vignettes, they implicitly supported ideas about the projection of truth, honesty, and confidence through a close connection with their notes. Bank profits increased the longer that notes stayed in circulation and bankers believed that visually appealing paper money would earn more of the public's trust and stay in use longer.[7]

The American artistic community also recognized the connection between the skill of engravers to produce beautiful and sophisticated designs and the public's appreciation of art. An article in *The Crayon* on the "History and Progress of Bank Note Engraving" declared that, when the work of engravers is done properly, "currency is furnished, which is well calculated to diffuse throughout the community a refined taste, and a love for the beautiful in Art." An 1854 profile of bank note engravings in the *Illustrated Magazine of Art* remarked that Americans might initially be attracted to paper money designs because of their beauty, but such appreciation brought important economic ramifications. The article detailed the artisanal labor involved in bank note creation and singled out a special new "geometrical lathe" that could only be operated by Cyrus Durand, who was then employed at the firm of Danforth, Wright, and Company. Bank directors, bank note producers, and the artistic community agreed that the quality and the beauty of a vignette mattered for the successful circulation of a bank note, but how did this affect the actual appearance of paper money? The short answer was that the parties worked together to craft something memorable the public could connect with.[8]

Sometimes it was not a particular image that bank directors sought to display to consumers; it was an emotion. In 1837, Timothy Tredwell, the president of the Bank of Ypsilanti, wrote a colorful letter to John Horton Jr., the cashier of the Michigan State Bank, in regard to his design ideas for the bank's new notes. He exclaimed, "Get a real furiouso plate—one that will TAKE with all creation—flaming with cupids, locomotives, rural scenery, and Hercules kicking the world over!" Scantily clad classical female figures graced Tredwell's own Bank of Ypsilanti notes, but that did not necessarily help their circulation. The bank closed in 1839 after just three years in business. Horton did ultimately take some of Tredwell's suggestions; the final version of his three-dollar bill included a vignette of Ceres, the Roman god of agriculture, holding sheaves of grain and another of an allegorical woman with her arm around a bald eagle and a liberty shield.[9]

Many factors influenced bank note creation and not all operations had the same commitment to quality and long-term security; while some banks paid extra to create lasting, recognizable images, wildcat institutions out for fast profit seemed more concerned with minimizing expenses. Not all paper money was equal when it came to production costs. Edwin and Charles Starr's 1824 "distypographic" bank notes featured anti-fraud technology, which included a watermark woven into special paper of their own design, so that the "mark is only visible on holding the note up to the light." The resulting secure bank notes were not cheap; the Starrs charged $100 for initial black-and-white specimens with a $1 charge for every 400 notes printed thereafter, while initial color notes went for $250 with a subsequent charge of $2.50 for each additional 400 notes. Bills with colored ink did not suit every situation, but for the Orange Bank in the County of Essex based in Orange, New Jersey, the branding opportunity of orange notes was worth the extra amount. The Philadelphia firm of Fairman, Draper, Underwood, & Co. sold quality engravings of four notes with vignettes on a copperplate from $300, but also offered a cut-rate version of the same plates without the vignettes for $200. The firm specified that all payments needed to be made in secure notes receivable at Philadelphia banks.[10]

Banks also saved money when they reused vignettes from other bills. After the time and expense to craft an image for an institution and design a bank note with identifying markers that the public would recognize, engravers retained the property rights to most of the vignettes they created. Banks could save money and engravers could save time and energy when they combined a collection of generic images into a new note instead of producing something from scratch. Some vignettes became so familiar to the public that they were repurposed on noncurrency items, such as commemorative envelopes or stationery. Engravers stockpiled thousands of vignettes of presidents, cherubs, and dogs that bank officials assembled into visually pleasing notes to convey whatever message they wanted to send to the public. These vignettes even survived the collapse of engraving firms as other producers rushed to buy up leftover copperplates to add to their catalogs. When one of Cyrus Durand's partnerships dissolved, for example, engraver and possible counterfeiter Waterman Ormsby accumulated many of its images.[11]

One problem with reused vignettes was that any original meaning held by the image became confused or lost in a different application. Early in the 1860s, the Egg Harbor Bank ordered a one-dollar bill from the American Bank Note Company that featured an unlabeled portrait of a small boy.

FIGURE 9. Engravers like Durand & Company issued specimen sheets to provide bankers with a catalog of images from which they could construct new bank notes. Courtesy, Library of Congress Prints and Photographs Division, LC-DIG-pga-13735.

The child was Philip M. Wolseiffer, the first baby born in Egg Harbor City, New Jersey, after its incorporation in 1857. Wolseiffer's father laid out the community's streets and his son's image projected civic pride for the new town and its bank. However, after the notes entered circulation, the American Bank Note Company held on to the image and reused it on several other bills, including one-dollar samples from the New York County Bank, Bank of Germantown, and Farmers' & Mechanics Bank of Shippensburg, Pennsylvania. It even landed on a hundred-dollar bill from Union Bank of Tennessee in Nashville. Noteholders must have wondered who the little boy was, but the lost connection to the original bank and community probably did not hurt bank note circulation. There were other examples where compromised branding severely cost an institution.[12]

Since the public identified a bank through its bills, failure to protect the security of those vignettes could devastate their visual profile. On June 2, 1850, a small gang led by an English burglar, Jack Wade, used explosives to rob $29,036 in notes from the Dorchester & Milton Bank in Dorchester, Massachusetts. Even though authorities apprehended Wade in Buffalo and sentenced him to sixteen years in Charlestown State Prison, he had also stolen Dorchester & Milton's engraved bank note plates. Wade sold the missing plates to counterfeiters before his capture and they were never recovered. Soon, authentic, but illegal notes from the Dorchester & Milton Bank began to circulate in great number. Forced to deal with the untenable situation of being responsible for notes that they had not issued and a related crisis of identity, the bank's directors changed the institution's charter and in 1851 opened the new Blue Hill Bank complete with all new bank notes.[13]

Before starting a formal analysis of the vignettes, it is useful to first focus on the words that graced paper money. The fine print mattered and not just when the makers of unregulated shinplasters sought to evade legal liability with phrases such as "This is not intended as a circulating medium." Banks utilized several textual conventions to inspire confidence in their money and convince consumers of their stability. From boasts about an institution's assets to explanations of its liability, confidence-boosting language played on the public's comprehension of the finer points of the banking system. It was essential to understand the legalistic phrases on paper money to determine a bill's type (bank note vs. unregulated shinplaster), the institution's capital reserves, and any protections against bankruptcy.[14]

After New York legislation created a Safety Fund that served as deposit insurance to guard the value of notes from bankrupt institutions, newly printed paper money broadcast whether particular banks were member institutions. Banks that paid to join the fund, like the Albany City Bank, alerted the public of their new security with the phrase "New York Safety Fund" across the top of the bill. The fund struggled to protect noteholders after the Panic of 1837 led to multiple bank failures, but customers liked the promise of government-backed redemption. While only those with a deep knowledge of state banking regulations mastered the nuances of the complex legislation, the public clearly understood enough of the law and its benefits. Caroline Kirkland, in *A New Home—Who'll Follow?* (1839), a semiautobiographical novel about a family's move to the Michigan frontier, mentioned that any migrant to the backcountry needed "a reasonable supply of New-York Safety-Fund notes, the most tempting form which 'world's gear' can possibly assume for our western, wild-cat-wearied eyes." The statement was insightful about the poor condition of frontier Michigan banking, where spurious wildcats ruled. Likewise, Kirkland casually cited banking regulations without expectation that the "Safety Fund" or other terms needed an explanation or a definition. Her mostly female readers were familiar with Safety Fund notes and understood why they would have been of value even five hundred miles west of New York State.[15]

Other institutions utilized text to highlight features of their individual charters and promote their solvency. Amid the insecurity of the Panic of 1857, the Dubuque Central Improvement Company issued bills that read: "stockholders individually liable for the payment of this note." The promise was not unusual, as the phrase "Individual Property of Stockholders Liable" appeared on numerous bills, but what was unique was a list of the names of its twenty-nine stockholders on the back of the note. When the Dubuque, Iowa, economy soured and the Central Improvement Company lost its landholdings, it paid off the notes (to avoid lawsuits) to the financial ruin of some of the stockholders on the list.[16]

The skill to navigate paper money text was just part of Americans' need to make rapid judgments about the currency placed in front of them when they were involved in early republic market transactions. It was also critical for individuals to develop keen visual skills. The young nation's emerging urban marketplaces forced participants to investigate their surroundings, even as new forms of commerce attempted to obscure what they saw around them. When it came to paper money, this meant that everyone had to learn how to view and decipher bills, especially as bank note producers made more sophisticated products over time. Bank officials, engravers, and printers modified currency to make something both seemingly secure from counterfeiting and economically stable; consumers analyzed what was presented to them to ensure that it was wise to extend their confidence. This process depended, first and foremost, on the ability to read paper money vignettes.[17]

Any attempt to create a grand unified theory of bank note vignettes is misguided because all notes did not fit into the same banking strategy. Some bank notes' mélanges of unrelated dogs, Roman gods, and geometric patterns did not seem to make much sense. Sometimes engravers produced vignettes simply for their comic potential or titillation. Anyone could pick up a one-dollar note from the Bank of Wisconsin or five-dollar bill from the North River Banking Company in New York and possess pictures of topless women in relaxed poses. Such bills offered the public easily portable risqué images without the stigma of carrying illicit material. The fraudulent Commercial Exchange Bank of Terre Haute, Indiana, put out a two-dollar note that circulated for years in the Midwest. Designed by a colorful character, Waterman Ormsby, it included an intricate geometric design on its reverse side made up of concentric circles of little red "2" characters, but when held at arm's length, its pattern revealed a pair of breasts.[18]

However, for all the mischievous cherubs or half-clothed women in classical garb that served as cheap, discrete sources of pornography, some important patterns developed in how banks assembled the imagery on their paper money. It is useful to analyze these patterns to explore how Americans viewed and engaged with early republic paper money. In 1856, George Peyton detailed the information and visual skills necessary to assess paper money's trustworthiness. He argued that "[it is] manifest that an intimate acquaintance with the engraved illustrations, aided by the explanatory text connected with them, will insure a skill in judging of bank notes." Issuing institutions utilized vignettes that depicted regional economic stereotypes, scenes of geographic and historic significance, or national or local celebrities with the hope that American consumers would emotionally connect with the note's imagery and use that bond to infuse the bill with their confidence.[19]

Perhaps the most prevalent bank note trope was the portrayal of economic activity. With a few exceptions, these images utilized generic symbols of industrial progress (railroads and steamboats) or more specialized portraits of agricultural, artisanal, industrial, or resource extraction labor. Some notes paired railroads or other technology with Native Americans "giving way to the modern commercial road," to put a fine point on the depiction of white advancement and dominance. Occupational scenes did not merely champion the nobility of labor; they created and maintained regional commercial stereotypes. Contemporary observers believed that there should be a link between the type of economic production pictured on a note and the location of its bank of origin. One anti-counterfeiting pamphlet warned about fake bills that purported to come from northeastern institutions "bearing upon their face scenes representing negroes cultivating cotton, sugar mills, and many Southern plantation views; some with

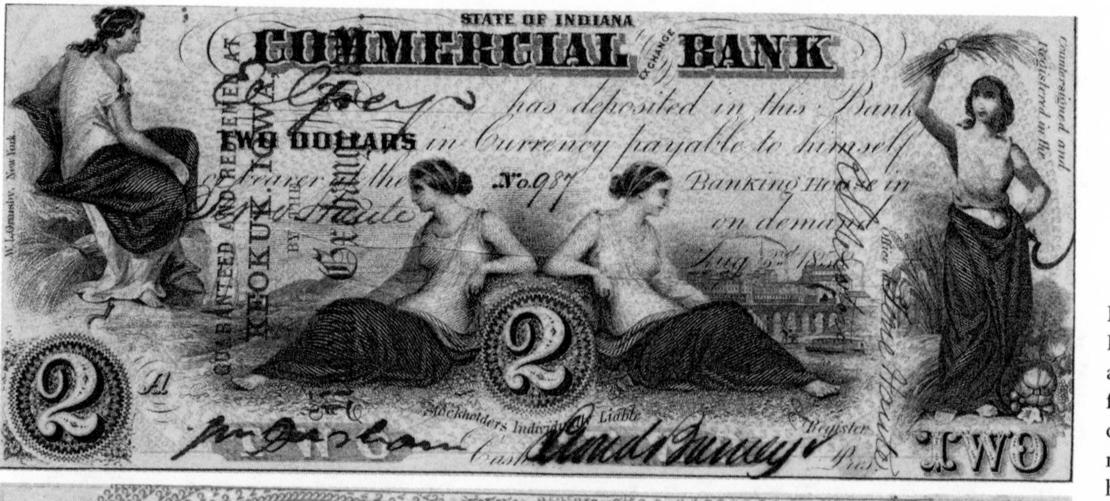

FIGURE 10. Risqué images and topless figures appeared on a variety of notes. Shown here are the obverse and reverse of a two-dollar note from the Commercial Exchange Bank. Author's collection.

Western river-steamers, buffalo and wild-horse scenes; and various other absurd alterations," that only passed when the public failed to pay attention to their misplaced content. Properly executed depictions of labor linked banks to their region's production and served multiple constituencies. A local audience responded with pride to the representation of hometown industry, while the same image advertised those industries to consumers and businesses across the country. Such vignettes moved past local boosterism to tie approval of a particular economic achievement with confidence in the issuing institution. The visual argument was simple: a region with thriving industrial or agricultural production must have a prosperous financial sector as well.[20]

It is impossible to discuss all the economic depictions on bank notes, but it is useful to look at both typical and unique examples. Farming vignettes abounded in all regions with some differentiation by crop type, labor force, and use of technology. Wheat farmers appeared on notes from Kentucky to Michigan to New York; they showed men with plows at work in the soil or farmers with sickles or mechanical reapers involved in the harvest. Other notes included the cultivation of corn or hops. The Bank of Washtenaw in Ann Arbor, Michigan, capitalized on two midwestern occupations with both a depiction of wheat farmers and the resource extraction of lumberjacks. Coal miners graced bills across the Appalachians, like five- and ten-dollar examples from the Allegany County Bank in Cumberland, Maryland. More mining scenes appeared on notes from the pointedly named Anthracite Bank of Tamaqua, Pennsylvania. The Oil City Bank might have been located in a town described as having "the most disgusting *name* in all Petrolia," but the bank's beautiful twenty-dollar bill included a detailed vignette of men at work on an oil derrick.[21]

Northeastern factory workers and craftsmen appeared in bank note vignettes that highlighted particular types of regional labor. Early nineteenth-century bills from Paterson, New Jersey, and North Providence, Rhode Island, featured male workers in rudimentary textile production, while later notes from across New England, like an 1861 bill from Sanford, Maine, showed more sophisticated machinery run by young female operatives. Other vignettes focused on specialized industries or depicted unique local manufacturing. Thomas Dyott's Manual Labor Savings Bank ran up against persistent criticism from Philadelphia authorities during its checkered existence, but his notes included intricate images of glassblowers at work in Dyottville, a four-hundred-acre factory and housing facility in the northern part of the city. Not all northern industry occurred on such an expansive scale. Several notes, like a one-dollar bill from the Mount Wollaston Bank in Quincy, Massachusetts, showed the intimate family production of artisan shoemakers. The neighboring Randolph Bank skipped the scene of fabrication and just included a drawing of newly completed shoes and boots.[22]

These northern bank note vignettes featured triumphant visions of workers, whether agricultural or industrial, but mercantile or financial labor was largely absent. While bank buildings appeared on numerous bills to promote institutional strength and stability, banking as an occupation was not depicted on paper money. Americans preferred producerist bank notes that championed honorable hard work rather than reminders of who really profited from the bills. White-collar work in general was rarely shown, with the exception of various surveyors and a Revere Bank of Boston two-dollar note with an interesting vignette of an architect showing his building plans to a stonecutter. Even here, the viewer entered the scene from behind the stonecutter.[23]

A different picture of labor relations proliferated on bank notes from the South, where few bills featured industrial images. One outlier from the Bank of Yanceyville in North Carolina included an elaborately rendered scene of a tobacco factory interior by artist Alfred Jones. In this precise depiction of the Yanceyville factory workflow, enslaved young African Americans sorted tobacco and prepared a large machine press under the watchful gaze of white overseers. The vignette especially highlighted the labor and power hierarchy between these individuals; one boy, with his shirt sleeves rolled up as he carried a heavy load, appeared directly adjacent to a formally dressed overseer, wearing a coat, who looked relaxed as he leaned on his elbow with one leg crossed in front of the other.[24]

From the Bank of Lexington in North Carolina to the Mississippi Union Bank in Jackson, most southern bills with economic imagery highlighted the production and transportation of cotton and emphasized the role of enslaved labor. While few early nineteenth-century bank notes included pictures of enslaved men and women, the images expanded dramatically during the increased sectional tension of the 1850s. Such presentations of African American bodies and cotton on bank notes showed the public more than just depictions of regional economic production; they captured the centrality of white supremacy and slavery to the Cotton Kingdom's wealth and credit. However, because it was so easy for bank officials to tailor bank

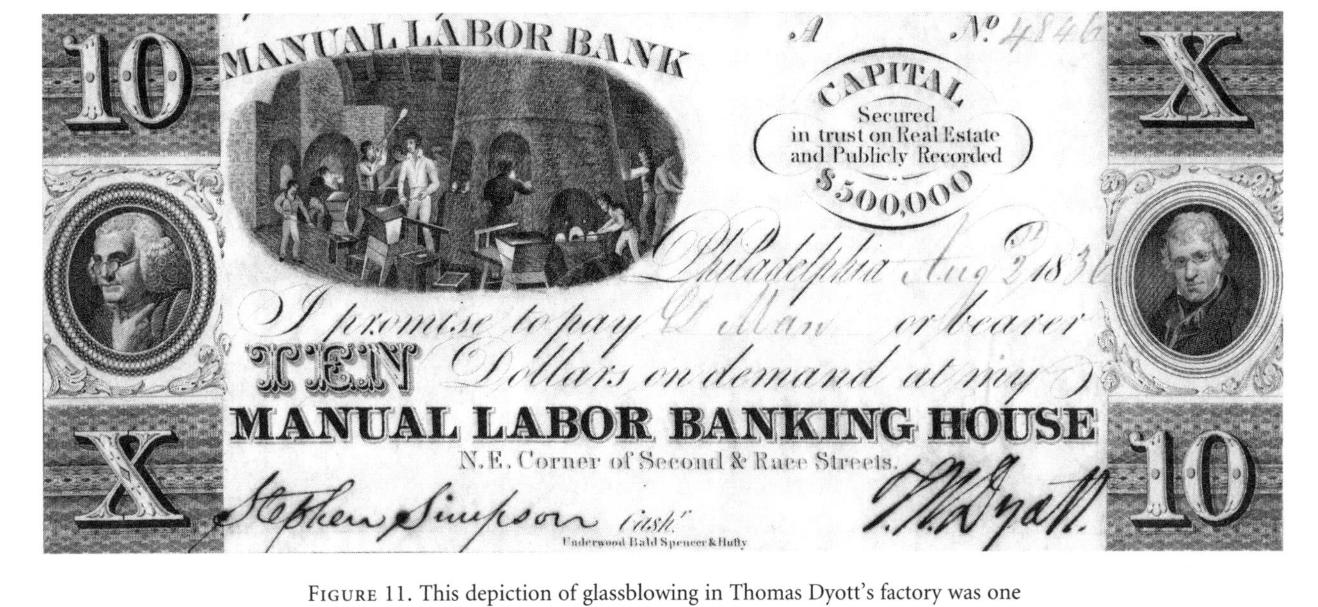

FIGURE 11. This depiction of glassblowing in Thomas Dyott's factory was one of many images of local industrial production on bank notes. Author's collection.

FIGURE 12. Most bank notes that featured industrial images came from northern states, but this vignette of a tobacco-processing factory appeared on several 1850s notes from the Bank of Yanceyville in North Carolina. Courtesy, American Antiquarian Society.

notes to suit their personal vision, not every vignette of African American labor displayed a southern view of race and regional economics. The Conway Bank in Massachusetts opened in 1854 and issued five-dollar bills that featured both a vignette of white female mill workers and their looms and an enslaved African American man with a bushel of cotton along with others picking cotton in the background. Viewed strictly through the lens of late 1850s economic categorization, the images represented two separate types of regional production, but the third vignette on the note, a portrait of James Scollay Whitney, neatly united them. A member of the Conway Bank board of directors and manager of the Conway Manufacturing Company and cotton mill which bought and processed more than 300,000 pounds of cotton in 1855, Whitney was a dues-paying member of the American Colonization Society and a Democratic politician who supported James Buchanan. Taken as a whole, the Conway Bank note projected a message of North-South unity and reconciliation and reflected Whitney's business and political views. However, the bank issued bills with this design well into the 1860s after young men from the Conway area had already

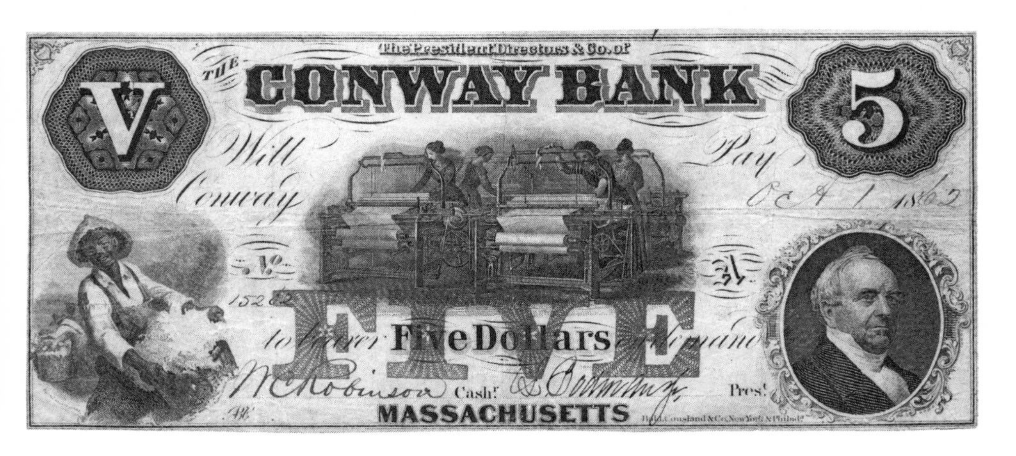

FIGURE 13. The Conway Bank of Massachusetts mixed depictions of slavery and textile manufacturing on a note that highlighted the economic connections between North and South. Collection of the Massachusetts Historical Society.

fought and died in the Civil War. Whether the bills stirred anger or resentment in 1862 or 1863, it is hard to believe that the image went unnoticed.[25]

Just as bank note images of economic production helped create Americans' regional stereotypes and reinforced them at the same time, a second category of vignettes concerned geography or history and instructed as they glorified. Since bank notes traveled far from their home institutions and consumers often encountered money from distant locations, geography became a prominent paper money theme as institutions forged regional reputations. Using maps or clues to their location, banks situated themselves within the national landscape and proclaimed their authenticity in a nation filled with elusive wildcat institutions. The use of geographic themes on paper money highlights the project of Jedidiah Morse, Noah Webster, and others who pursued nation making through the connection of language and cartography, while expanding their effort to include numeric and monetary literacy.[26]

Several banks embraced topography and cartography as part of their geographic vignettes. A ten-dollar bill from the Hadley Falls Bank in Holyoke, Massachusetts, created an effective bond between a bank and a location with an expansive view of the area's waterfalls spread across its entire face. According to a pamphlet on how to recognize counterfeit bills, such images helped inform consumers about a note's authenticity. Just like the observation that a regional economic portrait needed to match its place of issue, the authors stated that "in most cases the vignettes and designs on bank-notes indicate the location of the banks (unfortunately this system is not properly adhered to); for instance, a view of the Falls of Niagara indicates an institution located in that section of the country."[27]

Striking, specific landscapes did not suit every bank, so maps often tied together geography and banking institutions. Bills from the Bank of Delaware printed in the late 1850s included a center vignette of a detailed Ohio state map flanked by a Native American woman and a white woman. Such images literally put banks on the map and declared to those unfamiliar with small towns like Delaware, Ohio, that they should not be skeptical of money from the frontier. Observers responded positively to the maps, like when the *St. Charles City Intelligencer* informed its readers about a new "beautifully executed" ten-dollar bill from the State Bank of Iowa that contained "a map of Iowa with all the counties distinctly marked." Given the level of detail, noteholders could use these bills as guides when they traveled. Pocket map use only began to grow in the late eighteenth century, so map vignettes on bank notes certainly could have served as what one scholar calls "ambulatory maps," which allowed individuals to connect their lived experiences with specific cartographic information.[28]

Of course, a map or well-drawn landscape was not the only way to indicate an institution's location. Thomas Dyott's Manual Labor Banking House's bills pinpointed its address in Philadelphia at the "N.E. Corner of Second & Race Streets." Likewise, many merchant and corporate shinplasters served double duty as currency and advertisements that included the location of the business. F. R. Harris, for example, issued ten-cent notes that placed his hat shop "opposite the post office" in Portland, Maine. A related text-based location appeared on paper money from Clark's Exchange Bank, a family-run national network of banking and exchange houses originally established by Enoch White Clark in the 1830s. Twenty years later, the firm printed notes in Springfield, Illinois, that included a large seal detailing their multiple locations and kinship ties. Made up of fathers, sons, brothers, and brothers-in-law in offices in Philadelphia, Boston, New York, St. Louis, and Burlington, Iowa, Clark's paper currency created a virtual map of American finance through their connections.[29]

A few banks situated themselves within their particular ethnic communities through the circulation of foreign language notes. There were not

FIGURE 14. The Northampton Bank paid tribute to its local ethnic population with one of the few bank notes printed in a language other than English. Collection of the Massachusetts Historical Society.

many of these bills, but the Louisiana Bank in New Orleans printed bilingual five-dollar notes with English text on the left and the French translation on the right, while the Lumberman's Bank in Warren and Northampton Bank, both in Pennsylvania, printed bills wholly in German. To drive home their appeal to the local Swiss German community, some Northampton Bank five-dollar notes included a central vignette of three men ceremonially swearing allegiance to Der Bund bookended by images of poets Johann Lavater and Christian Gellert. In this case, German history and culture meshed with the German text to create American paper money that clearly and discretely appealed to an ethnic enclave.[30]

Bank notes that linked geography with history would have seemed familiar in the early republic because they played on concepts already in use by some of the nation's leading educators. Emma Hart Willard, a best-selling author of historical textbooks in the era, adapted the graphic appeal of maps to her study of the American past. Her popularity partly derived from how she moved away from pure narration to a visual form of storytelling to illustrate the past through maps and other pictorial representations of time and space. Paper money engravers followed Willard's approach when they designed historical vignettes that embraced graphic nationalistic detail to fashion memorable images. Bank notes that depicted important historical events created mental associations between banking institutions and moments of national pride and confidence.[31]

A fundamental event in American history like the Battle of New Orleans appeared in three or four separate vignettes on more than a dozen bank notes from the 1810s to the 1850s. The banks hailed from every region of the country and included more than one fraudulent business that floated spurious bills as a moneymaking endeavor. Aside from nationalism, there were some noticeable connections between the locations of the banks and the famous 1815 event. Three Tennessee banks played on the tie between Andrew Jackson's home and the battle, while another one from Providence, Rhode Island, was called the Jackson Bank. However, it was odd that none of the many New Orleans banking houses employed vignettes of the battle. Some scholars claim that nationalistic imagery on bank notes transitioned to more regionally specific vignettes as sectional politics took precedence toward mid-century, but the diversity of banks across the decades that used the Battle of New Orleans meant that a straightforward pattern may not be so simple. Politically charged vignettes engaged viewers on multiple levels and in turn operated on national, regional, and local sympathies.[32]

The story is more complicated for bank notes that featured local, rather than national, historic events. Such images elicited civic pride near home, but they may not have received the same recognition the further the money traveled from the bank. Provincial residents easily recognized particular revolutionary memorials—like the Rhode Island Agricultural Bank's depiction of the Burning of the Gaspee or the Battle of Monmouth from the Bank of Monmouth, New Jersey—but what did they mean to Americans from other states? When the image of the Battle of Monmouth, engraved by the firm of Asher Durand, Cyrus Durand, and Charles C. Wright, also appeared on a ten-dollar note from the Bank of Cheraw in South Carolina, did it convey the same feeling or simply strike viewers as a generic military scene? Likewise, how many antebellum consumers picked up a two-dollar bill from the Syracuse City Bank and quickly identified the unlabeled center vignette's depiction of the signing of the 1784 Treaty of Fort Stanwix?[33]

What muddled local history scenes was the fact that engravers sometimes emphasized or deemphasized specific parts of the vignette. Several Boston area banks included a depiction of the Battle of Bunker Hill, but not all the vignettes looked alike. The engravers Toppan, Carpenter, and Co. reworked one version of John Trumbull's famous painting, *The Death of General Warren at the Battle of Bunker's Hill, June 17, 1775*, to create an image on an 1850s Monument Bank five-dollar note that included a black soldier, perhaps based on Peter Salem. African American abolitionist William C. Nell commented that "in some engravings of the battle, this colored soldier occupies a prominent position, but in more recent editions, his figure is *non est inventus* [not to be found]. A significant, but inglorious omission. On some bills, however, of the Monumental [Monument] Bank, Charlestown, and Freeman's Bank, Boston, his presence is manifest." This vignette served as a counterpoint to a Planters Bank of Fairfield, South Carolina, note that altered an image of white wheat farmers into one of enslaved men in a cotton field. Race was added, subtracted, or altered in images of regional economic production and history as engravers and bank officials highlighted certain political expressions.[34]

Related to triumphant historical vignettes, a third category of bank note images was the depiction of celebrity, although this category included a wide range of possibilities because the concept of American celebrity was in transition. In colonial America, following convention, certain people achieved civic, military, or religious success and even though, supposedly, they had not sought out fame, it had found them. Early republic characters like the daredevil Sam Patch represented something different: a modern type of celebrity who wanted to be famous and achieved notoriety for his or her deeds. Both types of celebrities graced bank notes, from the nationalistic founders who embodied a classical celebrity, to others who captured the excitement and popular appeal of modern, overwhelmingly masculine adventurers.[35]

No one in the early nineteenth century conveyed more stability and honesty than George Washington, who appeared on hundreds of bank notes including more than 140 in New York State alone. Washington made an ideal bank note subject. Aesthetically, he satisfied what one art historian calls the "appearance of truth" that guided late eighteenth-century American portraiture. This fact guided antebellum engravers who applied classical and authoritative vignettes to bank notes by reusing well-known images of Washington painted in the nation's formative years by Charles Willson Peale (ca. 1779–1781), John Trumbull (1790), and Gilbert Stuart (1796). Politically, Washington's nonpartisan reputation also meant that his image functioned well across ideological divides. Other politicians appeared on paper money specifically because of their party ties or regional association. For example, the tragic presidency of William Henry Harrison led to a wave of more than one hundred bank note appearances in the 1840s, but most

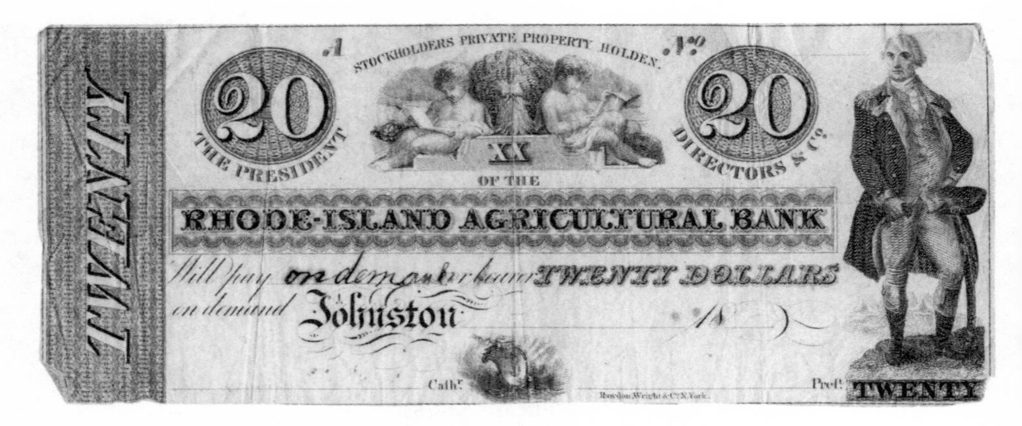

FIGURE 15. Hundreds of bank notes featured portraits of George Washington in an attempt to co-opt his authority and stature. Author's collection.

of these were in pro-Whig strongholds or institutions connected to Harrison, such as the Tippecanoe Bank in Winnemac, Indiana. Other political celebrities proclaimed regional identity in a way similar to vignettes that depicted specialized economic production. Daniel Webster became a common sight on Massachusetts notes like the Webster Bank in Boston, but he graced only one bill in South Carolina, the Farmers' and Exchange Bank of Charleston. In contrast, John Calhoun was a favorite with sixteen South Carolina banks and others across the South, but only two in Massachusetts.[36]

Portraits of politicians appeared frequently on bills, but a newer sort of swashbuckling adventurer inhabited the most vivid and exciting images. Bank officials hoped to inspire public celebration and nationalistic pride when they placed famous individuals on their bills, but a particular mixture of adulation and pride was reserved for new celebrities in the Sam Patch model. One example was Dr. Elisha Kent Kane, who earned national fame during a series of dramatic Arctic adventures in the 1850s. Kane received extensive newspaper coverage and his book, *Arctic Explorations*, cemented his fame. Even before his premature death in 1857, tributes ranged from "Dr. Kane's Arctic Polka" to portraits in the global press. In this context, bank note engraver Alfred Jones produced an elaborate image of Dr. Kane as he resolutely led his Arctic voyage. The vignette appeared on at least ten

FIGURE 16. Dr. Kane's exploits in the Arctic provided dramatic material for a bank note vignette. Courtesy, American Antiquarian Society.

bills in the 1850s and 1860s even though it did not appear on any bank notes in Kane's hometown of Philadelphia. Instead, the snowy image was favored by northern banks—three in New England and another five in Wisconsin.[37]

Not all celebrities depicted on bank notes rose to the popularity of Dr. Kane or Daniel Boone (who appeared on a Georgia bank note next to St. George slaying a dragon) or represented the same manly frontier ethos. On its one-dollar bill in the late 1850s, the Harvard Bank in Cambridge featured an image of Gore Hall and a portrait of a man named Thomas Dowse. Like other geographic vignettes, Gore Hall symbolized Harvard University and Cambridge specifically. The building served as the school's library from 1838 to 1913 and is still emblazoned on the town seal. Dowse was an artisan with no formal connection to Harvard, but he was described around Boston as the "literary leatherdresser" and known for his impressive private library of over five thousand volumes. After his death in 1856, Dowse donated his collection to the Massachusetts Historical Society where it still resides in a room with a portrait of Dowse that served as the basis for the bank note image. What message did the Harvard Bank proclaim when it placed a

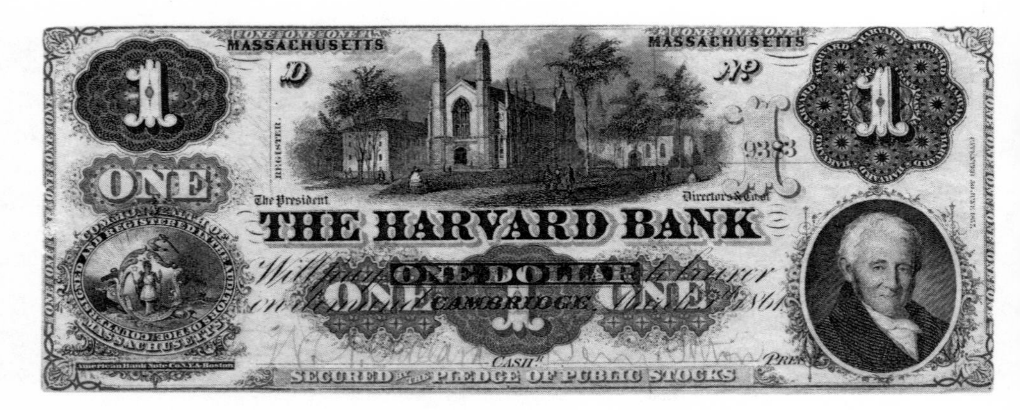

FIGURE 17. Local personalities like Thomas Dowse graced numerous bank notes even if their identities might not have been known where the bills circulated. Collection of the Massachusetts Historical Society.

portrait of a marginally noteworthy individual on a bill? If the overall goal of bank officials was to create a paper instrument that maintained its circulation, why did they think a picture of Thomas Dowse would help? Would local residents recognize Dowse and trust the bill more because of his likeness and, at the same time, would consumers further outside of town look past his portrait to the image of Gore Hall which they invested with confidence because of its connection with Harvard? Any and all of these reactions could have existed simultaneously.[38]

Whatever drawback the placement of a minor figure like Thomas Dowse created for a note, the idea to feature someone on a bill whose persona complicated notions of honesty and confidence could be greater. The most poignant example of this came from a five-dollar bill issued by the Pequonnock Bank of Bridgeport, Connecticut. The note featured a portrait of legendary singer Jenny Lind; another of P. T. Barnum, Bridgeport's most notable resident and Lind's promoter; and a detailed center vignette of Iranistan, Barnum's massive neo-Moorish residence. Barnum also served as president of the Pequonnock Bank from 1851 to 1855 and signed their early paper money personally. Barnum's position attracted publicity in 1854 when John Thompson, publisher of a bank note and counterfeit reporter, sent him a letter accusing the Pequonnock of having insufficient funds to cover its bank notes and threatening a negative rating in Thompson's publication. Barnum, a frequent target of blackmail schemes, refused to pay Thompson the money he requested and instead publicized that he would personally redeem any Pequonnock notes should the need arise. The scandal did not ruin the bank, but between September 1854 and January 1855, the institution's circulation shrank from over $195,000 to less than $115,000 as it sought a healthier ratio of paper liabilities to cash reserves. Barnum's name and likeness conjured up the specter of a humbug, exactly the wrong visual cue for a bank note, but his mansion and Jenny Lind's presence simultaneously reinforced a sense of wealth and prosperity, reassuring imagery for paper currency. Both John Thompson and P. T. Barnum seemed aware of this tension and how easily one message challenged the other as information spread to the public.[39]

A picture of a celebrity on a bank note meant to inspire confidence was not the same thing as a stable, solid bank with sufficient deposits; the wrong selection of images could expose a dissonance between the real and projected health of an institution. In the midst of the prolonged economic downturn that followed the Panic of 1837, the Farmers' Bank of the State of Delaware issued a note that featured weighty images of George Washington and Benjamin Franklin. However, the bill's face value of 6¼ cents did not broadcast the same level of confidence as the vignettes themselves. Twenty years later, a rough-looking Franklin appeared on a badly made shinplaster released during the Panic of 1857 that caused the *New York Times* to lament the note "we saw shabbily engraved on wood—about half the size of a bank bill. The vignette was an ark on a troubled sea. On the left side was FRANKLIN'S head—shame!—and on the right corner the kakographic [*sic*] sign of one who sells cakes and coffee." The irate reviewer pointed to a number of alarming aspects of the shinplaster, but principally to the disconnect between a poor likeness of founding father and printer Benjamin Franklin and an even more terribly rendered advertisement for a bake shop. Separate from the images themselves, the physical quality of the note failed to provide any confidence in the issuing operation.[40]

Americans understood that bank notes and even shinplasters functioned as circulating currency and could not do so if they failed to look or feel like money was supposed to look and feel. There was a distinctly material component when someone decided to trust the bill in front of them. One critic remarked on the inferior feel of paper money and its inability to physically "confer a distinct gratification" when he explained why misers preferred to hoard specie. Gold was better for the "seeing, touching, and handling pleasures," while a "bank-note can no more satisfy the touch of a true sensualist in this passion, than Creusa could return her husband's embrace." Specie promised an immediate tactile reassurance; bank notes were subject to further material inspection. Separate from financial data or the text and images on its face, the touch and appearance of paper money conveyed information about its value. The process started with the paper on which the notes were printed.[41]

While not all stable banks used the same type of paper to print their money, writers of counterfeit detectors universally informed the public of a direct relationship between the strength and integrity of a bank and the condition of its paper. In one 1852 bank note guide, Henry C. Foote explained that "genuine bank-note paper is made of linen or silk or a mixture of both, of a firm texture and of a superior quality." Illegal or wildcat notes, he continued, were printed on "slazy or half cotton paper" because only respectable institutions could afford or obtain the better stock. In reality, anyone could print their currency on high quality paper, while many well-capitalized institutions used nearly translucent, so-called onion-skin paper. The confusion over whether an institution's paper stock should be trusted meant that such information joined the unending flow of data that passed between banks and the public. The Goshen Bank in New York, for example, alerted the community in 1858 to refuse any notes from their bank printed on bright white paper (their notes were usually a dull, light brown) because some of their samples had been stolen.[42]

Whether it was a shinplaster printed on crude paper or a legal bank note on fine stock, the movement of paper currency from person to person around the country eventually led to a noticeable deterioration of the bills. Moreover, commentary about the physical state of a bank note almost always paralleled its financial state. A poem in the *Scientific American* specifically questioned the value of a note from the Bank of St. Clair in Detroit when it called attention to its shabby physical appearance. It began, "I will not take the *ragged* elf, / In payment for my labor; / Your villainy's revealed itself, / You've robbed myself and neighbor." Just a few months after the poem ran, Bank of St. Clair notes traded locally at a 65 percent discount.[43]

Literary sources captured the deterioration of notes, both physically and financially, in more evocative language. In Caroline Kirkland's second book about life in Michigan, *Forest Life*, she described one transaction where she lost out after she received a payment "in wild-cat money, that turned to waste paper before we got it off our hands." The title character in the satirical *History of a Little Frenchman and His Bank Notes: "Rags! Rags! Rags!"*

likewise suffered one humiliating paper money transaction after another until all that was left was "a parcel of ragged dirty bills, pregnant with filth and disease." The Frenchman's statement was a good reminder that the material condition of paper money mattered partly because of the personal nature of its circulation. Between the moments when bills needed to be held, they resided in individuals' pockets, purses, and wallets, while some kept them safe and concealed in their hat or boot. However, as nineteenth-century public health reformers could attest, the American public was not that clean. All of this time spent on and around people's bodies transformed once clean, crisp paper currency into dirty rags.[44]

Antebellum doctors who observed interactions between bodies and bank notes questioned whether they might be responsible for the transmission of certain diseases, especially smallpox. Soiled and smelly notes were more than a nuisance. They potentially carried serious health risks as they circulated through the population. Such speculations built on earlier episodes where disease and paper money coincided, like during the Revolutionary War, when North Carolina moved its currency production from New Bern to Wilmington because smallpox threatened to compromise paper money manufacturing. Despite one publication's satirical call for readers to send them bank notes to test an inoculation plan, most antebellum observers accepted the potential relationship between paper money and communicable disease. Newspapers recounted the details of a bank teller from the Clinton Bank in Columbus, Ohio, who contracted smallpox and claimed that his infection came from a batch of notes as they moved from Cincinnati to his institution. *Peterson's Counterfeit Detector* warned people who "handle bank notes, not to wet their thumbs while counting the bills" because if the "thumb comes in contact with the tongue after handling a note from the pocket of a man infected with the small pox, the infection is as sure to take effect as the inoculation of a child."[45]

One public health study tied disease to banking policy and argued that the rise in small-denomination notes that followed the Panic of 1837 altered who touched paper money and what they spread to the notes. A patient with smallpox, for example, usually stayed in a hospital with money still in their pockets and when they desired a treat sent "a note saturated with the poison, and having perhaps the very Sea-tick odour of small pox, to a confectioner, who takes it of course." That same patient paid their hospital tab with the infected bills, which in turn traveled to the market to buy hospital provisions. The reporting physician concluded that it "would be impossible to conceive any better mode of distributing the poison of a disease, known to be so very highly contagious and infectious" because, given how closely individuals interacted with their money, it was no different than if they had distributed the "clothing of small pox patients." A comparison between bank note circulation and the purposeful application of germ warfare was alarmist, but it highlighted how paper money served as a physical extension of the body. Ralph Waldo Emerson's maxim "Money is another kind of blood" summed this up nicely. Far from impersonal scraps of undifferentiated paper, bank notes existed as intimate appendages in people's lives.[46]

Whether it was through disease, dirt, or dazzling beauty, bank notes' materiality affected how the American public connected with the market economy. Bank officials and engravers recognized this when they crafted paper money designs with an eye toward their connection with consumers. They clearly succeeded. In some odd scenes, the physical appearance of paper money mattered so much that it inspired passionate responses. One case concerned a young Philadelphian who was so taken with a bank note that he fell in love with the woman depicted in the portrait. The man wrote to the bank cashier to find out if the image was invented or "the representation of a breathing woman." The cashier then asked the note's engraver, who told a fanciful tale about the model being a former school teacher from a small New York town where she became a local celebrity when she saved a group of children from a fire. The narrative eventually devolved into speculation about the teacher's current location and marital status. In the end, the young man pledged that if she was real, "he was determined to have her, or die in the attempt" even if the search took him "to Kamtschatka."[47]

The young man's story was probably invented to provide whimsical material for a newspaper, but it worked as an anecdote because of its message about how Americans interacted with banks and bank notes. The proliferation of financial institutions did not create a marketplace where anonymous cash moved seamlessly from stranger to stranger; paper money was the physical and visual face of early republic banking where each bill possessed an identity of its own. As consumers accumulated financial sector and currency data, they latched on to any information that helped them navigate market relations. Paper money was particularly useful in this task because it provided an easily accessible way to probe the character of often distant institutions.[48]

Americans sought physical, emotional, and intimate connections in the marketplace and bank notes helped forge them. As the young man in love with the portrait on the bill attests, this relationship was not passive. Individuals did not accept whatever rates someone else offered during a bank note transaction; they utilized their monetary knowledge to actively negotiate and make the bill as useful for themselves as possible. Similarly, the public did not just accept bank notes in the form that financial institutions pushed them into circulation. Chapter 4 examines the way Americans physically engaged with paper money and manipulated bank notes by ripping them in half, lighting them on fire, or writing all over them.

CHAPTER 4

Bank Notes and Queries

THE ECONOMIC BOOM that followed the close of the War of 1812 meant new small-town businesses like the Jefferson Bank, which was chartered in New Salem, Ohio, in 1816. In an attempt to instill some grandeur in their institution or separate themselves from the other questionable banks that formed at the time, bank directors issued a variety of notes with unique, striking vignettes of patriotic scenes. Created by renowned Philadelphia engraver Richard G. Harrison, the images captured important national and regional events such as Oliver Perry's victory on Lake Erie in 1813 (three-dollar bill), Andrew Jackson's forces at the Battle of New Orleans in 1815 (one-dollar bill), and even Ohio legislators as they signed the state constitution (five-dollar bill). As part of the guarantee of confidence and authenticity from bank officials, each note contained the signatures of bank president Dr. George Duffield and cashier Robert Baird. The practice hardly ensured solvency, but it tried to replicate older face-to-face networks with an offer of personal assurance and a designation that specific individuals were legally responsible for the bill's redemption.[1]

Within months of its opening, questions arose about the Jefferson Bank's health; this led one noteholder to have difficulty passing a bill. Duffield and Baird ensured that large quantities of the notes pushed their way into the local economy, but that did little to help one man once rumors of insufficient funds at the bank started to circulate as well. The holder responded to the failed transaction on the back of the bill with some disgruntled poetry that indicated his exasperation. It called out the bank officials by name:

This note will pass
You stupid ass

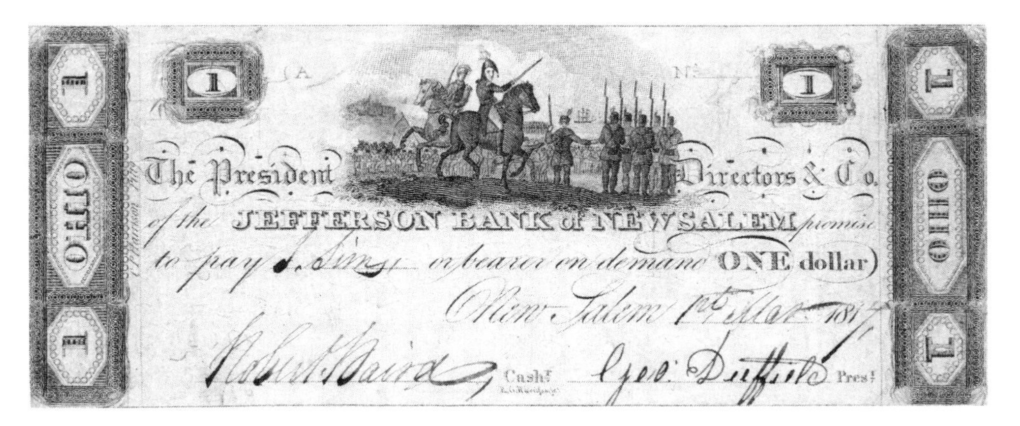

FIGURE 18. Notes from the Jefferson Bank of New Salem, Ohio, presented a confident facade with lively vignettes of historical events and bold signatures of bank officials. Author's collection.

For George & Bob
Have signed it

It is not clear whether the poet ever got someone to take the bill, but the naysayers were right about its quality. The Jefferson Bank went bankrupt less than two years after it opened and lawsuits against George Duffield to recover funds from unredeemed notes soon followed. The trial, held in 1818, also proved memorable when an argument between Dr. Duffield and prosecuting attorney David Redick spilled into the street and turned physical. Redick lunged at the banker/doctor, who defended himself with his surgical lance, stabbing the lawyer in the neck. Redick died from his wounds, but a subsequent trial cleared Duffield, who also escaped any real punishment for the bank collapse. Years later, the court seized Robert Baird's desk as the only remaining asset of the institution. After he found a bundle of worthless Jefferson Bank notes in a desk drawer, the sheriff used one to light his cigar before he returned the singed bill to the pile and closed the story of the bank.[2]

The Jefferson Bank narrative highlights how bank notes and shinplasters were more than mere scraps of undifferentiated paper that served to represent distant wealth. Americans engaged with paper money as specific physical objects whose images, words, and textures were vital to their circulation and how much confidence they inspired in the economy. Individual interactions with the bills should not be discounted, but rather seen as a vital part of the way that consumers utilized paper money to mediate market relations. Chapters 2 and 3 detailed the ways that Americans used currency transactions and bank note imagery to accumulate financial information about issuing institutions and their relationship to the national economy. This chapter picks up on that conversation to show that one of the ways they applied that information was to manipulate the bills by ripping them, burning them, and scribbling all over them. Paper money men designed the state bank note system for personal gain, but the public did not just capitulate to a currency regime that was not of their own making. When they materially altered cash to suit their own needs, consumers shaped the nation's paper circulation. This discussion also demonstrates how Americans' empirical understanding of banking and currency was inherently physical. Paper bills were not just fiat currency in the early republic; they had meaning and use separate from the value they represented or any goods or services that they could purchase.

An important feature of the bank note system was that the public engaged with bills not merely as banks had produced them, but also as paper instruments that they could manipulate. Americans repurposed paper currency in ways that showed both their ability to navigate the system as it was intended and their employment of accumulated financial knowledge to make discrete adjustments. This process mirrors what one historian has called the "village enlightenment" that occurred across America after the Revolutionary War as new citizens produced and consumed all sorts of print sources and material objects such as clocks, globes, and furniture that transformed individuals and communities alike. Paper currency functioned the same way as early republic Americans used bank notes both to understand the market and to engage with it.[3]

In order to challenge notions of how the market worked on a micro-level, it is critical to identify the ways that individuals used paper money experiences to make connections to the emerging capitalist economy. Scholars debate the effect of market forces on ordinary people and whether advancements in transportation, communication, and finance brought Americans closer together or functioned to isolate them from one other. Most acknowledge that steam engines and new sources of credit, for example, enabled the economy to grow rapidly, but not without a cost to the individuals involved. This moment contained a tension between depersonalized transactions devoid of humanity which forced producers and consumers to deal with unfamiliar people at a distance and more personal experiences where individual choices mattered as they shaped the marketplace. One way that consumers re-created those lost familiar and tactile associations was to utilize paper money that moved from person to person. Americans who infused cash with individual characteristics could facilitate distant or anonymous transactions and still feel an intimate connection to the market. Bank notes or shinplasters that were ripped in half or written on before they were released into the economy countered the supposed anonymity of the capitalist market and helped individuals construct a direct, physical connection.[4]

It was easy for early nineteenth-century Americans to view bank notes as more than just random paper scraps because of their long history with personified money. Throughout the eighteenth century, it-narratives (adventures of a pin, adventures of a cat, adventures of a pen) included examples of money that lived and communicated as it traveled around the countryside. Typical was a *Worcester Magazine* collection of stories that ran in the 1780s; written from the point of view of currency, it covered a range of economic, religious, and political topics. One satirical piece in the series, "Paper Money, Raised from the Dead, Speaketh for Itself!," championed paper money's commitment to the Revolutionary War cause: "I was born, lived and died for the salvation of America." These stories questioned the viability of paper money debts and ultimately the nation's credit in the face of untrustworthy and unstable bills and governments. This made sense in the revolutionary and post-revolutionary years when such questions of confidence related to the survival of the new nation and states that printed the bills, but by 1800, the paper money supply consisted mainly of bank notes. Questions of confidence became fragmented among the hundreds of note-issuing institutions and cemented the view that different types of paper money embodied different characteristics. There were good, trustworthy notes and ragged, dubious bills.[5]

The subtext of nineteenth-century currency narratives questioned the health of a financial system that included paper instruments issued alternatively by solid or questionable banks, but the content of the stories focused on the physicality of the bills themselves. One newspaper article, "Autobiography of a Fip Shin-Plaster," followed the circulation of a small-denomination note during the Panic of 1837. After it initially left the hands of a corporate clerk, the bill was tied together with others and placed in a "greasy pocket-book." When it fell into the possession of an old maid or a good housewife, she would attempt to preserve his "clean face"; one even "ironed me out smooth and nicely." However, the note complained that an old beggar had "kissed me rather roughly" and a miller had "crushed me into one corner of his pocket," before his corner was burnt by a clerk. In addition to the diversity of individuals who touched the notes, such narratives stressed the physical relationship between paper bills and their holders. Money did not simply exist to purchase goods or services, it functioned as a material object manipulated by its owners in their daily lives.[6]

In a few rare cases, this intimate treatment of money crossed over into fetishism where paper money became both animated and the object of desire. An extraordinary story in the *Literary Harvester* by C. D. Stuart, entitled "Meditations over a Bank-Note," recounted a dream in which the narrator obtained a Bank of the United States note from a miser who addressed the bill in question: "I have thee, and thou shalt escape no more." The young dreamer finally acquired the note and observed its "docility," while he conducted a scientific examination of its "name, age, characteristics, and the climate in which it was reared." His probe didn't end there, but instead turned to phrenology to "feel of its bumps, in order to ascertain somewhat of the habits and traits of character, if any it had." The story ended with a warning about trust based on appearance and the damage caused by the note and its compatriots from the Bank of the United States.[7]

Not every story of a physical interaction with paper money was so high-minded. After stage driver Washington Wilbur lost five dollars in an Albany tavern in 1855, he believed he had glimpsed the note in the possession of William Teelin. Wilbur called the police, who checked the bar and strip-searched Mr. Teelin. Before he left, the officer jabbed his finger into Teelin's mouth to dislodge his chewing tobacco. He found the five-dollar bill "neatly imbedded in the narcotic weed" and arrested Teelin. Stories like these that highlighted the tactile nature and the ease of physically manipulating paper currency furnished plenty of ammunition for lame jokes and bad puns. One typical attempt, called "Epigram for Wall Street," included the line "Take a bank note and fold it up, / And then you will find your money in creases!" Jokes like this provided humorous filler in the cultural landscape, but also reinforced the fact that bank notes existed as constant companions in Americans' physical lives.[8]

Such anecdotes showed an American public that was comfortable with the idea of paper money as active with personality, rather than passive and nondescript. Unlike gold or silver coins, whose permanence was part of their appeal to individuals interested in monetary constancy, paper money was inherently alterable. The pastor and economist Francis Wayland specifically argued in favor of paper currency because "if stolen, [it] is more easily identified, and, hence, more easily recovered." Any holder who glanced at the "marks of a bank bill, may safely swear to its identity; but, inasmuch as coin is intentionally all alike, this would be impossible in the case of specie." Bank note diversity came not just from its multitude of designs, but also from the various ways noteholders purposely manipulated them. If it was necessary to rip, eat, burn, or write on paper money in order to maximize its efficacy or satisfy a personal need, that is what the public did.[9]

It may seem odd to tear one's money, but paper bills were regularly ripped apart in the course of their life cycle. From their initial production, bank notes and shinplasters were made to be cut. Printed on sheets, individual bills had to be separated before circulation. In a bank this occurred behind the scenes, but for some unregulated shinplasters the process might take place in the open. After 1846, Iowa laws prevented banks from issuing currency, and without a local supply of bank notes, questionable shinplasters proliferated in towns like Dubuque, where one gentleman was seen "carrying in his [high silk] hat whole printed sheets resembling bank bills [and in] his vest pocket a pair of scissors, so that whenever and where-ever he was met on the street or other place, he was prepared to pay in this currency for wheat or pork." This sort of behavior raised eyebrows because of how transparently it presented questions about the value of the bills being supplied in such a cavalier manner. An English traveler likewise expressed his alarm when he looked through a window on Wall Street and witnessed men "with long scissors cutting and clipping the quires of new pretty pictures, and making them into bundles." He only later discovered them "to be new bank notes, on which they were intent upon raising the wind!" Those who saw notes cut in their initial creation could not help but ask whether the process was acceptable, but it became more commonplace to see bills torn in half once they entered circulation.[10]

It confounded some people, but on occasion it was practical to cut a bill to aid a transaction. During his travels in the 1810s, Englishman Henry Bradshaw Fearon stopped in Washington, D.C., where he tried to buy a pair of fifty-cent gloves. The shopkeeper would not take his one-dollar Philadelphia bank note without a large discount, so Fearon paid with one from a Baltimore bank one hundred miles closer. However, when the merchant could not make fifty cents in silver change, he "took a pair of scissors and divided the note between us." Although initially suspicious, Fearon learned that it was common practice and later noticed that "demi-notes are a common circulating medium." This practice persisted for decades. Just as shinplasters might circulate to address a local shortage of small change, demi-notes from legal, stable banks seemed to also fill the gap. Unused demi-notes also found value for their paper; during a charter election in Detroit, worthless "$5 notes of the Wild Cat Banks were cut in two and used as ballots."[11]

The most frequent reason to rip a bank note in half was to securely send it through the mail to conduct a long-distance transaction. When Anna Briggs Bentley asked her brother Isaac to send some money from Maryland to Ohio in 1826, she mentioned that as a precaution he should "procure as large notes as thee can, in United States or Baltimore notes, cut them in half, send one half and retain the other till thou hears from us, keeping a particular description of them and the half of but 1 note at a time." She hoped that a bill divided into two pieces meant better odds than one letter with a complete bill in case it was stolen or lost in transit. Of course, the extra cost of multiple envelopes could add up and the method did not actually guarantee safety. In the early 1840s, one newspaper described the practice as a ridiculous "ancient custom," which only succeeded in "doubling the postage, and *taking two* chances instead of *one*, to lose the note." This made sense before 1845, because each bank note sent through the mail was charged as a separate sheet of postage. Postal reform legislation lowered rates and by 1855 Americans had sent $100 million dollars through the mail.[12]

So many demi-notes traveled through the mail that it created a hassle when incomplete bills arrived without their partners. In 1847, administrators at the Botanico-Medical College of Ohio agreed to collect the mail for one of their students, but they did not know what to do when only one-half of three bank notes sent to him from Georgia arrived. After they wrote to the banks in question, they received a detailed response from H. W. Maer, the cashier of the Planters' Bank in Savannah with the institution's rules for the "payment of halves of bank notes." The guidelines stipulated that the half presented for redemption needed to have the signature of either the cashier or president and then the customer had to present proof that the note had been destroyed or lost, advertise in a newspaper for three months as to the details of the missing half note, and present a bond to secure again some later redemption attempt by another party. The college administrators took exception to the bank rules as unwieldy and impossible to fulfill. How, they asked, could they prove that the other half had been destroyed or lost? "May not the rogue who stole them have them yet? Suppose it were a post office clerk, may he not still be looking for the return of those halves to the office whence they came?" Likewise, they objected to the cost of three months' worth of newspaper advertisements given that if the bill was under ten dollars, its value would be largely eaten up by the process.[13]

Lawsuits quickly followed when holders of half-notes tried to recover their face value from the banks that issued them. A typical case involved John and Isaac Reynolds, respectively from Ohio and Maryland. John cut three notes from the Farmers' Bank of Virginia that totaled $210 and sent them through the mail to Isaac in two separate letters. The first set of half-notes arrived, but their matching pieces never materialized. After newspaper advertisements from Washington to Cincinnati failed to produce the lost notes, the men submitted the remaining pieces to the Farmers' Bank along with evidence of their ownership and even a security against any later appearance of the absent halves. The bank refused, but a judge upheld their claim and awarded them the funds. In this and other rulings, courts acknowledged that it was perfectly acceptable for bank note holders to tear or manipulate bank notes in ways that suited the public, even if the issuing institutions objected to the role consumers played in shaping the physical form and circulation of paper money.[14]

Just as easily as the public ripped a note in half, they could paste the pieces back together again. Evidence in one trial about the recovery of lost money included a Bank of the United States bill "which had been cut in two and pasted together, and looked dirty," while in California a lack of small-denomination notes resulted in two demi-notes from different banks being pasted together to create a new bill. The necessity of cutting and rejoining notes highlights the adaptability of American consumers to the material realities of their currency, which eventually led to new products like "Currency Adhesive Paper!" that was "Neat, Durable and Cheap." A sample advertisement promised that it was "superior both in quality and texture to anything heretofore invented for repairing bank bills." It was also finer aesthetically: "[It] is prepared perfectly transparent, which renders the reading as legible as before applied. It is THOROUGHLY ADHESIVE, and yet flexible, and will not break or crack in folding the Bill, Scrip or other parts applied."[15]

The public's comfort with bank notes being cut in half and reattached offered unique opportunities for fraud. A case from Alabama in the 1850s featured A. W. Marsh, who sued the Bank of Mobile to redeem a mutilated twenty-dollar bill that had been torn and pasted back together. While he claimed the note had come into his hands in the normal course of business, a bank teller testified that several similar notes had come to the bank, all "less in length by seven-eights than the original." The witness concluded that six notes had been cut and reattached to create a seventh note with the help of a counterfeit bill featuring the same classical vignette of a woman holding scales and a lion featured on the genuine bills. This time the court ruled for the bank and deemed the pasted money worthless. This anecdote is more than just an example of how individuals could use the idiosyncrasies of paper money to try and cheat others. It shows how the manipulation of bank notes was so ingrained in the bank note system that there was not necessarily anything unusual about a bill that had been torn or reattached; it took the expert eye of a bank cashier to spot a truly fraudulent example.[16]

Of course, not all plans to manipulate bank notes had to do with market exchanges. Sometimes it was about the enjoyment of playing around with the paper. Uriel Hayward wound up on trial in 1813 after he gathered up several notes from the Hallowell and Augusta Bank in Maine, tore them into long strips, and united them into a new note. The supreme judicial court of Massachusetts found Hayward not guilty because it judged that he had not intended to raise the value or circulate the end product of his project, but rather wanted to experiment with the design of the money for his own edification. The bank notes in question utilized elaborate plates made by Jacob Perkins, and Hayward's interest developed when he played around with the intricate designs contained in the pattern on the bills. Perkins himself liked to experiment with the physical properties of his own bills and reportedly once printed some bank notes on paper made from asbestos, "which were incombustible and served to surprise his friends." Bank notes that served as a party trick prop or artistic experiment seemed a far cry from their intended function, but they underlined the range of ways that individuals interacted with paper money. Such experiences were inherently physical and intimately tied noteholders to their notes. Even when they made remote purchases through the mail, Americans handled currency in personal ways. When a note was ripped in order to send each half in a separate envelope or when those pieces were pasted together, individuals were not detached from the market, they were actively engaged with it. This was not just about torn bank notes; there were numerous ways to manipulate a paper bill, including burning it.[17]

Most Americans did not play with asbestos like Jacob Perkins or light their cigars with broken bills like the sheriff in the Jefferson Bank case, but there were times when bank notes needed to be burned. Regulators understood that paper money's physical form made fire the best way to destroy unwanted notes, so when it came time to remove old bills from circulation many state resolutions called for broken bank notes to be burned with public notice. The process was labor intensive. It took more than five days in 1851 for the New York Treasury to burn $1.5 million in old bank notes that their office had accumulated. The problem was how best to physically manage a pile of bills equal to one thousand reams of paper. Officials first tried "placing them in a large strongly heated stove, but this was found to be a very tedious operation; the notes were so closely packed as to prevent the fire penetrating between them." They eventually chopped up the bills with a straw cutter to accelerate the burning. That seemed to do the trick. The spectacle must have pleased satirist James K. Paulding, who once wrote that he received a note of such poor quality that he could not pass it, so he threw it "into the fire, out of pure revenge against the bank from which it issued!" State regulators did not have much power over the antebellum money market, but a public burning sent a clear signal that they were doing what they could for the community.[18]

Physical interactions with bank notes included ripping, eating, or burning currency, but the most common way that early republic Americans manipulated paper money was stamping or writing all over it. While there were exceptions, especially in the 1850s and early 1860s, most bank notes were printed on one side with nothing on the reverse. This provided an opportunity for postproduction marks on bills that ranged from the mundane to the poetic. The blank space on the back of a bank note or shinplaster functioned equally as an advertising billboard, handy piece of scrap paper, or political broadside. Whether the reason was financial, practical, or lyrical, the shear amount of writing on the back of paper currency shows us that individuals were not shy about using bank notes to connect to the outside economy and society. This approach to bank notes compares favorably to the way antebellum Americans interacted with other textual sources; even readers of fiction engaged texts in ways that transcended an often-solitary act. Like reading a novel, using a bank note became a social experience. This is vital to our understanding of the early republic economy because it offers one more piece of evidence about how paper money functioned not to drive people apart, but to bring them together. Whether in the context of a formal banking procedure, a commercial transaction, or a personal meditation, Americans enhanced paper money with their own writings as part of the process by which they crafted wider economic relationships.[19]

Signatures, endorsements, or stamps used by professional paper money men to track bank notes through their life cycle humanized paper currency and demonstrated that it was more than just a lifeless signifier of wealth. The first time a bank note was marked after production was when the bank's officers signed it and pushed it into circulation. As shown in the case of the Jefferson Bank, signatures carried real value to project confidence to the local community and create a persona for paper money. Especially in small towns where most residents would have known bank officers by name, if not in fact, it was vital to tie bills to real people with their own reputations. However, bank notes did not always stay near their issuing institutions. So how did bank officials' signatures operate on notes far from home? Ideally, personal signatures ensured the bill's authenticity and provided a layer of security against counterfeit or fraudulent currency. For this system to work, individuals who were not connected with the bank or its local community needed to be able to recognize a cashier's or bank president's signature by sight. However, it was impossible to identify all these names, especially when the number of banks in the nation climbed to over a thousand. Enter *The Autographical Counterfeit Detector*. The book reprinted bank president and cashier signatures from almost every institution in the nation (the 1852 edition went on for sixty-five pages) to provide a guide for curious merchants, consumers, and bankers. As might be expected, this security measure quickly became a tool for counterfeiters who used the magazine as a handy reference for their labor.[20]

Inspired by early republic theorists who claimed that an individual's distinct penmanship revealed their inner characteristics, the public took it upon itself to analyze the physical aspects of the signatures. Like other shifts from Enlightenment rationality to Romanticist emotionalism, such analysis even posited that handwriting could betray hidden truths about the self. Taken to its most Romantic extreme, such displays of individuality could be part of a resistance to the perceived homogeneity of the market economy. However, it would be folly to claim that with a personal signature on a bank bill a cashier or president struck a blow against the evolution of systematic financial capitalism; it is also clear that the rise of the bank note system did not simply turn bankers into machines who sucked the humanity out of the economy. Signatures and other official marks brought life and character to paper money while they provided important information for consumers.[21]

Just as signatures on the front of a bank note began its life in circulation, a name or date on the back could end it. Not every woman or man who redeemed a note wrote an endorsement, but it was common to see "C. Baldwin 5/6/62," "Mrs. Simon," or just the elegantly drawn initials "B. B." Sometimes bank clerks wrote statements on the back such as "Presented by Chas. R. Young" or "Presented 14th April 1840 and specie payment paid." Clerks also identified problematic notes from defunct institutions and labeled them as broken. Not every consumer knew that the Exchange Bank in Brunswick, Georgia, failed in 1842, but they could accumulate critical financial knowledge if they came across one of their notes that read: "Presentation acknowledged payment refused 26th June 1843 Jas Moore cashier." The text prevented the circulation of this particular broken bill and conveyed vital financial data to anyone who came in contact with any notes from the Exchange Bank.[22]

Some notifications about a questionable bill's trustworthiness were more than informational alerts; they were explicit warnings meant to identify counterfeit bills and remove them from circulation. When this process occurred at the powerful Suffolk Bank in Boston, the institution used its unique role as the quasi-central bank of New England to provide added authority to the label on a bad bill. When a clerk at the Suffolk Bank noticed that a five-dollar note, purported to be from the Warren Bank in Danvers, Massachusetts, was actually a fake that had been altered from the Blue Hill Bank, he stamped it "Counterfeit Suffolk Bank" to declare it unfit for circulation and inform any future party that it had been recognized and decommissioned by the imposing figure of the Suffolk Bank. In the late 1850s, when the upstart Bank of Mutual Redemption challenged the Suffolk's exchange authority, the new bank followed suit and added "COUNTERFEIT/A.B./BANK OF M.R." stamps to fake notes presented at their counter. Outside the presence of the Suffolk or Bank of Mutual Redemption, the community looked to peer support for declarations of bad bills. One inscription merely read "Of Isaac Fletcher Counterfeit so say all W. Stevens."[23]

While these paper money markings largely aided banks as they tracked currency, they also provided a wealth of information to the public about the institutions and their notes. Recent studies describe the power of nonhuman bureaucratic or business ephemera, such as accounting books, in ordering capitalist knowledge and behavior. Ledger books or mercantile accounts usually resided within an individual's or firm's business sphere and did not travel through the wider community, but paper money was designed to operate across such borders and without limitations. When bank officers added stamps or text to their bills, they interacted with those members of the public who would subsequently possess and use the money. Such connections remind us that even seemingly mundane pecuniary information about redemption locations or rates existed as part of the interpersonal human exchanges facilitated by paper money.[24]

Like bankers with their stamps, the general public used the blank reverse side of bank notes for practical concerns such as a ledger to identify how the money had been spent, as a billboard for advertisements, or just a piece of scrap paper to jot down some remarks or words. The backs of paper money made convenient receipts for consumers, merchants, landlords, or any other individuals who sought to keep a personal accounting of their notes. One Burrillville Bank note contained endorsements that detailed its activity in Providence on "July 17, 1841" and the "Dedham Turnpike July 28, 1843." While the bank actually failed in 1832 and the Dedham Turnpike was free to travel on after 1838, the notations show the movement of the bill over time and space and how some holders attempted to catalog its usage. Similarly, the back of a New York Exchange Bank three-dollar bill indicated that it was "Rec'd for Rent" from a "Mr. Mathews." Another just stated that it was "To pay the rent." Other notes detailed longer histories, including a ten-dollar note made out to J. Smith that was issued from the Woodstock branch of the Vermont State Bank at the bank's founding in 1807. He still possessed the bill more than fifteen years later when he tried to redeem it, but unfortunately for Smith the overextended and badly run bank had closed its doors in 1812. That did not stop a Mr. Lyman who signed the back of note in 1824 and wrote that he took it from Smith for seven dollars in cash. Such markings offer tantalizing clues to recreate the movement of individuals and cash within the market economy, but, more importantly, they show how early republic Americans tried to rationalize or keep account of their own lives.[25]

While not as dramatic as the "adventures of a bank note" stories, some bills wound up in the middle of extraordinary circumstances retold on their backs. When Baltimore constable George Riggs arrested N. S. Jacobs in

1849, he also seized a fraudulent hundred-dollar bill from the Farmers' Bank of Seneca County. Jacobs had obtained the note from his former roommate William Thomas Green Morton, a con man and later medical pioneer known for his use of ether as a surgical anesthetic. Morton skipped town, but he left behind a trunk that contained the questionable currency. To retain any evidentiary value that it might have for future legal proceedings, a witness, F. J. Streeter, cataloged a brief history of the bill on its back: "Rec'd from Mr. Riggs, as one of the Bank certificates taken by him on the arrest of Jacobs, and the seizure of W. T. G. Morton's trunk. F. Streeter Balto. June 1849."[26]

Likewise, E. B. Moore, a former printer and soldier in the Mexican War, crafted a narrative on the back of a note from the Granite Bank in Exeter, New Hampshire, that created a synergy between his experience and the bill itself. He obtained the one-dollar bill in Boston in 1844 and, after holding it for four years, sat down to catalog its adventures. He had taken the bill through the southern states before it accompanied him "in every batt'e from Vera Cruz to the city of Mexico . . . [over] the length of the Mississippi and Ohio rivers." After all these "imminent dangers and hairbreadth 'scapes," he restored the note to circulation with his "best wishes." While not stated explicitly, Moore may have held on to this particular bill because it included a vignette of a bustling industrial scene in Exeter, New Hampshire, just down the road from his home near the mills on the Merrimack River.[27]

Bank notes that featured advertisements projected less information about a bill's past narrative and more about a business's hopes for its future circulation. Merchants who stamped the backs of paper currency to promote themselves calculated that whatever time and labor it took to apply the stamp would more than be repaid with new customers. Leonard Bond certainly embraced innovative strategies to publicize his hat warehouse. He offered free hats to ministers, "free hat ironing on Saturday," and over the four decades he operated in New York, placed hundreds of advertisements in newspapers like the *New York Mirror*, the *New York Evangelist*, and the *Subterranean, United with the Working Man's Advocate*. Toward the end of his career, Bond adopted an underground advertising campaign and stamped notes that came into his shop: "Bond's Hat Warehouse 156 Canal St. NY." One example of this stamp is particularly curious because of its inclusion on a note from the New Jersey Manufacturing and Banking Company of Hoboken, dated July 4, 1828. The Hoboken bank folded a year

FIGURE 19. Merchants stamped advertisements on the back of bank notes so they could cheaply reach a wide audience as the bill moved around town. Shown here are the obverse and reverse of a three-dollar note from the New Jersey Manufacturing and Banking Company. Author's collection.

later, when Bond's shop was located on the Bowery and not at 156 Canal, where he operated over fifteen years later. So either Leonard Bond advertised on a bill that circulated decades after the issuing bank had closed or he repurposed old notes for billboard advertisements. Either prospect offers an interesting lesson for how merchants used bank notes as canvases on which to speak to the public.[28]

Another colorful advertisement popped up on a note from the Newport Bank of Rhode Island. It was stamped:

Chinese Billiard Rooms
The Largest & Most
Elegant in the World
539 & 541 Broadway, N.Y.
G. D. & C. F. Miles
Proprietors

In the late 1850s, most New Yorkers were already familiar with the Chinese Rooms. Known for its minstrel shows, Chinese jugglers, and casino, the building was famous even before it housed Barnum's New Museum. Was the advertisement meant for out-of-towners or the many newly arrived immigrants to the antebellum city? It is hard to know whether stamped ads increased business, but the frequency with which they appeared on bank notes clearly shows proprietors' willingness to try to connect with the public.[29]

Not all bank note scribbles were for business purposes; the backs of bills also made ideal, portable writing surfaces. By the end of the eighteenth century, most middling Americans took for granted that they could obtain stationery supplies from booksellers in any large town. However, such materials usually remained in one's home. Bank notes became a ready source of scrap paper in a pinch. When the need arose to jot down random words, names, or addresses, people grabbed whatever paper was handy and bank notes were always around. So, when one holder of a ten-dollar Rhode Island Agricultural Bank bill needed to calculate some figures, she or he wrote on the back:

3.30
5.
1.70
10.00

While this was a simple equation, its inclusion on the back of a ten-dollar bill provided concrete evidence of an individual using this specific piece of paper in multiple ways. The note was both money to be spent in the market and a physical space to calculate what that money could buy. This note also highlights how bank note holders manipulated the paper object in front of them for their own personal purposes. Yes, bills bought goods and services,

FIGURE 20. The backs of bank notes doubled as convenient scratch paper. Collection of the Massachusetts Historical Society.

but they could also be used to help consumers organize their thoughts or express their views.[30]

Some holders created bank note writings that were less practical and more lyrical; they crafted poetic, personal, or political statements to engage the wider community. Such partisan quotes or wry observations are best explained as a mixture of marginalia and graffiti. When antebellum readers encountered fraudulent literary sources, some reacted with displeasure or outrage and felt compelled to immediately respond within the pages. These demonstrations were not just a show of taste, they were readers' attempts to issue a judgment on the truthfulness of the material before them. One reader wrote "A great lie" next to a particularly unconvincing story of a man who treed a bear a la Davy Crockett. Bank note marginalia similarly commented on the quality of the currency and whether it was able to inspire confidence. The ruling written on the back of a note was then pushed into circulation to provide financial information to the community.[31]

Other messages on paper money functioned like graffiti that explicitly sought to make connections to the wider community through expressive, philosophical, humorous, profane, or sentimental words. On a wall or other public surface, graffiti functioned to literally write an individual's name, story, or ideas onto an otherwise indifferent landscape. Bank note endorsements that emotionally exclaimed political views or thoughts on financial policy fulfilled the social commentary aspect of this formula, while autobiographical accounts about hardship or loss shared personal narratives with the public. Each bank note inscription represented a step taken by its author to be recognized in the midst of an expansive and supposedly isolating market; the author had put pen to paper money to make a connection with whoever the bill would meet as it circulated.[32]

The fact that a bill's purchasing power was not tied solely to its face value, but rather to society's confidence in it, manifested in a desire to celebrate a good bill or indict a bad bill on the back of the note itself. One overly excited owner of a five-dollar bill from the Exchange Bank of Tennessee exclaimed, "This is a damn good Bill." Given that the note was produced in 1854 and the bank failed just four years later, it is possible that the holder wrote the declaration to convince a skeptical party and not just as a triumphant salute.[33]

Perhaps this type of response is best seen on a couple of Panic of 1837–era shinplasters issued by Ohio builder Thomas Morrison, whose bills proliferated in Dayton after a wave of local bank closures resulted in a lack of available small change. At least one individual seemed to lament that development on the back of a 6¼-cent note when he wrote, "Oh! the gold and silver currency." Morrison didn't help his standing in the community when he skipped town just as the state passed an 1838 law that prohibited shinplasters, even though he did post a public notice entitled "Shin-plasters in Danger!" Claiming that he had to leave Dayton for a job, forty miles away in Greenville, Morrison wrote, "I am not the man under any circumstances to take advantage of a law by which the State allows me to act the rascal. I intend to redeem every note I have put into circulation, and that as soon as I return, and will do it with pleasure and satisfaction." He continued, "I desire my fellow citizens and all who have confidence in my word of honor not to refuse to take them until my return, when every cent shall be paid with the addition of six per cent. interest." Apparently, no lawsuits were filed to hold Morrison accountable and at least one later source claimed that he did return to Dayton to fully redeem his shinplasters.[34]

As evidenced by a message on one of his 12½-cent bills, not everyone was satisfied with Thomas Morrison's unregulated paper currency. Using the builder's shinplasters as a basis for a wider discussion of the era's monetary policies, it read, "Ever since Van Buren has been president the Country has been infested with this trash. Jackson tinkered with the currency so much it robed the people of a metalig kind that they had and these damd rags was necary to be printed. huza for democracy. Signed A holder." The message uniquely attacked Democratic presidents Van Buren and Jackson, while simultaneously tapping hard money beliefs that paper money, especially small-denomination notes, deprived the economy of more stable specie. The expansive text showed the direct connection many noteholders made between the actions of specific politicians and their daily use of poor-quality paper money.[35]

Such arguments about financial policy became commonplace on bank notes as the Bank War and the Panic of 1837 took their toll on the nation's confidence in paper money. Some featured partisan attacks like the questionable Urbana Bank notes inscribed with "Fruits of Whiggery," "Anti-metalic or Whig Representative," and "go it ye cripples." More often, it was boilerplate anti-banking slogans ascribed to William Henry Harrison, Andrew Jackson, or another leading politician. A standard Daniel Webster attribution on the back of a two-dollar note from the troubled Bank of River Raisin in Monroe, Michigan, read, "Of all the contrivances for cheating the laboring classes of mankind, none have been more effectual than that which deceives them with paper money. It is the most effectual invention to fertilize the rich man's field with sweat of the poor man's brow." Attributed quotes were not always accurate, but they provided noteholders with an authoritative voice for expressing opinions about the fraudulent state of early republic currency.[36]

One person whom individuals turned to for authentic anti-banking political quotes was William Leggett, the editor and inspirational leader of the anti-monopoly Loco Foco Party, who inveighed against bank notes in the pages of the *New York Evening Post*. Leggett implored his readers to use the notes themselves to challenge the system and declared that, since "paper money is fingered by a great many hands," it offered a unique opportunity for cheap, but effective protest. He suggested that his readers "write upon the back of every bank-note which should come into their possession, some short sentence expressive of their sentiments. For example—'No Monopolies!' 'No Union of Banks and State!' 'Jackson and Hard Money!' 'Gold before Rags!' and the like."[37]

Some scholars have questioned whether Leggett's readers ever followed his advice, but his was not the only voice that advocated such protests. Just two months earlier, *The Man*, an anti-bank New York newspaper aimed at the city's workers, included a letter from "Peter Pincers" with suggestions for bank note commentary based on the bill's vignettes. His example for those with "a dog laying on the key of the strong box" (seen on a three-dollar bill from the Bank of Orleans, a one-dollar Phoenix Bank note, a five-dollar bill from the Stueben County Bank, and others): "Why place a dog upon the key? Say, was it meant to frighten me From getting out a silver dollar, Lest puppy-dog should show his choler?" Peter Pincers concluded his opposition to paper money with the argument that even if they were clever, such endorsements would not give "Bank notes *durability*, *solidity*, and *worth*." He instead suggested "a brick or corresponding block of wood for every note." He believed the added weight would limit their circulation, but sarcastically worried that the banks would just profit by using the new notes to monopolize the brick and wood business.[38]

The Hecker brothers (John, George, and Isaac), who worked as bakers during the day and Loco Foco politicos at night, definitely took Leggett's message to heart. George Hecker later explained in detail:

> When we were bakers the money in common use was the old-fashioned paper issued by private banks under State charters. We were regularly against it. So we bought a hand printing-press and set it up in the garret of our establishment. All the bills we received from our customers, some thousands sometimes every week, we smoothed out and put in a pile, and then printed on their backs a saying we took from Daniel Webster (though I believe it was not quite authentic): "Of all the contrivances to impoverish the laboring

> classes of mankind, paper money is the most effective. It fertilizes the rich man's field with the poor man's sweat."

Hecker's description of the brothers' conscious and labor-intensive effort to manufacture anti-banking propaganda on the back of the money that came into their bakery shows a fascinating choice of protest. Once they set up a printing press, they could have been content with the Loco Foco broadsides they also printed and posted around the city, but they made sure to bring their message to the community on its paper money. Like Leggett, they identified the medium as important for this particular anti-banking message.[39]

Bank notes tagged with political slogans became so popular that Philadelphia bookseller James Davis sought to make the process easier for the public. In the early 1840s, Davis sold a booklet of "ten such 'endorsements'" that were "printed with good, large type, on fair paper." For one dollar his customers received quotes from William Leggett, Henry Clay, John Adams, Andrew Jackson, John Tyler, and others, representing a variety of political parties: "Old Federalists and Modern Whigs, Democrats of the olden times and Democrats of the modern times." The customer just had to tear out the quote of their choice and paste it onto a bank note in their possession. Prefabricated quotes were not as personal as ones written by hand, but like a graffiti artist's stencil, they provided a tool for allowing a message to be transmitted from a noteholder to the community.[40]

While political messages written on bank notes often followed a predictable script, others straddled the line between political and personal. One five-dollar bill from the Farmers' Exchange Bank in Glocester, Rhode Island, contained this cryptic phrase: "Col. Lucifer with his imps of Fudderalism on the lying scout election squad." While the immediate meaning of the unsigned text is obscure, it seems to be an attack on the Federalist Party traced to Dedham doctor, diarist, and fervent Republican Nathaniel Ames. Even though, or maybe because his brother Fisher was a leading Massachusetts Federalist, Nathaniel relentlessly attacked what he called the "Fudderal" party in the early years of the century. Like the Lucifer comments on the note, Ames even bemoaned a Federalist electoral victory when he wrote "Devilism reigns!" in his diary. Completely deciphering Ames's quote is not important by itself, but what is interesting is his choice to place the phrase

FIGURE 21. Whether personal or political, bank note inscriptions allowed paper money holders to communicate with others in the market. Collection of the Massachusetts Historical Society.

on the back of a Farmers' Exchange Bank note sometime after it began circulation in April 1808.[41]

The Farmers' Exchange Bank was not just any bank; it failed spectacularly in the spring of 1809 when Boston financier Andrew Dexter Jr.'s scheme to get the bank to print hundreds of thousands of dollars of unbacked notes crashed and burned. Maybe Nathaniel Ames held the note when the bank went under and, like others, blamed Federalist politicians like Samuel Dexter (Andrew's uncle) for the debacle or maybe this was a personal message placed on a bank note he sent to his brother. There are numerous possibilities for why Ames wrote the words, but what the message does show is that any act of scribbling on the back of a bank note could be both personal and part of a larger political conversation between the writer and the public.[42]

Political attacks did not have to be aimed at politicians; high-profile bank officials made useful targets. Anti-bank tensions ran especially high in Baltimore, especially after the collapse of the Bank of Maryland in 1834. It was not an economic downturn that led to the institution's downfall, but rather scandal and fraud among several of the bank's officers. The public's anger grew and boiled over during a three-day riot in August 1835. The backs of notes captured some of the anti-banking strife in the city, such as the snarky comment on a Baltimore Savings Institution bill that declared "Stopt pay Sept. 9th 1840 Presdt. ran away." A detailed comment on a shinplaster from John Clark's Lottery and Exchange Office offered advice on how to stop city bank closures:

> The way to make the Baltimore Bankers pay
> specie—just erect a Gallows in front of
> every Banking house in the City and show their
> officers a *Hempen Rope*—then they will fork it up.

Threats of violence were not common in bank note writings, but given the history of riot, incarceration, and anger experienced by members of the Baltimore populace, it was not a surprise to see individuals seeking outlets to express their feelings.[43]

Rather than restrict themselves to political issues, bank note authors often utilized personal narratives when they engaged with the public. A frequent topic was loss of money, so that the note that served as the platform for the words also represented the end of their funds. The back of a Planter's Bank twenty-dollar bill made specific reference to a lost cotton fortune: "Go, go!—12 months ago I was worth two thousand of your amount, but alas, to-day I am now not worth one dollar.—Oh, Cotton! Cotton!! Cotton!!!" A similar primal scream from a failed speculator on his last note exclaimed "cotton, cotton, cotton." One newspaper editor credited the outburst as an homage to Greek orator Demosthenes's famous quote "action, action, action," but this might be giving a bit too much literary credit to the speculator. More standard bank note lamentations included "The last of a large fortune spent on drink" or "After keeping this for ten years, it is gone at last. Such is life." These sentiments were conscious musings on the multilayered connection between the author and the physical paper on hand. The loss of wealth was not abstract, but rather experienced through the potential absence of the actual bank note from his or her presence.[44]

Another related genre of bank note writing specifically referenced gambling losses and the role that paper money played in a gambler's luck. Joseph Cross included painful words (and even an invocation of death) on the back of a Northern Bank of New York five-dollar note dated March 14, 1849, from Fort Independence, Missouri. Cross found himself in unfortunate circumstances after he had set out for California from the East Coast with $450. He got to Missouri and gambled heavily and unsuccessfully. Down to his last five dollars, he mourned, "God only knows where I will get more. I part with it as though it were my last friend." In this sad case, the bank note both provided Cross with his last physical connection to a hopeful life that was almost gone and the space to leave a lasting record of his failure. Perhaps he thought his story could act as a warning for naive Forty-Niners. Another despondent gambler exclaimed, "Gentlemen, this is all I have left of a fortune of $50,000. I owe it all to gambling. Oh, the vice!" However, on the same note a different writer answered his gloomy lament with a hopeful suggestion: "If you get this bill again try your luck; for I bet it on a horse trot, and won it, at Waterville, Me." While it was unlikely that the bill circulated back to the initial inscriber, this colorful exchange speaks to how bank note authors viewed paper money as a collective billboard within a public forum. Likewise, when gamblers reached out to the community through their bank note writings, they played on an unspoken aspect of the conversation that compared illicit gambling on cards or horse racing to the risk taken by anyone using questionable paper money.[45]

Statements of loss could move beyond gaming debts to read like a last will and testament for both the note and the note holder. One message, supposedly "written in an elegant business hand," declared, "Here is a $5 bill which I intend to toss out of my window, in Norfolk, as soon as I have written this. I am now no lover of money. I hate it most cordially, for it has been the ruin of all my family. I will beg from door to door eternally, rather than own another cent one hour." The pain was not just his own. He continued, "[Paper money] made my grandfather a suicide, my father a murderer, my mother the victim of a sorrow that sunk her early to the grave, my brother a gambler, and myself a convict in the state prison four years." This was an overly dramatic account, but it highlighted the way that paper money served as both the symbol of an individual's relationship to the wider economy and their physical connection to it. A writer who placed his last thoughts on a note meant to be discarded made an attempt to sever ties to the market that had brought bad tidings, but not before he made one last attempt to communicate with others through that same bank note.[46]

Not all bank note writings hinged on drama and calamity; sometimes authors used humor or sarcasm. A note signed J. D. offered the following prayer: "I will be married to-morrow. God help me!" Another wedding featured in a message by James S. Slidell, a disgruntled justice of the peace. He declared on the back of a note from the City Bank of Beaver Dam, Wisconsin, his annoyance that "this one-dollar bill is all I received for performing the marriage ceremony between John Gibbs and Mary Wallace, of the town of Salem, Wisc., after having traveled five miles in the cold and paid two dollars and fifty cents to the livery stable." Here again, the effectiveness of using the bank note as a broadside to jot down an immediate complaint or gripe hinged on the dual role paper money served as a circulating representation of value and as a physical object itself. Knowing that the City Bank bill would continue to move around the Wisconsin economy, Slidell used the paper instrument both to vent his emotions and to transmit information about Gibbs and Wallace to the community. If James Slidell did plan a bit of public shame for the skimpy compensation, he certainly achieved it. The anecdote was picked up by the press and reprinted in newspapers from Boston to San Francisco in the summer and fall of 1859.[47]

Statements on paper money offered the public everything from valuable financial information about the bills in their hands to pithy observations on politics and the community, but not everyone appreciated the tone or the content of paper money graffiti. When the Hecker brothers turned their New York bakery into a Loco Foco print shop to mark bills with anti-banking slogans, officials attempted to stop their work. George Hecker explained that "they tried to punish us for defacing money, but we beat them. We didn't deface it; we only printed something on the back of it." No official records explain how the authorities tried to punish the brothers, but George Hecker mentioned that any penalty was withheld because, like most bank note writers, they only stamped the blank back of the notes. However, two decades later, a young man ran into trouble when he tried to redeem notes at a bank counter, because he had literally defaced the vignette on the front of the bill. His transgression occurred when he "affixed a pipe to the mouth of the venerable" Edward Ermatinger, president of the Elgin County Bank, whose portrait graced the note.[48]

Other objections came from those who did not like the blunt language or the use of words like "damn" or "ass" that littered the notes. The *Baltimore Sun* decried the fact that one-third of the city's shinplasters contained "the *witticisms* of low blackguards, which render them unfit to enter the hands of any respectable persons. Low, indecent and obscene language is written on the back of them, and the sooner they are expelled [from] the community, the better for the morality of the rising generation." The comment both identified the large number of bills with writing on the back and acknowledged the cross-class circulation of notes within the city. Individual notes moved easily around town from person to person, so any message written on the back came into contact with a variety of viewers. Bank note authors recognized these patterns and chose to mark up paper money specifically because it enabled them to communicate with the wider public. Rather than isolating or atomizing individuals in the growing market economy, bank notes and shinplasters helped facilitate associations.[49]

One final example demonstrates the power of manipulated bank notes and how Americans utilized these discrete scraps of paper money to connect to a wider economy and society in the antebellum years. In 1836, as the Bank of the United States concluded its run as the nation's central bank in the wake of Andrew Jackson's veto of its recharter, Boston merchant Henry Plympton held a five-dollar bill from the institution. He attached an endorsement to the note to link the national banking crisis to his personal fortunes: "The enclosed Bill I intend to keep till the re-establishment of another U.S. Bank." A pledge not to spend five dollars was a pretty small wager on the bank's ultimate success, but this modest step emphasized Henry Plympton's choice to not simply acquiesce to the fiscal policies of distant politicians. The public did not just pass along notes in the way that banks or the government intended, but instead made the currency their own when they marked it up or tore it in half as they used their accumulated financial knowledge to actively engage with the banking system.[50]

Henry Plympton's pledge was not just a statement about the Bank of the United States; it was an attempt to translate his personal paper money practices into action related to the government's political decisions. Chapters 3 and 4 have explored the numerous ways people interacted with their paper money on a daily basis. They gathered monetary information through a material connection to bank notes and then manipulated those same bills as part of that relationship. However, life within the bank note system did not end with buying and selling in the market. Americans sought various ways to connect their personal currency experiences with the national and state policies that shaped the economy. Chapter 5 examines how people like Henry Plympton used their lived experiences and understanding of the paper money economy when they entered into political debate and action.

PART III

Political Economy

CHAPTER 5

Getting Money into Politics

EVEN THOUGH IT occurred in the midst of a major economic downturn, the election of 1840 is remembered more for its display of popular democracy than its serious policy debates. The campaign featured parades, floats, barbecues, and songs about log cabins and hard cider along with "Tippecanoe and Tyler Too." Meanwhile, Whig candidate William Henry Harrison gave more than twenty major speeches that covered banking, currency, and slavery on his way to a short stay in the White House. At an appearance in Dayton before a crowd estimated at over fifty thousand people, Harrison explained that because the nation's hard money (specie) supply could not meet commerce demands he was "in favor of paper money," but that did not mean that he trusted it. Harrison's wariness of the financial system came from his own experience: "I am not a bank man. Once in my life I was, and they cheated me out of every dollar I placed in their hands." He instead called for a "safe" and "properly devised banking system" with the "capability of bringing the poor to a level with the rich." There was nothing specific or original about his comments, but the audience's "tremendous cheering" indicated their approval. An anonymous bank note holder who reprinted Harrison's "I am not a bank man" line on the back of a suspect two-dollar bill from the Bank of River Raisin in Monroe, Michigan, seemed to agree as well.[1]

The daily adventure of using uncurrent notes, wildcat bills, or worthless shinplasters colored Americans' opinions of the marketplace and spilled over into the political arena. Paper money transactions provided individuals first-hand lessons in how currency functioned and grounded entry into debates over fiscal and monetary policy and legislation. This did not necessarily mean a causal relationship between one's bank note dealings and voting preferences, but lived experiences mattered for political engagement. Individuals did not bring one type of bank note empiricism to the political arena, but rather reactions that ranged from outright hostility to an embrace of paper money.

Because individual experience played a critical role in shaping ideas about currency policy, such debates did not always follow blind political ideology and could cut against expected partisan loyalties. While Loco Focos embodied a near-universal opposition to paper money and chartered banking, Whigs occasionally called for legislation to restrict bank notes and Democrats sometimes favored measures to expand the paper money supply. Moreover, groups of nonpartisan actors banded together to seek more fairness in the currency system. This chapter examines three discrete paper money debates to demonstrate how Americans' political rhetoric and activities related to how they read, manipulated, and negotiated bank notes. Few people who used paper money believed that it operated efficiently and fairly; almost everyone wanted the system changed in some way, from the issuance of more bank notes to the elimination of paper entirely.

During the Bank War, large crowds vigorously objected when Andrew Jackson's removal of federal deposits from the Second Bank of the United States (BUS) led Nicholas Biddle to contract the bank's credit supply. The havoc that resulted in the nation's money markets elicited calls from around the country for the federal government to exert its authority to guarantee stability and uniformity in the currency system. Underneath these public cries was the general agreement that state banking regulations did not sufficiently ensure the quantity and quality of the nation's paper money supply. Not everyone looked to a paper increase to resolve money market problems. Hard money advocates believed that fairness in the currency system meant a prohibition on paper money. Groups like the Loco Focos, intellectually led by William Leggett, cited workers paid in poor-quality bank notes to call for a specie-based economy with stable, face-value currency that could not be manipulated. Other individuals pursued a middle ground monetary policy to bring specie's stability to the most vulnerable members of society; at the same time, merchants and bankers would be left free to assume the increased risk of using paper bills. The banker and Whig/Republican politician Samuel Hooper personified the push to prevent small-denomination bank notes under five or ten dollars, while larger bills would continue to circulate for business purposes. These small note regulators waged a state-by-state campaign that targeted minor changes to existing banking law rather than pushing major systematic disruptions.

One year after Andrew Jackson vetoed a measure to recharter the BUS, the conflict between the president and the bank's director, Nicholas Biddle, entered a new phase when the Treasury Department removed the government deposits that usually made their way to the national bank. The policy change now sent hefty sums to select state-chartered institutions (nicknamed Jackson's pet banks) instead of the BUS. In response, Biddle called in loans and stopped the bank's flow of credit in a move that sent waves through the nation's money market from the fall of 1833 to the summer of 1834. Bank War historiography is extensive if not particularly recent; most scholars investigate the relationship between partisan politics and the financial struggle or how the nascent Whig Party and Democrats debated banking ideology. While the wider conflict was not exclusively about currency, this episode was all about paper money. Biddle's decision to squeeze the nation's money supply deprived even those Americans who did not directly seek bank credit of cash they needed for daily necessities and simultaneously created a ripple of fear through the market that even good bills would not circulate. The bank note system required confidence and the crisis meant that even a pet bank that never stopped its specie payments, like the Agricultural Bank at Natchez, saw the discount on its notes in New Orleans rise from 4 to more than 25 percent. This point is often missing from descriptions of the so-called "Biddle contraction," but it is vital for a holistic explanation of how citizens translated their daily paper currency experiences into political engagement during the Bank War.[2]

Credit was neither an abstract concept nor something that most Americans personally obtained from the BUS or even a local bank; credit meant available cash and that meant bank notes. Artisans, laborers, and farmers did not generally have access to bank loans in the 1830s, but they understood the connection between the money market for individuals who received bank credit and the money supply for everyone else who utilized bank notes. Americans confronted Biddle's credit crunch as less an ideological battle about the fate of the nation's central bank and more an immediate shortage of necessary currency that their families and businesses needed to pay for essential goods and services. It was in this context early in the Bank War that Philadelphia type founder John Ronaldson explained that everyone should pay attention to monetary and financial policy and turn their personal narrative into political action. Under the name "A Friend of the People," he argued that "all of us—the poorest, as well as the richest citizens—being deeply interested in the *currency* of the country, which affects every transaction of our daily business,—we all have the right to investigate its laws, and the practices connected with it; and to point out the good, or expose the evil influences of Banks in relation to this." People heard the message and when Biddle's contraction seized up local money markets, the outcry was swift and loud.[3]

Public meetings and rallies around the country demanded a currency fix and sent strongly worded memorials to Congress pleading for a legislative solution. More than seven hundred petitions from every state except Jackson's home of Tennessee arrived in Washington during Biddle's contraction with about 70 percent opposed to the removal of the deposits. The documents reflected the fact that, even in the midst of the Bank War, there was still space for political expression outside of a binary conflict between two partisan models of capitalism. Committed Democrats and proto-Whigs played critical roles in the credit contraction debate, but they did not account for all the voices. Much of the American public engaged the Bank War on a personal level, concerned about access to needed paper money, rather than simply as partisan pawns in a political battle engineered by Nicholas Biddle and Andrew Jackson. The story of hatmaker Leonard Bond provides a useful example.[4]

Just after his twenty-third birthday and just before he got married in 1823, Leonard Bond opened a retail and wholesale shop on the Bowery in New York where he manufactured and sold a variety of beaver and elastic waterproof hats. His bestselling "Rutgers' cap" was made especially for students of the recently renamed Queen's College in New Jersey. Bond's forty-year career lasted until his death during the Civil War as he operated on the fringe of success in a life filled with several triumphs and numerous setbacks. It was not from a lack of effort or pluck. As mentioned in Chapter 4, Leonard Bond was a tireless promoter. He placed hundreds of advertisements in local newspapers and directories and stamped the back of bank notes with an announcement of his shop's address to spread the word. Bond's knack for publicity reaped early rewards as he earned a commendation from Governor DeWitt Clinton and his shop was the subject of a beautiful 1828 watercolor by illustrator and famed architect Alexander Jackson Davis. However, overexpansion forced him to file as an insolvent debtor just one year later. A recovery in the 1830s came to a halt during the prolonged financial downturn associated with the Panic of 1837. Bond temporarily left the city for nearby Rye, New York, and declared bankruptcy in 1842. A couple of years later, he reemerged downtown to try his hand at new business ventures and open new warehouses over the last twenty years of his life.[5]

As the owner of a shop in New York City, Leonard Bond had plenty of paper money experience. His waterproof hats sold for between $4 and $5.50 in cash and generated a constant flow of small bank notes in and out of his pocket as evidenced by the time he lost his calfskin wallet at a barber shop. Along with a "literature lottery" ticket and some other papers, the wallet contained more than fifty dollars in "bank notes of various banks of the state." Leonard's paper money business also informed his voluminous public advertisements. An 1826 notice for Bond's shop announced "Hats always sold cheap when cash is offered" and, in particular, "Vassalborough Bank Notes taken at par for hats." While a lower cash-price incentive was commonplace, the appeal for specific out-of-state notes from one institution required some explanation. Incorporated by the Maine legislature in 1825, the Vassalborough Bank immediately raised public suspicion for its aggressive paper money issues, its remote village location, and the fact that one Hallowell family supplied almost all its initial capital. While not technically in violation of Maine's banking laws, the family used the Vassalborough as their private treasury to obtain loans paid out in paper money that they dumped in distant markets like New York City to prevent redemption. After a state investigation observed numerous "irregularities in the management," the institution moved to Hallowell where it changed its name to the Central Bank and operated into the 1840s.[6]

Why would a New York City hat manufacturer like Leonard Bond advertise to happily accept dubious bank notes at his shop without any discount on their face value? There was little question about the public's lack of confidence in the bills. The same week that Bond ran his advertisement for Vassalborough notes, the local money market discounted Maine banks across the board and listed nearby Hallowell and Augusta banks as broken. However, Leonard Bond tried to drum up some business with Vassalborough noteholders as an outlet for their unwanted bills. A clue to Bond's behavior stems from the contingent of his family that lived in Hallowell, Maine, just ten miles from the Vassalborough Bank. These relatives included his uncle Elias Bond, another hat manufacturer. Leonard Bond owned property in Hallowell and could use his family connections to send the Maine bank notes back for easy, cheap redemption. It was just one small anecdote, but it highlighted how Bond navigated the complicated early republic bank note system.[7]

Leonard Bond participated in the bank note economy, but how did his familiarity with paper money relate to his engagement with the political arena? Late in 1833 and a few months after the Treasury Department started to remove deposits from the BUS, Bond became a member of a Tenth Ward Democratic Party Vigilance Committee. However, the following March, he appeared on a list of Tenth Ward Independent Republican electors. This group coalesced with others to form the New York Whig Party later in 1834. By May 1835, Bond's position in the neighborhood business community had led the Board of Alderman to appoint him as clerk of the Washington Market, one of the city's largest. Perhaps this was a belated reward for political service, but it came well after his defection from the Democratic Party, which seemed to be precisely timed to the disruption of New York's money market during Biddle's contraction.[8]

A hatmaker, businessman, and consumer, Leonard Bond did not take part in the Bank War purely as a partisan ideologue, but rather as an individual with years of accumulated personal knowledge about the fraught bank note system. As early as December of 1833, Bond changed the wording of his newspaper advertisements to reflect new money market developments. In addition to the usual language that trumpeted his famed "Brush Hat," the text now specified that he had resisted the pressure to raise prices and continued to sell the hats for five dollars, "the price which they had always been sold." It was a subtle change, but one directed at a community in the midst of a cash shortage. Two months later, Leonard Bond attended several public meetings about the credit contraction and removal of the deposits and signed two petitions bound for Congress. The memorials sent by New York's merchants, traders, and dealers expressed their alarm about the bank note supply and the "present deranged state of the money market." They cited the "distresses of the community" and called for a "sound, secure, and stable paper currency." What most troubled the signatories was the fact that the problem appeared to be self-inflicted. They prayed for Congress to find a solution to the sour relationship between the administration and the BUS.[9]

Leonard Bond sold hats for bank notes and while that provided an important context for his political activity in 1834, it did not determine who he supported in the Bank War. Small New York hatters like Bond enlisted on both sides of the dispute. Just a week after Bond initialed his petitions, James Clohesey signed a memorial of merchants and mechanics "against the renewal of the charter of the Bank of the United States," while fellow hatmaker P. C. Willmarth joined nearly three thousand "mechanics and artisans" concerned about the "present deranged state of the money market." Noticeably similar language in the opposing memorials recognized the "unusual pressure of the commercial community" and Congress's need to restore confidence to the people. Individual empiricism, not just partisan loyalty, affected political engagement for these hatters. Similarly, while it is unclear how much Leonard Bond discussed his political actions with his extended family, Leonard's hatter uncle Elias also signed a memorial bound for Congress in the spring of 1834. This one came from a "meeting of inhabitants of Hallowell, in relation to the currency"; they decried the removal of deposits from the BUS and utilized similar language to the memorials Leonard had signed a couple of months earlier.[10]

It is an overstatement to say that reactions to Biddle's contraction avoided partisanship, but the moment brought together some strange political bedfellows. Aside from their Quaker heritage and residency in Wilmington, Delaware, Wilson Pierson and James Canby did not have much in common. Pierson was a mechanic and founder of the Association of Working People of New Castle County, the nation's second Working Men's Party. More electorally successful than other early labor parties, it captured thirteen of eighteen offices in Wilmington in 1830 when Pierson served as organization president. The New Castle working men called for an "abolition of chartered monopolies such as banks" as well as "the establishment of a system of free public education" meant to create an informed class of voters. Pierson's initial statement on behalf of the association distilled their particular brand of political economy down to "the poor have no laws; the laws are made by the rich, and of course *for* the rich." Alternatively, James Canby was born into a prominent merchant family and became the owner of several flour mills and president of the Wilmington and Baltimore Railroad. Canby was also a prominent banker who served as president of both the Bank of Wilmington and Brandywine and the Union Bank of Delaware. In New Castle county politics, he occupied a seat on the borough council in the 1810s and 1820s.[11]

What brought Wilson Pierson and James Canby together was their reaction to Biddle's contraction and their attendance at a February 1834 meeting in Wilmington. The gathering of "Farmers, Manufacturers, Mechanics,

Traders, and Citizens" from New Castle County debated the removal of deposits from the BUS and the bank's restriction of credit and then drafted a memorial signed by nearly seventeen hundred men, a majority of the voters in the county. The group was occupationally, economically, and politically diverse, with scores of farmers, shoemakers, laborers, and painters mixed together with doctors, scriveners, and manufacturers. The document's rhetoric was grounded in the experiences of individuals familiar with the bank note system who hoped for the restoration of the public deposits and "the permanent establishment of a sound and uniform currency." They explained that what had started as a want of circulating money had evolved into a depression of prices and an "almost total suspension of all productive business." A central feature of the New Castle memorial was its explicitly nonpartisan posture. Signatories disclaimed "partisan or political feelings" and directed their appeal to all members of Congress as the "constitutional and exclusive guardians of the currency of the country."[12]

After the New Castle meeting, a committee of eight representatives including James Canby traveled to Washington to present the memorial to the Delaware congressional delegation and meet with Andrew Jackson. Their forty-five-minute encounter with the president illustrated a fascinating disconnect between partisan political concerns in Washington and the daily lives of people outside the capital. Jackson ranted against the BUS as a "Monster of corruption" and Nicholas Biddle as a criminal, while the party from Delaware said that they did not care to "decide a question of party politics," or relitigate the BUS's constitutionality, but wanted instead to learn "what course would be adopted for the relief of the country in the present deranged state of the currency." To personalize their case further, they noted the lack of a BUS branch in Delaware and explained that they only cared about the institution "giving to the country a sound currency." Jackson spoke past his visitors to argue that "the laboring classes were injured by paper money" and that the removal of the deposits from the BUS was part of his plan to use state banks to create a "better currency." He also tapped into both a hard money argument and a desire to prohibit small-denomination notes, telling the Delaware memorialists that, empowered by the additional deposits, the pet banks would drive from circulation "all bank notes under $10, then under $20." This would allow farmers and laborers to use specie "for the common purposes of life."[13]

James Canby and the committee reported back to a mass meeting in Wilmington how surprised they were that Jackson underestimated the public's fluency with bank notes and their level of sophistication with the paper money system. They explained that "our countrymen generally know how to read, and the people of our own State can distinguish a *One* from a *Five* dollar note," adding that "our citizens" were not "so ignorant as to render silver and gold the only intelligible representatives of value." It was not the physicality of currency in its paper form that was the issue; it was the lack of enough money at fair value that prompted their distress. They did not believe that there was enough available specie in circulation to fulfill their needs and argued that the removal of bank notes from the economy would create a dangerous lack of tangible cash in the market. Laboring men received their wages and farmers sold their wheat and corn for paper money. The committee's report of their meeting with the president concluded with their doubt that the political system could solve their monetary problems.[14]

The attempt to eschew party politics and focus on money market and currency stability was a laudable, if fraught goal. Reactions to the removal of the deposits and the credit contraction in Philadelphia—the home of Nicholas Biddle and the BUS—provide one last complicated example of how individuals brought their lived experiences to this part of the Bank War. The economic downturn associated with the contraction hit Philadelphia hard. After five hundred "excellent workmen, with large families, wholly dependent on them for support" lost their jobs on New Year's Day, 1834, one employer regrettably told the press that the men had worked for him for a decade, but that he had laid them off because of "his former customers being, from the state of the money market, unable and unwilling to buy." Episodes like this led to mass meetings to investigate the "suffering and pecuniary distress" in the city and the nation. Those in attendance included "mechanics, merchants and tradesmen—friends and foes of the administration—and those who take no part in politics whatever." Not all public meetings opposed to the removal of the deposits or critical of Biddle's contraction were harmonious nonpartisan events, but participants' attempt to characterize them as such reflected how they preferred to frame the Bank War.[15]

The complexity of the situation can be seen in how individuals self-identified alongside the thousands of signatures on the memorials that came from the mass meetings. Categories included "Jackson man," "original Jacksonman," "a republican," "supporter of Jackson," and "an original supporter of Gen Jackson." William J. Benners labeled himself a "Jacksonman," but added that he was "no vetoite," while Joseph Lacost declared himself "now for Jackson, but not governed by interest, but the welfare of the country." It was not clear whether Thomas Mellon was a Jackson supporter, but he did claim to be "one of the defenders of New Orleans, 8th Jan. 1815." Other identifiers contained more nuance, like George S. Warren's claim that he was "a Jackson reversed" or Albert S. Mendenhall's explanation that he was "a Jacksonian until September last," exactly the time that the credit crunch first hit Philadelphia. A. C. Peixotto just declared that he was "no party man." These self-imposed labels demonstrate how Americans' personal circumstances and conception of themselves did not always match up with simple partisan rhetoric as they reconciled their lived experience and political engagement.[16]

The Philadelphia memorials also provided evidence of how individuals' economic realities informed public debates about monetary policy. Signatories followed the advice of type founder and fellow Philadelphian John Ronaldson—quoted above as "A Friend of the People"—to learn more about banking and paper money and get involved. Incidentally, both John and his brother Richard Ronaldson signed a petition concerning the "disordered state of the currency." Memorialists not only included their occupation next to their names; they sometimes explained how events in their own lives motivated their participation. Master brassfounder Owen Colton wrote that he "employed five journeymen, all discharged" since Biddle's contraction began, while cork manufacturers Elliot & Stevens explained that they "have been compelled to discharge 2/3 of our hands." These employers blamed the removal of the deposits since they could see no other "cause that has contributed in the slightest degree to the present disastrous condition of the country." Jacob Wunder and George Youkin came to their political activity from the other side of the employment story. In consequence of the market, they described their occupation as "doing nothing," while G. Carter elaborated that he was "doing nothing for want of money." Finally, J. P. Limeburner explained his lack of occupation was because he was "suffering for want of money." None of these comments excluded partisan motivation, but they should be seen as an attempt by the memorialists to draw a direct line between recent monetary policy, the effect of those policies on their personal economic experiences, and their entrance into the political arena to ask Congress to stabilize the currency system.[17]

Most congressional petitioners during Biddle's contraction sought a uniform and sound currency even if it meant an increase in the volume of circulating notes, but another group of Americans believed that true stability would only come when metallic currency replaced paper. Nicknamed Loco Focos by detractors and inspired by newspaper editor William Leggett, members of the Equal Rights Party developed the most vocal political case in opposition to paper currency in the 1830s. The group highlighted the experiences of workers and laborers to argue that monetary transactions should be conducted with specie rather than bank notes. They claimed that gold and silver coins possessed immutable face value, while paper money was easily manipulated and subject to compromised purchasing power. Loco Focos presented their case as a commonsense solution to the daily injustices experienced in using paper money and managed to influence national financial policy even as they remained a small electoral force.[18]

Usually described as an anti-monopoly movement, the Loco Focos' decision to splinter from New York Democrats and form their own party in 1835 also derived from their anti–paper money stance. At the Tammany Hall meeting where Equal Righters challenged pro-bank nominees and theatrics with Loco Foco brand matches earned them their nickname, protesters carried signs with the slogan "We go all gold, but Ringgold." The banners singled out assembly nominee Benjamin Ringgold, described as a "bank and legislative 'go-between,'" but more importantly signaled the Loco Focos' attack on bank notes in favor of hard money. The resolutions produced at that first meeting guided the party through its short existence and included the statement that "for all amounts of money, gold and silver are the only legitimate, substantial, and proper, circulating medium of our country." In reality, coined money was not perfect; the products of the United States Mint and the men who created them still had to earn the public's confidence. However, even though Loco Foco agitators overstated specie's stability and accessibility, their currency preference was not blindly ideological. It sprang from observed firsthand problems that occurred when workers dealt with bank notes.[19]

Just as Americans' physical relationship with bank notes informed their engagement with the wider market economy, Loco Focos argued that specie's form and value was more substantial than bills printed on poor-quality paper. William Leggett encapsulated this discussion of bank notes when he referred to them as "sickly, worthless trash which has so long supplied the place of constitutional money." Bank notes were not just unconstitutional in this formulation; they were decrepit and weak. When Leggett told his readers to write anti–paper money messages on the backs of uncurrent bills, he also stressed the contrast between strong metal currency and flimsy bank notes. His suggestions "Gold Before Rags!" and "Jackson and Hard Money!" directly celebrated the material strength of specie. Even his opponents recognized that hard money attacks on paper usually commented on its poor physical features. One Whig writer claimed that Loco Foco calls for a "*better currency*" always came paired with images "in the shape of a eagle cut, a cider barrel, or some other vignette, fringed with the mummery of '*I promise to pay*.'" This line of protest was not just an aesthetic argument about which currency looked or wore better; it argued that hard money was actually strong and valuable rather than something easily manipulated that merely represented possible value.[20]

Leggett and his acolytes sought to expose paper money's dangers, because if a malleable dollar was not really a dollar, then the currency system was built on promises and lies rather than inherent value. This conviction led to Loco Focos' reputation as self-righteous crusaders for monetary justice and earned them a position as convenient foils in sarcastic portraits of bankers. In *Specie Humbug*, for example, hard money Loco Focos thwart Ferret Snapp Newcraft's plot to issue bank notes based on "public credulity" rather than actual capital reserves when they force mass redemptions of his unbacked bills. Printed in William Gouge's *Journal of Banking*, the multipart "extracts from the private diary of a certain bank director" likewise feature hard money scolds. The bank director writes of a visitation by Satan, who appeared in the form of a Loco Foco (it made sense in context) to argue against bank notes. He invokes "the importance of a fixed standard of value—that it would be as absurd to be always changing the size of the bushel, or the length of the yard stick, as to be always changing the value of a dollar." A separate non-Lucifer Loco Foco in the diary explains that money "was not only a medium of exchange, but also a *standard* and *measure* of value, and that when it was metallic it had a value in itself independent of what it derived from its use as a commercial medium." These satirical sources captured the Loco Foco conviction that bank notes needed to be opposed because, unlike specie, their value was always in flux. This was not just an abstract worry; Loco Focos believed that they and their families disproportionately suffered from bank note manipulations.[21]

From his platform as the editor of the *New York Evening Post* and later the *Plaindealer*, William Leggett personalized the dangers of paper money to his readers. He traced uncurrent bank notes as they circulated through the city at a discount to the benefit of monopoly institutions and at the expense of hardworking laborers and their families. Leggett railed against this manipulated paper money as "a direct and infamous fraud upon the working classes." It is worth quoting his description at length:

> It is a common practise [*sic*] with employers when they pay off their hands on Saturday, to go into Wall street and purchase of some broker for the purpose, a lot of notes of depreciated value, varying from a half to one and a half per cent below par. These notes they palm off upon their workmen as money. If a master mechanic has a thousand dollars a week to pay to his hands, it is clear that he pockets every week by this operation some ten or fifteen dollars; and it can be shown with equal clearness that those in his employment are defrauded out of this sum. . . . *The entire sum paid for the discount of depreciated bank paper falls on the mechanics and labourers, and is wrung out of their sweat and toil. Nay more: they not only lose the amount which is actually paid for discount to money changers, but they also pay a per centage on that amount equal to the average rate of profit which merchants charge on their goods.*

The picture Leggett eloquently painted captured the weekly experience of workers in New York and across the nation. Pushed to take discounted bank notes for already completed work, they scrambled to get as much value as they could from the bills. In true Leggett form, the tragedy he portrayed was not just that bankers and money brokers defrauded mechanics and laborers, but that they reaped financial benefits without doing hard work.[22]

The fraudulence that robbed workers of their rightful earnings did not even require malice; it was baked into the paper currency system. Leggett explained that a small grocer might receive one hundred dollars in uncurrent bills a week, but without the ability to redeem them at the bank, had to seek out a broker who turned them into "ninety-eight dollars in bankable money." Over the course of a year, the grocer lost one hundred dollars and rather than bear the loss himself, passed it along to the "carpenter, the bricklayer, and the labourer, when they [bought] a pound of tea, or cheese, or butter, or any other article in his line, to take home to their families." This meant that "every article of consumption is now charged from two to three per cent higher than it ought to be," whether or not the grocer wanted to gouge his customers. Of course, Leggett printed plenty of stories where greedy vendors manipulated bank note transactions, but even these highlighted the inefficiency inherent in the system.[23]

Loco Foco depictions of uncurrent bank notes as both a systematic and an immediate household danger gave hard money advocates a framework for understanding and challenging the paper money system based on personal observations. Even though scholars claim that Jacksonian-era opposition to paper money alternatively sprang from adherence to literalist constitutional readings, belief in Gresham's Law that bad money drives good money out of the market, or an allegiance to the political economy of British writer David Ricardo, these sources were not where most Americans looked for monetary policy analysis. It was Leggett's more personal explanation of how bank notes defrauded hardworking members of society that inspired the call for a hard money economy. His bank note editorials did not mention Gresham or Ricardo; they spoke to the injustices that his readers witnessed with their own eyes. Hard money advocates around the nation reiterated Leggett's message with appeals grounded in similar terms. When the editors of *Loco Foco*, in Swanton, Vermont, complained of workers getting paid in merchant shinplasters, they didn't look to erudite economic treatises, but explained that a local man received "but fifty cents per day for his labor, and that in merchandise—in miserable trash on which his family could not subsist, and for which he had to pay double its real value." Such a charge could have come from Leggett himself.[24]

Warnings about paper money explicitly tied monetary practice to electoral outcomes. An 1837 appeal to "laboring and working men" sought to turn individuals scammed by poor-quality bank notes into a voting bloc. It asked these victims of an unjust currency system "to discover the politics of those men who want to pay them shinplasters, and when they do, just vote against them at the next election. Let the polls in November next, speak in a voice of thunder against the irredeemable paper factories of all sort and sizes." This was a direct call for political action based specifically on the quality of money used to pay workers. The inaugural issue of the Buffalo *Loco Foco* similarly issued a pointed attack on mainstream Democrats who were too aligned with financial interests. The editors observed that "the Van Buren Party is the Bank Party" and asked their readers, "How does the Safety Bank Fund Electorial Ticket suit the Loco Foco's?" For all that soaring rhetoric, the Equal Rights Party only achieved a couple of minor campaign victories in its short existence before most of its members folded back into the Democratic Party. However, the influence of hard money beliefs was seen in several 1830s monetary policies, most notably the Specie Circular.[25]

As one of the most visible Jackson administration hard money directives, the Treasury Department issued the 1836 Specie Circular (or Clause) to require specie payments for most federal land sales. The Specie Clause had little overall effect on the nation's economy because the purchase of federal land accounted for only a small percentage of total spending and bank notes just moved to other purchases, but it became a lightning rod in paper money debates. The "working men of New York," who called a mass meeting in City Hall park in the spring of 1837, identified the Specie Clause as evidence of progress toward a hard money economy. They believed that "gold and silver being demanded for the PUBLIC LANDS" had curtailed the "desolating influence of PAPER MONEY" and had led to specie "being paid to the farmers, mechanics, and other useful classes of society." This enthusiasm was short-lived as the collapse of the financial sector and the refusal by banks to redeem their notes during the Panic of 1837 resulted in a shortage of both hard and paper money by the summer.[26]

Critics pounced on the Specie Circular as a failed Loco Foco promise that had exacerbated the nation's currency woes. Whig politicos took advantage of the situation and attacked hard money policies on the same terrain that Loco Focos used to oppose paper money. A lithograph sketched during the Panic of 1837 depicted an unemployed artisan and his hungry family confronted by two agents at their door seeking rent payments. Asked by his children if they could eat some "Specie Claws," the man had nothing left in his toolbox to give except "Loco Foco Pledges." This was not all just partisan bluster. Even privately, Whigs argued that the banking crisis exposed the material reality that not enough gold and silver coinage circulated in the United States to support economic demand. Writing to his nephew Richard S. Varnum in Michigan, Whig representative Leverett Saltonstall exclaimed, "So much for the gold system—the hard money currency, as it is called, which has left us without hard, or any other currency. So much for the delightful visions of gold and silver—the yellow boys peeping through network purses—coin flowing up the great rivers of the west." Modest policies that aimed to create a specie economy had failed to drive paper money out of circulation; gold coins and good paper money had become scarcer than ever.[27]

The Loco Foco agenda to abolish bank notes and champion the supposed security and stability of hard money ran into the material realities of the

FIGURE 22. Whig political cartoons released in the wake of the Panic of 1837 mocked Loco Foco hard money policies as dangerous for working families. Courtesy, Library of Congress Prints and Photographs Division, LC-USZC4-3240.

specie supply and alienated even some radicals. Robert Dale Owen, a former leader of the New York Working Men's Party and current Democratic member of the Indiana legislature, declared in 1839 that he was "not a hard money man" and advocated a paper money compromise. He compared bank notes to steamboats as "very dangerous things . . . apt to blow up," but remarked that to rely on a specie economy was no more practical than "Mike Fink's primitive boat, urged up stream by force of pole or aid of bush." It was safer, but a quaint option that could not satisfy the modern economy's demands. The best course was to use wisdom and regulation to prevent explosions. Maybe not all paper money needed to go away, just the most dangerous bills.[28]

Many Americans empirically understood the problems with the antebellum paper money system, but like Robert Dale Owen, fell between boosters who believed that a proliferation of bank notes would solve scarcity problems and hard money advocates who longed for the fairness of a specie-based economy. Those in the popular middle ground called for a narrow ban on small-denomination bills. Denominational limitations allowed merchants to use large bank notes to transact their business while they blunted the proliferation of small notes that adversely affected ordinary workers and farmers who lost out to inflation and devalued currency. Whether defined as bills under one dollar, five dollars, or ten dollars, the attempt to prohibit small notes seemed like a sensible regulation that would shield vulnerable members of society from the most pernicious aspects of paper money, while it retained those benefits that contributed to economic growth.

As soon as banks started to issue paper money, the debate began over small-denomination bills. Almost every state passed some prohibition on small notes between the 1790s and 1860s, although many subsequently repealed these laws as they tried to curtail abuse of the paper money system and get the right balance of small currency regulation and market flexibility. Massachusetts provides a useful example. In 1799, the commonwealth passed a law that forbade issuing bank notes of under five dollars based on the notion that a recent influx of foreign specie would cover the local economy's needs. When that specie dried up in Boston, local merchants, desperate to help their customers, began to issue shinplasters as small change. The importers Trott & Blake, for example, saw the bills as a marketing opportunity and produced branded notes with a small elephant vignette to represent the Indian goods for sale in their warehouse. The circulation of this questionably legal private money demonstrates the weakness of a currency market that did not meet local demand. Even more difficult to spend than a devalued bank note, the shinplasters raised the ire of the community. By 1805, the legislature responded to the "popular voice" and overturned the small note prohibition. The cycle repeated itself when another local specie shortage after the War of 1812 led to the proliferation of "fractional bills, less than a dollar" which the legislature banned in 1818.[29]

The Bank War brought more currency woes to Massachusetts and another debate about the place of small-denomination paper within the economy. A new law refined small note circulation: "Every bank within this Commonwealth may issue bills under five dollars, to the amount of one quarter part of its capital actually paid in, and no more; but no bank shall issue bills of a less denomination than one dollar, under a penalty of one hundred dollars for each offense." Banks could issue notes between one and five dollars, but they had circulation limitations based on their capital reserves. When some banks stopped paying out specie during the Panic of 1837, the rules changed once again to allow for a temporary circulation of small notes to help get the economy back on its feet. The evolution of small-denomination regulations in Massachusetts demonstrates the precariousness of the early republic paper money system. Economic and political developments on the ground regularly pushed citizens to call for changes to paper money law that would make their daily transactions more just and restrict bankers from their desire to issue whatever currency they wanted.[30]

A prominent voice in this cyclical debate belonged to merchant, banker, and politician Samuel Hooper. Born into a family of Marblehead merchants and bankers, Hooper's economic education took off in the 1830s as a junior partner in his father-in-law's Boston firm, Bryant and Sturgis. Samuel's early business correspondence showed a persistent lack of cash and a disrupted currency market around New England. A typical letter to Hooper from Casy & Co. warned that the "pinch in the money market is very severe here"; there was not enough specie available to fulfill the needs of the business community, let alone retail customers. In later years as a financial insider, Samuel understood how paper money men used currency shortages to unleash waves of small notes to gain an advantage and ensure institutional profit. He wrote that banks would "offer easy discounts if bundles of their small bills will be taken to be carried out of the State as far as possible, so that they will be a long time coming back, or if the receiver will promise, at all events that the bills shall not come back within a specified time." Based on his observations as a banker and merchant, Samuel Hooper believed that the proliferation of poor-quality small-denomination notes crowded specie out of the economy and punished consumers. Any Loco Foco or Working Men's Party member knew this was not an original analysis, but as an influential Whig and later Republican inside the financial sector, Hooper was in an advantageous position to challenge small bills.[31]

Writing from Boston in the 1850s, Hooper could have relied on the Suffolk Bank to police bank note circulation and ensure small note values, but as a banking insider he understood that the veneer of stability created by the Suffolk system cloaked what actually happened within the New England bank note market in the 1840s and 1850s. For years, the fact that most New Englanders could use bank notes without large discounts on their face value was enough to manufacture confidence in the local money supply without regard to bank officers' management of specie holdings, loan decisions, or note issuance. Underneath the surface, the Suffolk Bank did not restrain the circulation of bank notes and actually expanded the currency supply because bank officials and the public became convinced that the money market was healthier than it was. Hooper argued that the Suffolk system merely enabled mischief. He observed growing numbers of small bills from New England banks on their way out to western states where "on account of the stability supposed to be given to these banks by the Suffolk system of mutual support, they enjoy a credit superior to the issues of the local banking establishments, sometimes, with good enough reason, called wildcats." Small notes shipped out west created the long-term problem of an "enlarged power of circulation, tempting the banks to speculate too deeply in the manufacture of money for foreign as well as home use." He worried that this would eventually "defeat the Suffolk Bank system or greatly curtail its benefits."[32]

The Suffolk Bank's decision not to use its oversight abilities to reign in small-denomination notes made it complicit in the bad behavior of its member institutions, because it provided cover while they increased their circulation and devalued their currency. Hooper cited figures that showed New England banks held $4 million in specie, but they had $25 million in bank notes in circulation. This was a better ratio than the wildcat banks out west had, but it was untenable for a conservative Boston banker. The small note debate resulted in laws that prevented "bills of a less denomination than one dollar" or "any fractional part of a dollar," but Suffolk-aligned bankers lobbied for the Massachusetts legislature to reject more significant small-denomination regulations. Samuel Hooper wanted more ambitious restrictions for the commonwealth and during the 1850s pushed for a law to prohibit all bank notes under ten dollars. The risky bankers ultimately prevailed.[33]

It was not just how his fellow bankers shifted small notes around the economy that worried Samuel Hooper; it was also the material nature of the bills themselves. Due to bank notes' "porous and absorbent nature," they retained the smell of everyone and everything they touched. Hooper argued that "with every roll of small bills, a man puts in his pocket more stinks than Coleridge discovered in Cologne, none of them much resembling that favorite article of perfumery which took its name from that celebrated city." Small-denomination notes became particularly soiled because of where they traveled. Hooper explained that "bills circulate every where—

the smaller the more widely—in shantees [*sic*] as well as in palaces—in grog-shops redolent of every abominable odor—in houses of still worse fame—in the abodes of filth and of pestilence." This statement acknowledged the medical consensus that paper money served as a vector of illness to spread diseases like smallpox, but it was also a moral judgement of the people who used small-denomination notes and the places they resided.[34]

Hooper might not have been bothered that small notes circulated in grog shops and houses of ill fame, but he understood how bills moved through the market. He worried that diseases would spread across class and gender lines "from the pest-house to the delicate fingers and rose-scented porte-monnaie of the sensitive lady." Even the "blooming belle, who prides herself on the spotlessness of her attire," could not always use new or clean money. They were forced to "shop with soiled rags, which water cannot wash, nor any ventilation or fumigation make decent." This argument specifically opposed small notes because of their physicality and the reality that Americans of all sorts intimately dealt with dirty pieces of paper on a daily basis. Why not, asked Samuel Hooper, devise a currency system that protected working women and men from disease and the devaluation inherent in small-denomination bills, but left options open for bank directors with access to good, clean paper money?[35]

While his political economy discussions sometimes veered into tariffs and how to maximize specie circulation, Hooper grounded his pamphlets in the personal experiences of the American public. One review even complimented his "practical observations and well matured reflections." Hooper pointed out that small bills, more than large-denomination notes, moved from person to person with such velocity that it was difficult to keep track of their value even for those with the best monetary literacy. Every transaction altered the value of a bank note, but the "public receive no benefit from these fluctuations of currency." Those who handled small-denomination paper money felt like they had played "Robin's alive," a hot potato–type children's game that involved a fiery stick passed around a circle until the fire went out. Bankers and brokers rigged this system for their own benefit, but, Hooper wrote, the public was "too cautious and timid to relish a game which to them seems similar to that of children when they pass round a firebrand." To play the game meant that someone eventually got burned and too often it was the most vulnerable members of the community who were left to hold the charred remains of something worthless.[36]

Hooper not only shared his views about small notes publicly; he also distributed his pamphlets to acquaintances to solicit their reactions. He circulated two of them—*Currency or Money* and *Small Bills*—to a who's who of New England Whig bankers and merchants and received generally positive replies. The politician and writer Samuel A. Eliot commended how the pamphlets addressed the "absurdities that are daily uttered & practiced in the community," which everyone knew about, but had not been studied with precision and skill. The pedagogical possibility of the tracts was not lost on Horace Mann, who asked Hooper for some extra copies because he was about "to teach a class on Political Economy before long" at Antioch College.[37]

These intimate exchanges offer a window into how leading political economic thinkers contextualized their discussions within Americans' daily monetary experiences even in their private conversations. The most eloquent example comes from an 1855 letter to Hooper from Francis Bowen—the Alford Professor of Natural Religion, Moral Philosophy, and Civil Polity at Harvard College—who suggested that removing all bills under ten dollars from circulation, coupled with a requirement that banks only issue three times the value in notes that they hold in specie (another Hooper proposal), would make the money market secure and stable. Bowen argued that a small note prohibition was a good middle-of-the-road measure and preferable to entirely "destroy[ing] *bank* notes." That would be ill advised because it would just lead to a proliferation of other paper instruments that could not be contained or regulated. Bowen used an example from his own life to explain what would happen to him on payday if there were no bank notes available for his employer, Harvard College:

> I should request the Treasurer of Harvard College to pay me my quarter's salary in personal checks, for fifty or one hundred dollars each, instead of taking the whole in coin, with the trouble of counting it and guarding it against thieves and fire. I would pay my butcher or grocer with one of these checks, and the retail dealer would pay a wholesale dealer with it, and the check might thus pay through a dozen hands before being presented for payment at the Bank. It would be *virtually* paper currency, redeemable at sight in specie. This is a *very small* instance; but the transactions among you merchants would supply cases of very large ones. Your own check might often circulate in this way, in spite of all you could do to

> prevent it, properly guarded by publicity and well devised legislative restrictions.

With a page from his own monetary life, Bowen expressed support for Hooper's small note regulations, but emphasized the delicate nature of the American currency landscape that could not function exclusively based on specie. Paper money was problematic, but inescapable.[38]

Other friends replied to Hooper's proposals with similar concerns. Edward Everett stated that he had "much doubt whether *any* benefit accrues to the community, in the long run, from a circulation of convertible paper;—certainly none which is not overbalanced by the necessary evils incident in it." Everett added that anyone who used paper money had noticed that the bank note system was broken and should be overturned for a more "metallic currency," but that "no violent charge ought to be made." This reality doomed the prospects for a legislative fix because, in addition to the "difficulty which exists in overcoming the apathy of the community in reference to all its practical intents, you would have all the Banks fall who depend upon them against you." Everett's latter point explained how someone like Samuel Hooper identified so many problems with paper money, but then used his political capital to fight for a minor prohibition on small-denomination notes, rather than a more systemic overhaul. Everyone who used antebellum bank notes understood how fraught they were, but inertia and resistance from those who benefited from the status quo prevented large-scale overhauls of the nation's currency no matter how popular they might be.[39]

Even with widespread support for his ideas, the disconnect between state regulations and national currency circulation meant that proposals for small note prohibitions like Samuel Hooper's did not work effectively. Little real punishment existed for those who skirted the law and if a prosecutor moved toward indictment, tiny fines or other pretrial deals did little to deter paper money men who profited from small notes. Those who opposed the elimination of small bills often cited the failure of previous legislation to curtail the problem. One Whig newspaper from Chillicothe, Ohio, looked into the consequences of New York's small note ban and found that the result was that "notes and shinplasters, under the denomination of five dollars, poured into the State, from Canada, Vermont, Massachusetts, New Jersey and Ohio." So "every intelligent man" found the law to be ridiculous and refused to follow it lest "he [be] black-balled as a malicious ignoramus who might have ventured to bring suit against a passer or receiver." The circulation of paper money required both the framework of state regulation and the deployment of public monetary knowledge. It did not matter that new laws were meant to solve problems that Americans experienced in their daily transactions; a legal change without buy-in from the public or a corresponding change in their behavior was bound to fail. For all the heat and light produced by monetary policy protests through the Bank War, Loco Foco opposition to bank notes, and the insider protests of a Whig like Samuel Hooper, circulation expanded rapidly in the 1840s and 1850s. Some small-denomination prohibitions passed, but they presented bankers with more of an annoyance than a real impediment.[40]

These varied moments of political engagement demonstrate how daily experience with the chaos and confusion of bank notes led Americans to contemplate changes to the relationship between the individual and the state in terms of monetary policy. Questions about who should be allowed to create paper money and how it should function in the marketplace were not just esoteric exercises for political debate, but rather essential matters for artisans and farmers whose households depended on whether a bill would be accepted and at what discount. Hard money supporters who felt burned by corrupt governance pushed a more libertarian viewpoint which tied the problem with bank notes to publicly chartered institutions—monopolies in the Loco Foco lexicon—rather than independent entities separate from exclusive state sanction. Conversely, in public meetings around the country, Americans opposed the removal of the BUS deposits and called for repairs to the money market, specifically appealing to Congress and the federal government to take a more active role in monitoring the money supply and ensuring its constancy. Those who sought small note prohibitions eschewed the difficult battles over federal policy and embraced more practical local regulation to offer justice to workers and flexibility to capitalists.[41]

The public's knowledge of monetary policy and its engagement in political debates derived from personal experiences with bank notes, but this did not necessarily mean that specific encounters simply pushed individuals to distinct political actions. Not everyone who lost money when they passed an uncurrent note became a Loco Foco or agreed with their hard money arguments. When George Henry Evans related the story of a "paper money manufacture" that had "blown up" in the first issue of his *Radical, in*

Continuation of Working Man's Advocate, he was already a well-known anti–bank note advocate from his time in the New York Working Men's Party a decade earlier. Now a Democrat living in the New Jersey countryside, he and a neighboring Whig farmer had gotten stuck with broken notes from the Farmers' and Mechanics' Bank of New Brunswick. Evans used the personal anecdote to rehash his traditional argument that the bank note system was an evil that served "to make the rich richer and the poor poorer." Even so, he did not know whether the experience that lost his neighbor the equivalent of "ten bushels of corn" had altered the Whig's attitudes about paper money. Evans expected it to be an easy decision, but it was a complex path from a lived experience with bank notes to advocacy for a particular monetary policy.[42]

Chapter 6 picks up this intersection of personal experience and political economy and examines what happened when the monetary system collapsed during the Civil War. If inertia and the political power of entrenched banking interests stifled radical challenges to the state bank note system in the antebellum period, the war presented an opportunity to remake the nation's currency supply. The need to fund the conflict, and the monetary chaos it unleashed, pushed the federal government to create a new currency structure and redefine the tenuous relationship between the individual and the state. The result was the creation of legal tender paper money and face-value national bank notes.

CHAPTER 6

Legal Tender Mercies

ON THE SECOND to last day of 1829, the Senate directed its Finance Committee to investigate the country's monetary system. The charge mirrored the previous day's referral to the House Ways and Means Committee to "inquire into the expediency of establishing an uniform National Currency of the United States." The probes followed Andrew Jackson's challenge during his first annual message that the Second Bank of the United States (BUS) had "failed in the great end of establishing a uniform and sound currency." Examination began to determine whether Jackson's pointed accusation properly characterized the monetary landscape, and to decide on the government's role to ensure a stable system.[1]

Both congressional committees produced lengthy reports on the "National Currency" in the spring of 1830, but neither one proposed ambitious or even incremental legislation to create a simplified paper money system. Released as politicians staked out positions for the upcoming Bank War, the documents seemed more concerned with whether to attack or defend BUS head Nicholas Biddle than suggesting monetary reform. The Senate Finance Committee, led by president pro tem Samuel Smith of Maryland, asked, "What is the soundest and most uniform currency?," before it quickly declared that the United States already enjoyed the most ideal legal tender currency: "gold and silver." Smith's report concluded that during the 1820s the government had utilized this system (with bank notes to stand in for specie) to process receipts of over $230 million and to pay its military and other debts. This worked just fine, Smith explained, so "if this currency is thus sound and uniform for the Government, it is not less so to the community." Americans who dealt with discounted and uncurrent bank notes on a daily basis surely disagreed.[2]

Thomas Mendenhall, a prominent Delaware merchant and banker, disappointed by the lack of congressional action, responded with *An Entire New Plan for a National Currency*. His pamphlet called for new government-issued paper notes that "will be a *legal tender* at its nominal value—and the only one in circulation." As the title suggested, this was not Mendenhall's first foray into currency proposals; under the name "a Citizen of Washington," he penned *National Money, or a Simple System of Finance* during the debate over whether to charter the BUS in 1816. His idea was to create Treasury Department notes that would "appreciate rather than depreciate" because they would be accepted for "all public dues." State banks would eventually adopt the government-issued notes, so they would become the "universal medium in trade, and one which [would] not depreciate in value to the injury of the holder." While it did not inspire any public response, this scheme sounded like the one he proposed in 1834.[3]

Written in the midst of the Bank War, Thomas Mendenhall's updated plan for a national currency utilized many of his original ideas and specifically addressed Jackson and Congress's charge to create a sound and uniform monetary system. He argued that to ensure that government-issued notes held their face value (unlike fluctuating bank notes), they must be made a legal tender. To defend their legality, Mendenhall cited James Madison's secretary of the Treasury Alexander J. Dallas, who had issued short-term Treasury Department notes during the War of 1812. Dallas declared that the federal government had the power to "supply and maintain a paper medium of uniform value." Mendenhall explained that this made his bills both constitutional and secure because "being the only money in circulation as a legal tender, its current value, stamped on the face of it, is fixed by the law of the land. Each bill is, therefore, the standard of its own value; and, as such, the most obstinate prejudices, foreign and domestic, can never work a depreciation." Backed by the power and authority of the government, Mendenhall concluded that his government-issued legal tender notes would be the soundest national currency possible.[4]

He stressed not only its soundness but also its physical uniformity. Mendenhall included images of his proposed national currency alongside the text in his plan. The left and right panels of the notes featured patriotic flag vignettes and slogans that read, "UNITED WE STAND," "DIVIDED WE FALL," "IN UNION there is STRENGTH," "Honesty is the best policy;—as it is by MORAL FORCE that our Republic MUST be supported," and "To Counterfeit is DEATH, AND THEN, WORSE PUNISHMENT!!" Under the heading "National Currency. By the Laws of Congress," the central text read, "This Bill of ______ Dollars, based on real property, secured by bond and mortgage, shall pass current as a legal tender, at its nominal value, in any part of the United States, in payment of debt and contracts, not otherwise specially provided for; and will be so received at the National Treasury.—Signed by order of the Trustees of the National Loan Office, Washington, D.C., July 4th, 1838." There was nothing visually striking about the sample notes, but their combination of nationalistic imagery and explicit legal tender pronouncement presented a model for uniform currency that had been absent in the early republic bank note system.[5]

Thomas Mendenhall was not alone in his desire for better paper money to replace the chaotic state bank note system. Separate 1830s plans by a Maryland merchant, Littleton Dennis Teackle, and a New York lawyer, George Sullivan, sought to tie existing local banks into a network that utilized federally issued paper notes instead of their own bills. The state banks and federal currency would work together to maintain a stable purchasing power because they could circulate "at par throughout the Union." Like Mendenhall, Sullivan included a mock-up of his proposed national bill to highlight its singular form. Whether any of these plans would have created a stable currency is questionable, but uniformity would have radically altered the type of visual literacy the public needed to assess paper money. However, during the antebellum period, none of these ideas for creating a uniform and stable paper currency gained traction.[6]

No matter how much the American public wanted better paper money, bankers' political and economic power combined with legislative inertia to maintain the status quo; it took a cataclysmic event to force a major change in the currency system. The remainder of this chapter examines how the pressures of the Civil War crippled the state bank note system and resulted in two new forms of paper money: greenbacks and national bank notes. Most scholarship places Civil War monetary legislation within the context of other wartime expansions of government power, but this discussion follows a different trajectory. Issued by separate entities and authorized under separate legislation, legal tender greenbacks and federally backed national bank notes received at par throughout the nation were not simply imposed on the economy by power-hungry politicians. Their creation addressed immediate wartime banking and financial problems and attempted to satisfy the public's demands for a uniform and stable currency. Bankers fought the government to maintain their notes; the people did not. This discussion highlights how the introduction of new currencies altered the ways Americans understood and used paper money. It was not just a political or financial expansion; it was a seismic cultural shift.

It is useful to briefly sketch out the relevant federal legislation before examining how Civil War developments altered the American public's relationship with paper money. The government struggled to craft a financial response to the outbreak of the war in large measure due to the Independent Treasury Act of 1846, a law that required the government to receive and make payments in gold or silver. Federal specie reserves resided at the Treasury and its subtreasuries around the nation, but the system was in trouble even before the events at Fort Sumter. In February 1861, only about $500 thousand sat in the depository and Congress had not been paid since December. The massive debt and poor credit meant few resources, little flexibility, and no time for deliberate planning when the fighting began. Without the ready cash, Congress passed a National Loan Act in July 1861 that raised $250 million through the sale of bonds and both interest-bearing and payable-on-demand Treasury notes in five-, ten-, and twenty-dollar denominations. Secretary of the Treasury Salmon P. Chase looked to fund the loan from New York, Boston, and Philadelphia banks and sell them interest-bearing Treasury notes in return. An amendment to the Independent Treasury Act gave Chase the authority to accept the bank loan in notes and drafts, but his hard money principles instead led to a plan to transfer $150 million in specie to the Treasury even though bank reserves only stood at about $70 million.[7]

Speculators and hoarders gobbled up gold as soon as it left the banks. In place of the missing specie, shinplasters proliferated and the public second-guessed the loan terms worked out between Salmon Chase and the bankers. The *Baltimore Sun* editors worried that it was a "step backwards for which no friend of a sound currency seems to be prepared" and expressed their alarm about the decision to remove most of the specie from large northeastern banks. When it sat in its vault, gold ensured confidence in circulating bank notes, but now that same gold was supposed to redeem the Treasury's demand notes. In the debate about whether federal currency expansion led to commodity inflation, consumers voiced their concern that bank notes could not retain their value if they were backed by the same gold supply that performed double duty for the Treasury. Bank note discounts ballooned and their overall purchasing power shrank from $205 million in 1860 to $202 million in 1861 even in the midst of a high volume of new military spending.[8]

Several types of money circulated simultaneously by December, but consumers had difficulty separating the good from the bad. One observer remarked that "Treasury demand notes, bank notes and credits, without regard to specie reserves, good-looking counterfeit notes, bad-looking shinplasters, worthless promises, undeveloped stump-tail, any thing that public credulity consents to circulate, is, for the time, a perfect medium of exchange." Secretary Chase's end-of-the-year financial report for 1861 indicated that the war required significantly more funding, but the Treasury Department did not have the specie to redeem additional demand notes. A week later, shrinking reserve levels pushed New York institutions to suspend specie payments on their bank notes. Banks across the North quickly followed.[9]

Early in 1862, a new round of monetary policy meetings between Secretary Chase and New York bankers led nowhere as Congress decided that the private institutions prioritized profit too much for wartime planning. This buttressed charges that bankers were a "great obstacle in the way of the general circulation of the new national currency." Salmon Chase and Congress turned away from the financial sector and pushed through the Legal Tender Act in February 1862. The result was $150 million in new legal tender notes—nicknamed "greenbacks" because of the green ink on their reverse side—guaranteed to be accepted for "all debts Public and Private except, Duties on Imports and Interest on the Public Debt, and . . . exchangeable for U.S. Six per cent Twenty Year Bonds, redeemable at the pleasure of the U. States after Five Years" without being tied to specific government specie reserves. Legal tender notes circulated apart from any path to redemption in coin, so their value hinged on the public's faith in the government and especially its success on the battlefield. By July 1862, the notes traded at ninety-one cents on the gold dollar, but the premium on gold grew to over 2 to 1 as the war dragged on. However, compared with the collapsing value of unredeemable bank notes, their relative success to pay for the expanding war effort meant that the Treasury released additional bills to bring the total to $450 million by their final issue in March 1863.[10]

Issued starting at $5 and later in $1 and $2 denominations, greenbacks introduced a large supply of new paper money into circulation in 1862, but they did little to solve the small change problem in the market. The author of one newspaper article, signed "Desperation," even asked for the government to issue $1.25, $1.50, or $1.75 bills to help with his family's "great strait for change." He added that his "wife complains terribly" about the small note problem. Consumers who could not find change and wanted to avoid shinplasters began using postage stamps. The universality of stamps and the stability of their face value even for denominations under one dollar seemed an obvious solution to pay for small fees. However, postage stamps were not physically designed to withstand the wear and tear of currency circulation. Even compared to poor-quality shinplasters, their unique form and the glue on the back presented challenges. Henry Russell Drowne, a late nineteenth-century numismatist, remembered his father's complaints about the time he used a stamp to pay for a Broadway stagecoach fare one winter night only to have it "stick to his wet woolen gloves." Once they were damp, they had to be held "carefully until they dried, before you could put them in your pocket book." Some businesses even curated their own stamp collections to facilitate their use as currency. So, instead of coins or shinplasters as change, a patron at "Gould's Dining Rooms" or "Joseph Bryan, Clothing Establishment" was handed a prepackaged, branded envelope with twenty-five or fifty cents' worth of stamps inside.[11]

In the hope of literally capitalizing on the public's confidence in stamps to hold their value, Congress formally created postage currency to solve the small change problem. Samuel Hooper, now a Republican member of Congress from Massachusetts, adapted his small note concerns to wartime necessities and managed the Stamp Payments Act that passed in July 1862. The vaguely worded law authorized the Treasury Department to make "postage and other stamps" exchangeable for United States notes and accepted in payment by the government for all dues less than five dollars. Simultaneously, the legislation prohibited the circulation of shinplasters by private corporations, banks, and individuals for amounts less than one dollar. Lost in its obscure language, the law did not actually authorize postage stamps to circulate as currency, but rather the creation of new "postage currency" notes in denominations of five, ten, twenty-five, and fifty cents that featured postal iconography. They were issued by the Treasury and could be exchanged for stamps at any post office or redeemed for greenbacks in five-dollar increments. Supporters of postage currency claimed it solved two problems: it relieved "the public of the nuisance of a scarcity of specie change, which has wellnigh become intolerable" and it furnished "a loan, of no trifling sum, to the Government" to meet war expenses. Seemingly a stopgap measure to infuse small change into the economy, Congress's postage currency was another federal government step to define what should be accepted or not accepted as legal money in the United States.[12]

The new law created problems almost immediately. Even before it went into effect on August 1, 1862, customers tried to pay for their purchases with regular postage stamps. Storekeepers refused them, "preferring to take shinplasters because the stamps stick to everything they touch and to each other, so that they have lost considerably by their use." Printing delays by the National Bank Note Company created widespread shortages and anger. In Cincinnati, postal officials cracked down after reports that $50,000 in misused stamps had circulated as currency, but Enoch Carson, the customs collector tasked to distribute postage currency notes, did not receive enough of the bills to satisfy local demand. A mob, "numbered between 5,000 and 8,000 persons," tried to force its way into the Customs House before military action dispersed the crowd.[13]

To head off similar problems, New York City's postmaster Abram Wakeman published a lengthy clarification to instruct the public on the difference between postal stamps and postal currency. He explained that the Post Office Department issued "*postage stamps*" that could be "used only for the pre-payment of postage," while the Treasury Department issued new "*postage currency* . . . expressly designed for a circulating medium." They could be used to purchase "*postage stamps*," but not for the "prepayment of postage." The confusion was not just about administrative classification or jurisdiction, it went to the heart of material differences between postage stamps and currency. Postmaster Wakeman clarified that stamps were "common paper, covered with mucilage on one side and paint on the other." They were not meant to circulate as money since stamps would quickly become "soiled, defaced and torn" when handled in that manner. Postage currency was of a much smaller size, but it was printed on bank note paper stock and therefore suitable for circulation.[14]

It was not a smooth process, but the Treasury Department managed to fund the war with new legal tender greenbacks and postage currency and without much help from the state banks that limped along after they suspended payment. Greenbacks pointed toward a future of uniform currency, but the public perception that they were a temporary measure, backed only by federal promises, meant that they never inspired universal confidence.

It would be necessary to get powerful bankers and their fourteen hundred state institutions to buy in to a national system for a long-term solution for sound paper. Abraham Lincoln addressed the currency matter in his second annual message to Congress, issued on December 1, 1862. The president explained that the "suspension of specie payments by the banks soon after the commencement of [the] last [congressional] session made large issues of United States notes unavoidable," and discussed the need for a "safe and uniform currency." He advocated for an "organization of banking associations, under a general act of Congress," that would "furnish circulating notes, on security of United States bonds deposited in the Treasury." As a bonus, the sale of government bonds to individual banks would encourage the financial sector to step up and support the war effort. The plan represented a compromise between the president's leftover Whig preferences for central banking and various existing state models of bond-supported free banking, especially the one used in New York.[15]

Early in 1863, Congress took up legislation to create a system of nationally chartered institutions that would issue a new currency to replace state bank notes. Led by Samuel Hooper in the House and John Sherman in the Senate, supporters had to overcome the objections of bankers and states' rights advocates as well as a population that had used the same familiar bank notes for generations. The precedent of greenbacks helped shake off some of that inertia, and the reality that Americans barely tolerated state bank notes provided political cover to push for something new. One of Sherman's central arguments in favor of a new uniform currency was its potential to thwart counterfeits. He explained that when a national bank note with just a few types of vignettes replaced those with thousands of variations, each American could detect the fakes and accept a bill with confidence from a stranger just as they would from a friend. Hooper spent the 1850s trying to incrementally solve the problem of small notes within the state bank system, but now as a Congressman galvanized by the banks' suspension of their obligations to redeem their own notes, he sought to craft a better regulatory regime. He did not just want a uniform currency. He wanted it to remain at face value, so he promised that the notes would meet the "demands of the public service, and at the same time provide for capitalists, bankers, and the people the means to prevent any depreciation of the currency." The key for Hooper was the fact that state rules allowing banks to flood the market with under par notes had outlived their usefulness. The national currency would follow stricter rules about how it was issued to maintain its soundness.[16]

FIGURE 23. Small-denomination United States Fractional Currency was receivable for stamps or exchangeable for greenbacks. Author's collection.

The congressional debate came together in February in the passage of the National Currency Act of 1863. The act allowed any group of five or more persons to form a bank within the national association provided they adhered to certain regulations in charters overseen by the Treasury Department and the new comptroller of the currency. In order to issue notes, each member institution had to purchase and deliver United States bonds to the Treasury. The comptroller would then issue uniform, numbered notes to the member bank where they were signed and circulated at up to 90 percent of the value of the deposited bonds. Unlike the patchwork state banking system, the new model imposed controls on total circulation. No more than $300 million in bills could be issued nationally. Additional rules set capital reserve levels based on the bank's size and location and ensured enough "lawful money" on hand to redeem at least 25 percent of their circulating notes and deposits before they made any new loans. By March 1863, the move to create a uniform currency even extended to small notes as new "fractional currency," similar in form to other federal notes, replaced postage currency.[17]

The National Currency Act of 1863 provided a framework for a new monetary system in the United States, but it was incomplete. In the rush to pass a currency measure to help fund the war, Congress had largely sidestepped the issue of existing state banks. A few groups created new institutions under the Currency Act, but there was no incentive and plenty of disincentive for existing banks to voluntarily accept the regulations to become a national bank. Laws in most states provided fewer tax liabilities and more opportunities for profit on loans, especially in New York. In some extreme cases, bankers even took steps to block the new national currency from entering financial markets. Signed on June 3, 1864, the National Bank

Act attempted to solve these bank tax and interest rate problems and provided a regulated pathway for state banks to become chartered members of the national banking system. The act allowed state banks to keep some aspect of their local identity when they converted to a national branch. Miller's River Bank, located in Athol, Massachusetts, for example, became The Miller's River National Bank of Athol with charter number 708 when it converted early in 1865.[18]

When taken together, the National Currency Act of 1863 and the National Bank Act of 1864 established a new financial and monetary structure in the United States. Rather than 1,500 separate banks' currencies with dozens of different state regulations, there would be one uniform national bank note individually branded by its issuing branch. In addition to its home, national bank notes were redeemable at face value in commercial centers across the country. The back of each bill declared:

> THIS NOTE is RECEIVABLE at PAR in all parts of the UNITED STATES, in payment of all TAXES and EXCISES and all other DUES to the UNITED STATES, except DUTIES on IMPORTS, and ALSO for all SALARIES and other DEBTS and DEMANDS owing by the UNITED STATES to INDIVIDUALS, CORPORATIONS and ASSOCIATIONS within the UNITED STATES, except INTEREST on the PUBLIC DEBT.

The statement spelled out how bank notes were used and their lawful standing in the economy but also contrasted the bills with Treasury-issued greenbacks because they did not mention legal tender.[19]

The decision to make national bank notes lawful money without a claim of legal tender status based solely on government decree was part of the congressional strategy to move away from the greenback model and toward an integrated public/private currency solution. The Senate legislative shepherd John Sherman wrote that "the public faith of a nation alone is not sufficient to maintain a paper currency. There must be a combination between the interests of private individuals and the government." National bank notes utilized this balanced approach and ensured face value protection through their redemption backed by federal bonds and ready convertibility across the country. This was an advancement from antebellum state banks that needed specie reserves to project confidence; a national bank note's security came from its place within a broad network of government-supported institutional deposits. The transition did not occur overnight, but more than 675 banks obtained national charters by the end of 1864. It was not easy to fund a war and craft a new monetary system, but the combination of greenbacks, national bank notes, and fractional currency enabled the federal government to muddle through.[20]

In the South, the challenge to pay for the rebellion and ensure a circulating paper currency was even more difficult. Before the first shot was fired on Fort Sumter, the new Confederate Treasury issued its own currency, optimistically promising payment either "six months" or "two years" "after the ratification of a treaty of peace between the confederate states and the United States." The notes were meant to project the Confederacy's strength and viability with vignettes of Southern statesmen like Jefferson Davis, Alexander Stephens, and Judah Benjamin alongside civic and economic scenes of government buildings, railroads, and of course, enslaved men and women. The display of images of black bodies at work alongside a formal portrait of John Calhoun also reinforced the centrality of white racial dominance to the Confederate project. Nicknamed "graybacks" in opposition to federal greenbacks, the open-ended post notes could be used at par to pay state taxes and public dues, but they inspired little confidence on the open market and failed to circulate in areas occupied by Northern troops. War costs necessitated more issues, so the Confederacy printed more than 680 million dollars even as their value plummeted and commodity prices spiked. Especially after Lincoln issued the preliminary Emancipation Proclamation, graybacks lost value in comparison to gold and Southern bank notes still in circulation until their purchasing price was less than ten cents on the dollar.[21]

While the context was different, the Southern banking system broke down even quicker than the Northern system as institutions stopped note redemption even before secession. Southern governments allowed the suspensions, but then required banks to accept Confederate Treasury notes in the hope that they could prop up the new unbacked paper currency. One report detailed Norfolk's currency distress in the fall of 1861: "The wealthier classes indulged in all the luxuries of the market. They had obtained possession of nearly all the metallic currency which was boarded away in their residences. To supply the void thus occasioned, the State had been flooded with shinplasters, which were looked upon with distrust, and received with grumbling by the lower classes of the community." In the wake of the rebellion and bank suspensions, the Southern economy was light on specie and inundated with graybacks, under-par bank notes, and numerous shinplasters.[22]

Southern shinplasters came in diverse forms as governments and businesses sought to facilitate trade. Consumers encountered a dizzying array of paper currency that ranged from five- and ten-cent notes from the municipal Corporation of Fredericksburg, Virginia, and merchant bills from Holcomb & Barnard's Drug Store in Fayetteville, Arkansas, to those issued in 1862 by the Cherokee Nation that promised to "pay to bearer FIFTY CENTS in notes of the Confederate States whenever the sum of 20, 50, or 100 dollars is presented at the office of the Treasurer" at their capital in Tahlequah. Shinplasters posed tough questions for individuals who tried to navigate the Southern economy, especially as inflation began to severely affect commodity prices. In the midst of a tense exchange, was it better to accept a questionable, postdated paper bill from a new national government that might not survive, a discounted bank note from an institution that had already given up its requirement to redeem its own bills, or a poorly printed scrap of paper from a local business? There was no simple answer to this conundrum.[23]

It was not government regulation or conservative banking ideology that ultimately threatened the proliferation of Southern paper currency; it was the lack of printing supplies. As early as 1861, a paper shortage "within the limits of Secessia," meant that "the only investment in capital is in paper and printer's bills, and these again are paid in shinplasters . . . presented on the points of secession bayonets, and the man who has corn, chooses between shinplasters and a halter." When new paper could not be found, currency was printed across the back of older unused notes. For example, three-dollar bills issued by the State of Louisiana on February 24, 1862, were printed on paper stock from the abandoned Exchange Bank of Holly Springs, Mississippi. Since such poor-quality notes circulated in large numbers, counterfeiters could more easily copy the bills than find the supplies to make forgeries. In fact, the constant shortage of liquidity led the administration to look at fake notes in a different light. Only a year into the rebellion, Confederate secretary of the Treasury Christopher Memminger asked Vice President Alexander Stephens to allow counterfeit notes to legally circulate alongside ones issued by the government. They did not fully embrace the forgeries, but they did eventually allow banks to include some fake graybacks among their assets. By accepting the fraudulent notes, the line between the Confederacy as a guarantor of sound currency and as a common counterfeiter became meaningless.[24]

The paper money market was even more complicated in border areas like Tennessee, which was caught between shifting front lines and opposing currency regimes. The lack of small change prompted Memphis businessmen to ask banks to "cut their notes into fractional parts, representing quarters and halves of dollars, for the relief of the trading community." A reporter who tried to purchase a quire of paper that was already marked up from the going rate of thirty to fifty cents was told that he would also be charged 40 percent on the change from his Bank of Tennessee note. He responded that this "inequality of exchange or want of uniformity in the relative values of currency and specie, and especially the depreciation of Confederate States money must soon produce an extraordinary derangement of financial affairs and business, and cause great distress." When the United States Army regained control of Clarksville, the population suddenly found themselves "transferred from one side [of] the line to the other" and stuck with large amounts of paper promises they had received from the "Southern Confederacy." Captain J. H. Putnam summed up the atmosphere in Nashville when he said that "the merchants are afraid of their own currency." This sentiment was shared by much of the American population during the Civil War.[25]

In the North and the South, wartime necessities pushed legislative fixes to a currency system that was already broken before the fighting started in 1861. Within a few years, Americans saw the creation of Treasury demand notes, legal tender greenbacks, graybacks, Southern state treasury notes, shinplasters, postage and fractional currency, and national bank notes in addition to the state bank notes that continued to circulate. Americans understood that this monetary upheaval had occurred within the context of the Civil War and observers quickly tied support for national currencies to support for the war effort. Northerners' stance on legal tender greenbacks became a loyalty test as even known hard money backers swallowed their personal views in the name of patriotism. Among other pro-administration publications, Philadelphia's Union League distributed copies of *The Old Continental and the New Greenback Dollar* in the month before the election of 1864. The tract asked legal tender note detractors whether it was possible to "have confidence in the Federal *armies*," and lack "faith in the Federal *currency*." Another snarky campaign pamphlet, *The Copperhead Catechism*, cited "postage currency and greenbacks" as the principal issues opposed by Northern Democrats who were critical of Lincoln and the aims of the war.[26]

This wasn't just about greenbacks. The introduction of uniform national bank notes forced Northerners to consider where currency and banking fit into the ongoing debate between federal authority and states' rights. Alexander Del Mar, the first director of the Bureau of Statistics at the Treasury Department, explained that there should be a clear relationship between the country's political culture and its monetary system. He wrote that, because "a *national* existence is claimed for the people living in the United States," the "National Banking system is essentially congruous with the times," while "State Banking systems [are] essentially incongruous." Del Mar believed that the war exposed not only the danger of states' rights ideas but also decentralized institutions that created an imbalance in regulations and organization.[27]

Southerners who contemplated the quick creation and demise of the Confederacy and its currencies confronted a different reality. The sense that there should be harmony between a nation's political and economic systems meant that the failure of the Southern cause represented more than just battlefield losses. Florida, for example, used its authority under Confederate regulations to issue state treasury notes that could pay government debts and purchase land. Between 1861 and 1865, the state issued more than $2.2 million in notes, but their value was undercut by graybacks that could be obtained more cheaply and also be used to pay state taxes or speculate in land. Considered unconstitutional state paper currency, the notes lost all value with the arrival of the Northern soldiers.[28]

One man mused on the connections between Florida's political, monetary, and racial systems when he inscribed the back of a soon-to-be-worthless ten-dollar state note. In reference to the bill's vignette of an enslaved man with cotton, he wrote:

> The "nigger" is free; there's not a doubt
> With "ourselves" is now on the level;
> So pull up your stakes, clear out,
> For now our State will go to the devil.

He lamented the shared fate of the Confederacy, the institution of African American slavery, and white superiority along with the states' rights power that enabled the creation of the Florida state treasury note on which his poem appeared. Like antebellum gamblers who poured out their stories on the backs of bank notes, Southerners wrote on defunct Confederate bills to signify the relationship between the material and spiritual end of their fortunes. Similar messages appeared with such frequency after the war that Margaret Mitchell included the trope seventy years later in *Gone with the Wind*. A Confederate soldier named Will shares a bill that features the poem "Lines on the Back of a Confederate Note," in which the note is referred to as "the pledge of a nation that's passed away."[29]

Self-referential reactions to Civil War currency were not limited to Southern poetry; green-covered pamphlets that analyzed legal tender notes put a fine point on the importance of the money's physical traits. One of these, *Green-back to His Country Friends*, purported to be a letter from an anthropomorphic bill to the members of Congress in 1862. A moderate argument, Green-back explained that he was comfortable with government-issued notes as long as circulation was limited and monitored to avoid depreciation. The overall message was to guard against "too much of a good thing." An 1864 pamphlet with a bright-green cover entitled *Money by Steam: John Law, His Body Moulders in the Ground, but His Soul Is Marching On* maintained that the national currency's text and iconography should convey messages of common interest. The author laments that each subsequent release of federal currency is like when "confidence weakens in handsome engravings." Firm limits are needed on circulation or "[the notes] will soon depreciate to the standard of works of art of similar beauty; as long as they can be doubled, quadrupled, or multiplied indefinitely, they are not money, have no value, and will be so regarded, no matter how great our loyalty." Within larger monetary policy debates, such tracts claimed that a bill's aesthetic qualities were central to its market value.[30]

For all the high-minded commentary about the legal tender bills' constitutionality or whether a national banking system properly challenged states rights' theories, the public reaction to greenbacks, postage currency, national bank notes, or new shinplasters often focused on their look and feel. As Chapters 3 and 4 have demonstrated, Americans' engagement with paper money was a physical relationship and its acceptance was contingent on its materiality. The introduction of new types of bills during the Civil War put this fact into stark relief. This did not mean that every neatly engraved bill immediately gained public approval. It meant that the public demand for a functional, sound, and uniform currency included calls to meet certain physical standards alongside details about redemption in specie or government backing. Even when they dealt in five- or ten-cent denominations, notes that fell apart easily, stuck together, or failed to present a strong visual imagery were unacceptable to the public.

Reviews of new postal currency in 1862 centered on its physical features especially when it was compared to noncurrency postage. While stamps "stuck to the fingers and the portemonnaie, and quickly got torn, dirty, wasted and uncurrent," the new currency would be "printed on stout, thick paper" and "will not be gummed." One commentator explained that even though it was "delivered in sheets, which are perforated like those of postage stamps," it was printed on bank note paper stock and was "therefore more difficult of separation than the old stamps." A Kansas newspaper warned the public to be "cautious when separating this currency, and not mutilate the notes," as they would be discounted if they were incomplete when redeemed. Some "evil disposed persons" utilized the similarities between postal stamps and currency to wash off the glue and alter stamps to resemble worn postage currency. This forced the Post Office Department to issue an order that "letters covered by soiled, defaced, or washed stamps, would be sent to the dead-letter office." The confusion demonstrated that, like other paper money, postage currency was not just a formless stand-in for value. The material appearance and feel of government notes mattered for how Americans used them and how much confidence they chose to extend.[31]

So, when the Treasury introduced greenbacks in 1861 as a new type of paper currency for a nervous nation, the public clambered for as much information as possible. The *Baltimore Sun* responded with an article titled "United States Treasury Notes—How They Are Made," which contained details about the paper, layout, and printing process for the new bills then in production by the American Bank Note Company of New York. The article indicated that the paper was of "the very best stock . . . durable and fit for general circulation" and detailed the placement of vignettes on the different notes, from the engravings of General Winfield Scott and Salmon Chase to "an Indian woman supporting the arms of the United States." The bills' most unique features came during the printing:

> On the face of the government notes two colors are used, black for the portraits, vignettes and part of the lettering, and green for the geometrical groundwork and certain portions of the lettering and general design. On the back, which is almost covered with geometrical-lathe work, the color is green. The object of using these

> two colors is at once to give a certain peculiarity of appearance to the government issues, and to guard against counterfeiting by photograph or otherwise. This end is effectively accomplished by the employment of the peculiar patented green tint, of which the American Bank-Note Company have the exclusive use.

The public appreciated such anti-counterfeiting measures, but it was the uniformity of the government-issued bills and their unique application of color techniques that most struck consumers. Greenbacks could be quickly identified; their appearance immediately marked them as a separate type of paper currency from the state bank notes and shinplasters still in circulation. The message behind the greenback design was that soon the American public would not need to spend time closely inspecting their paper money or divining whether it was a note worth trusting. The government would declare that it was.[32]

When they appeared a few years later, national bank notes entered a very different currency landscape. Rather than highlighting their unique qualities, supporters sought to demonstrate that the notes were uniform even though they came from a nationwide banking network rather than the federal government. Their contrast from state bank notes was apparent; a dozen images replaced thousands. To get buy-ins from the institutions that released and branded the notes, there were still small differences that balanced the banks' allegiance to the national system with touches of local color that let them retain some individual identity. For example, an oval vignette of the bank's state seal appeared on the back of one-dollar national bank notes. While these images varied based on the individual look of the seal, their similar placement and size within an otherwise uniform bill highlighted their connection to one another.

Attempts to commemorate the notes also stressed how the system brought together individual institutions to create unity. As part of an effort to raise funds for troops in the summer of 1864, the Western Illinois Sanitary Fair planned to "solicit from each National Bank throughout the country a specimen *Bank Note*." The notes would be "arranged in order under the names of the respective States from which they [had] come, and inclosed in a large and handsome frame and exhibited during the Fair." Organizers hoped the "valuable and interesting collection" would encourage donations, but the wider point was a celebration of the physical form of the bank notes and their message of national unification.[33]

It was not just an interested public that saw the importance of paper money's material features; Congress and the administration specifically crafted legislation with an eye toward how noteholders would interact with the new bills. The National Currency Act of 1863 created notes that projected an image of security and federal power manifested through a uniform nationalistic design, but also curtailed the sort of physical manipulation through personal inscription that was common on state bank notes. National bank notes featured a few large vignettes, a fair amount of text, and very little blank space. One hundred-dollar design, for example, included a female representation of Liberty next to the words "The Union Maintain it!" and a detailed engraving of Oliver Hazard Perry at the Battle of Lake Erie; a beautiful version of John Trumbull's Declaration of Independence appeared on the back of the bill rendered in green ink. With the addition of the bank note's identifying information on the front and long statements about redemption and a warning against counterfeiting or altering the note on the back, it was packed full of content. In addition to the elaborate design, Salmon Chase personally called for national bank notes with precise dimensions (exactly seven inches by three inches), ostensibly as part of an anti-counterfeiting measure.[34]

This layout altered the material relationship between Americans and their paper money. If someone wanted to write a poem, personal narrative, or political slogan on the bill, they were hard-pressed to find a place to put it. Language in the National Currency Act also threatened conviction for anyone "who shall mutilate, cut, deface, disfigure, or perforate [the notes] with holes." This included any attempt to "unite or cement together, or do any other thing to any bank bill." Coupled with the busy design of the notes, such cautions made clear that the types of personalization through physical manipulation that consumers regularly performed on state bank notes and shinplasters had no place in the new system. The legislation even included a provision to ensure that the comptroller of currency would "receive worn-out or mutilated circulating notes" and exchange them to ensure that Americans only used clean and proper bills. Regulated by the federal government, a uniform national currency would exist in a more controlled environment than its state bank note predecessors had.[35]

Public conversation about the appearance and function of greenbacks and national bank notes did not occur solely within congressional debates, newspapers, or political pamphlets. Prescriptive literature quickly incorporated the new currency into its story lines to teach lessons on representation, hard work, and fair exchange. The prolific children's author Jacob Abbott's *John Gay; or Work for Boys* (1864) told an extended tale about John, his younger brother Benny, and his cousin Mary as they created a pretend market economy. The kids did chores around the house and used homemade wooden currency to pay each other for their work. Great care and time went into the fabrication of John's "greenbacks." He chiseled different denominations in Roman numerals on each, "painting the backs of them green" and then fixed the color with "boiled linseed oil." Abbott explained that John's diligence in fixing the colors matched the production of real greenbacks, which made "them permanent and indelible, that they will not fade out or wear off by use, and cannot be effaced or altered by counterfeiters." Aside from lessons on mathematics and craftsmanship, the homemade greenback economy taught the children about monetary policy and circulation.[36]

In order to maintain his money's value after he paid Mary and Benny, John chose to pay down his debt before he spent any more. Jacob Abbott used the moment for a meditation on the nature of paper money: "It is true that bank-bills and real greenbacks, like John's imitations of them, look very pretty, and many persons attach a certain value to them on their own account. But they would soon lose all this value if people did not believe that they would be redeemed by something substantial when they were brought in, to those who issued them." Abbott's multilayered message to his youthful readers was instructive. He recognized the role that material appearance played in paper money's acceptance, but also argued that confidence in the paper could not be based solely on its physical beauty. A promise of redemption was needed. This was not a direct attack on Civil War greenbacks, but a reminder of conservative monetary policy and a signal of comfort with the national bank note model.[37]

Such prescriptive lessons were commonplace rather than aberrant because the move to legal tender paper was more than just a minor wonky alteration of the nation's currency policy; it was a major cultural shift. Legislative changes occurred alongside an outpouring of greenback-related literary production that informed the public what the new paper money was and how it worked. Even popular music and the stage reflected the developments. Plays, songs, and poems did not often introduce original analytic points about paper currency, but they brought the monetary issue to a wider audience. Sources that used satire or farce were not often favorable toward federal bills, but even critical cultural material normalized the notes and secured their place in the economic landscape. Taken together, positive and negative depictions of greenbacks and national bank notes provided a context for public acceptance of the federally backed bills more fully than any political speech or tract that debated the merits of new paper money could.

Legal tender note songs owed some of their success to an established antebellum market for music about currency that skewered shinplasters and uncurrent bank notes. In 1841, the Arch Street Theatre in Philadelphia staged an operatic burlesque entitled "Bank Monster, or Specie, vs. Shinplasters" that included parodies of popular songs and promised to "create quite a sensation in the *Money* market." One review invited the public to "go and look at specie contrasted with rags. What a difference," while another claimed that the performance was "a perfect delineation of broad grins—it has cured us of a liver attack of dyspepsia." Twenty years later, greenbacks became a similar target when their purchasing power dropped below face value. One satirist's epigram explained that "Chase and his money a mutual friendship show; / Chase makes false money—false money makes him so." Likewise, during the Bank War, customers at Cole's Music Store in Baltimore could purchase sheet music to "The United States Bank Waltz or A Squabble Between the Bank and the Government," which repackaged the day's economic news as a jaunty piano forte duel. During the Civil War, instrumental numbers with topical names such as "The Greenback Quick Step," "Secretary Chase's Grand March," "Shin-Plaster Jig," and "Legal Tender Polka" appeared in music stores. Their covers utilized brightly colored images of currency to promote the standard sheet music inside.[38]

The torrent of greenback-related cultural production represented the logical extension of earlier musical numbers that satirized shinplasters or other poor-quality bills, but they also familiarized the public with the new forms of paper money. While Salmon Chase and other federal officials bristled at the negative sentiment, each new song or joke that mentioned greenbacks further ingrained them in the national consciousness. Disapproval of federal notes was not the same thing as rejection. People did not need to like greenbacks; they needed to accept and pass them.

The most popular currency songs came from Bryant's Minstrels. "Greenbacks!" was written by troupe member and "Dixie" author Dan Emmett, and "How Are You Green-backs!" was crafted by E. Bowers, the author of the pro-Union "The Mudsills Are Coming." Both songs appeared

FIGURE 24. The "Legal Tender Polka" was one of many currency-related Civil War songs. Courtesy, Library of Congress Prints and Photograph Division, LC-USZC4-10799.

in 1863. "Greenbacks!" satirized the release of legal tender bills and the government personalities behind them. It exclaimed "Three hundred million more" are coming and "Chase he is a clever laddy, / But Father Abra'm is his daddy." "How Are You Green-backs!" was a reference to "We Are Coming, Father Abraham," an inspirational poem by abolitionist James Sloan Gibbons written in response to Lincoln's 1862 call for soldiers. Rather than rally troops for the nation, the satirical song explicitly described the arrival of the legal tender notes into the economy. It began:

> We're coming Father Abram, One hundred thousand more,
> Five hundred presses printing us from morn till night is o're:
> Like magic, you will see us start and scatter thro' the land,
> To pay the soldiers or release the border contraband.
> CHORUS. With our promise to pay, "How are you Secretary
> Chase?"
> Promise to pay, Oh! dats what's de matter.

The song appeared as part of a blackface minstrel walk-around and usually served as a performance centerpiece during the first act finale.[39]

"How Are You Green-backs!" attacked corruption and government profiteering, standard themes for minstrelsy's primarily working-class, white male audience, but was more ambiguous about the new federal paper money and the war effort as a whole. The song mentioned that greenbacks "line the fat contractors' purse, or purchase transport craft," but also claimed that "one hundred thousand more should help our Uncle Samuel to prosecute the war." It likewise supported a "march with gleaming bayonets upon the traitor's shore," but only if a "chieftain true" and "Generals on whom we can depend" replaced "Father Abram." While it did not support Lincoln's administration, greenback minstrelsy did champion a white working-class version of nationalism in defense of the Union. However, the monetary policy aspect of the song complicated this message. Minstrels promoted a vision of racial superiority and class hierarchy, but also begrudgingly acknowledged that their audience should accept a "promise to pay" from legal tender paper money that, by definition, leveled the demographic disparity in economic transactions. Unlike antebellum bank note negotiations that fluctuated based on socioeconomic power dynamics or the racial or gender characteristics of the buyer or seller, greenbacks promised a uniform and sound currency whose value did not hinge on the person who passed the bill or the one who received it.[40]

Even though it remained a popular minstrel number until well after the war, the power of "How Are You Green-backs!" to normalize legal tender paper money came from its ability to transcend a working-class, male crowd. Within weeks of its release by Bryant's Minstrels, other performers adapted the song for more varied audiences. At Laura Keene's Theatre in New York, Mrs. John Wood (born Matilda Charlotte Vining) added a version to her show that became her most "popular song and [was] nightly encored." A month later, in Washington, D.C., Miss Susan Denin made a special appearance at Grover's Theatre to "sing her new and popular song of "How Are You, Greenbacks!"[41]

Soon, "How are you greenbacks?" popped up in newspaper advertisements as a beckoning catchphrase. Bassler's in New York City used it to attract customers to purchase "Hats, Boys' Caps, &c., in exchange for greenbacks." It was also deployed by a Portsmouth, Ohio, committee selling land in Iowa to raise funds "to pay recruits to fill the quota of the 3d ward." Even the small-town *Luzerne Union* in Wilkes-Barre, Pennsylvania, employed the phrase in an anecdote about an old farmer who lost one hundred dollars because he did not understand how to use legal tender bills. When asked for help, an unsympathetic onlooker "put his thumb to his nose and said, 'How are you, greenbacks!'" as if the words themselves served as a threat to those who failed to embrace the new currency.[42]

The song title became a slogan throughout the nation and was picked up by partisans across the political divide to express their support for or derision of the administration. A Pittsburgh newspaper reported that, on a trip to Ohio during local elections in 1863, "How are you greenbacks" was a "complimentary salutation that frequently greeted Secretary Chase" as he campaigned around the state. The following year it popped up at the Sanitary Commission Metropolitan Fair in New York during a charitable fundraiser where individuals could pay one dollar to vote for their favorite general. The winner was presented with an elaborately decorated sword made by Charles Lewis Tiffany. For most of the contest, George McClellan led Ulysses S. Grant in what observers viewed as an 1864 election preview (with Grant standing in for Lincoln). When a wave of last-minute greenbacks came in through the mail for Grant, McClellan's supporters argued that Union League corruption had robbed the vote. The Democratic *Buffalo Evening Post* suspiciously exclaimed, "Grant won the sword at last! 16,000 majority. How are you Greenbacks?" These partisan Democrats might not have liked Lincoln, Grant, Chase, or legal tender notes, but their use of the phrase emphasizes how greenbacks had become entrenched in the economy and the popular consciousness.[43]

Cultural sources acclimated the population to new types of paper money, but the need to pay for the war meant that, outside of satirical songs, there was little space for effective opposition to legal tender currency. California's Specific Contract Law offered minor state resistance in April 1863 when it curtailed the use of greenbacks and allowed parties to a contract to specify payment in whatever form of money they wanted. The Supreme Court of California upheld the law in 1864 and ruled that, since the law did not question greenbacks but merely provided an alternative to using them in some agreements, it was compatible with federal legislation. Other western states quickly followed with their own Specific Contract Acts. Meanwhile, individual Americans who did not favor the currency changes sought redress in the courts. A combination of partisan judges (Republicans tended to support legal tender, while Democrats ruled against it) and lengthy appeals meant that no consensus was reached, but beginning in 1863, sixteen separate challenges worked their way through the process before a few finally reached the Supreme Court in 1870.[44]

Collectively known as the Legal Tender Cases, *Hepburn v. Griswold* (1870), *Knox v. Lee* (1871), *Parker v. Davis* (1871), and *Juilliard v. Greenman* (1884) resolved whether Congress and the president had the constitutional authority to create legal tender paper money. The court ruled against greenbacks in *Hepburn*, but in a fit of judicial whiplash, overturned that case a year later in *Knox* and *Parker*. *Juilliard* expanded on the court's pronouncement that greenbacks were constitutional in a sweeping final word over a decade later. Apart from the legal arguments made in *Hepburn*, *Knox*, and *Parker*, several odd circumstances colored the initial ruling and its quick reversal. The former secretary of the Treasury Salmon P. Chase participated in the cases not as a witness or advocate who guided the passage of the Legal Tender Act in 1862, but as the chief justice of the Supreme Court, a position he had taken over in 1864. Chase not only failed to recuse himself from the proceedings, he crafted the majority opinion against the constitutionality of legal tender notes in *Hepburn* and a fiery dissent in *Knox* and *Parker*.[45]

Likewise, observers questioned whether the five-to-three ruling in *Hepburn* was tainted by the condition of ailing justice Robert Cooper Grier. He survived three strokes and was only two days away from forced retirement when Chase read the decision. Grier's remarks during deliberation seemed to contradict his vote against the Legal Tender Act and some colleagues wondered whether he fully understood his actions. The timing of the decision also raised suspicions as two new justices joined the bench shortly after the *Hepburn* ruling. William Strong replaced Grier in February and Joseph Bradley followed a month later in a newly minted ninth seat on the court that created a pro-greenback majority.[46]

Apart from the judicial soap opera, constitutional historians and legal scholars have debated the arguments contained in the Legal Tender Cases for one hundred and fifty years. The court based its rulings on analysis of Article 1, Section 8, Clause 18 (Necessary and Proper Clause), Article 1, Section 8, Clause 5 (Coin Money and regulate the value thereof), the Tenth Amendment, and congressional war powers. However, many details in the legal tender test cases mirrored antebellum lawsuits pertaining to contractual obligation and arbitrage. State courts in cases like *Nashville Bank v. Hays & Grundy* (1834) ruled against creditors who tried to enforce the repayment of a loan of discounted paper money in specie or face-value bank notes because it was considered to be illegal usury.[47]

Rather than wade into the often-debated constitutionality of federal authority on monetary matters, it is useful instead to examine a separate aspect of *Hepburn* and *Knox* that scholars have overlooked. In these two landmark cases that decided the fate of government-issued legal tender bills, one of the plaintiffs (Susan Hepburn) and one of the defendants (Phoebe Lee) were women. There is no specific evidence that Hepburn and Lee's gender contributed to both of them losing their high-profile legal challenges, but who they were provides an important context for why they brought cases in the first place.

Let us start with the details of *Hepburn*. The story began on June 20, 1860, when Susan Hepburn gave a promissory note for $11,250 to Henry Griswold. She pledged to pay him on February 20, 1862, which it turned out was just five days before greenbacks became legal tender. Rather than make a timely payment, Hepburn allowed interest to accrue before Griswold filed a lawsuit to recover the funds. Hepburn attempted to satisfy the suit in March of 1864 with $12,720 in greenbacks, but Griswold refused to accept anything but gold. She instead paid the Louisville Chancery Court, which marked the debt paid. It is unknown whether Henry Griswold's gripe with Susan Hepburn's paper money would have been the same if it was her husband Hiatt's debt, but Griswold's reluctance probably did not come from a lack of faith in Susan's ability to secure the proper funds. She was a member of a prominent Louisville family and had locally managed and sold property and real estate for years. Her brother (and lawyer) William Preston was a former congressman and a Confederate brigadier general. Hepburn held leadership positions in the Ladies' Southern Relief Association of Louisville and the Ladies' Masonic Widows' and Orphans' Society.[48]

If it had been the 1850s, Susan Hepburn's status in Louisville might have helped in a tense paper money negotiation with Henry Griswold, but it would not have guaranteed success. Antebellum negotiations over state bank notes could hinge on the demographic profiles of the individuals involved as the fluctuating value of paper money provided an opening for social power dynamics to influence the terms of exchange. In the context of the Legal Tender Act, there was supposed to be protection for anyone who used greenbacks to pay a debt, so Hepburn was not satisfied to let Griswold set conditions on her method of payment. Her choices, first to pay the Chancery Court directly and second to bring a Supreme Court appeal after a loss in the Court of Errors of Kentucky, demonstrated her desire to utilize the power of government institutions to ensure an equitable paper currency exchange. Even a wealthy white woman such as Susan Hepburn could not formally press for better terms during the antebellum period; her insistence to do so after the war spoke to her conviction and the radical leveling power of federal paper money legislation.[49]

The specifics of *Knox v. Lee* were more complicated than the Hepburn case, but likewise concerned an affluent woman who utilized the court system to seek fair and equitable treatment with regard to currency valuation. Under the Sequestration Act against alien enemies, the Confederacy ruled in 1863 that Pennsylvanian Pheobe Lee was a loyal Unionist and confiscated 608 sheep she had left in Texas when the war began. The state of Texas then sold the sheep to William Knox. After the war, Lee successfully sued Knox to recover the value of her livestock, but the Circuit Court for the Western District of Texas ruled that Knox could make restitution in greenbacks. Lee objected, arguing that the sheep's value in specie was greater than in federal paper money. Knox eventually appealed to the Supreme Court to prevent any ruling that allowed proof of a difference between the value in gold and legal tender paper to affect repayment. Unlike Susan Hepburn, Phoebe Lee did not hope to use the legal tender status of greenbacks to achieve better terms for her paper money; rather, she tried to use the court system to seek an advantage in the valuation of her property because she opposed greenbacks' parity with gold. Unfortunately for both women, the shifting judicial ground beneath them meant that, even as they took up opposite sides in the legal tender debate, neither case was successful.[50]

As highlighted in Chapter 3, unequal power dynamics in bank note exchanges meant that women and people of color often had not achieved just outcomes in antebellum negotiations. The passage of the Legal Tender Act promised to end this imbalance and ensure market equality through uniform greenbacks that were regulated and backed by the federal government, but the short-term transition to the new paper currency regime did not always proceed smoothly. For Hepburn and Lee, their inability to achieve positive resolutions during private currency exchanges led them to file separate legal challenges to clarify how greenbacks would function in the real world. Hepburn hoped to acquire government support to ensure the value of her paper money, while Lee sought help from the court to protect value that she saw being compromised by those same notes. Before the Legal Tender Act, both women had to accept the best outcome that their monetary knowledge and status could negotiate; after the legal tender decisions, no negotiation over the value of their paper money would have been necessary. The cases enshrined the federal government's right to create legal tender. However, caught in the liminal moment between the old currency regime and the new one, Susan Hepburn and Phoebe Lee sought the aid of the legal system; this resulted in two of the most vital postbellum Supreme Court cases.

The parade of Legal Tender Cases generated a lot of heat and light, but *Veazie Bank v. Fenno* (1869), decided just weeks before *Hepburn v. Griswold*, proved more critical and enduring for the American public. The case dealt with bank notes rather than greenbacks and avoided the legal tender issue, while it affirmed the federal government's power to circulate paper money and set currency regulations. Just weeks before the end of the war, Congress amended the National Bank Act to impose a 10 percent tax on state bank notes set to begin on July 1, 1866. The measure was an attempt to compel resistant state institutions to obtain charters and join the national banking system. Since state banks issued their notes as loans, there was no way for them to raise rates high enough to cover the new tax and still earn a profit from their notes. Only if they became national banks would they survive as institutions that could issue notes. By August 1867, state bank notes vanished, but not without protest. The Veazie Bank of Maine disputed the bank note tax and its case against federal tax collector Jeremiah Fenno made its way to the Supreme Court in 1869. The ruling forcefully upheld the tax as lawful and cut off further challenges to the constitutionality of National Bank Notes.[51]

While bankers watched the case with interest, General Samuel Veazie could not enlist much outside help for his bank's suit. By the time the parties appeared in Portland before the United States Circuit Court in the fall of 1867, most state banks had already been rechartered as national banks. The legal challenge also suffered when the eighty-one-year-old Veazie died in March 1868 as the case was winding its way through the court system, a year and a half before it landed on the Supreme Court's docket. If the Veazie Bank hoped to gather grassroots public support for its cause, it had made a poor decision when it added Reverdy Johnson as one of its lawyers. Known for his defenses of conspirator Mary Surratt and Dred Scott defendant John Sanford, Johnson's high-profile career had included a lead role in the 1834 collapse of the Bank of Maryland, which left thousands of working people stuck with worthless bank notes. Public anger spilled into the streets during the August 1835 Baltimore Bank Riot and a mob ransacked Johnson's house. If the Veazie Bank case represented a last stand for the state banking system, the presence of Reverdy Johnson was a pointed reminder that the suit was about personal profit and bankers helping bankers rather than the public's legal rights.[52]

Outside of constitutional complaints and personal profit motivations, material concerns and ego might have contributed to Veazie's resistance to the National Bank Act. The legislation required the bank to replace notes that featured a portrait of Samuel Veazie with branded national bills designed with universal vignettes. While that fact was not explicitly mentioned in the proceedings, a separate argument about bank notes' materiality played a crucial role in the chief justice's decision to uphold the tax on state bank notes as a lawful excise tax. Chase used a detailed reading of *Hylton v. United States* (1796), a case that questioned a duty on carriages, to define the difference between an excise tax and an unconstitutional, unapportioned direct tax. Chase looked to the earlier court, which included several Constitutional Convention participants, and followed their view that only poll taxes and direct taxes placed on land needed apportionment. In this explanation, the carriage tax could be extended to bank notes or "all other objects" that were not land. A dissent written by associate justices Samuel Nelson and David Davis instead argued that notes in circulation were not part of a bank's "property but merely certificates of its debts" and as debts, rather than assets, they could not be taxed as such. Such a contention downplayed the materiality of bank notes and claimed that they were wholly representational. For Americans who had held and manipulated paper money for years, its physicality was one of its defining features. They did not need to be convinced that bank notes were more than just representational certificates. Newspapers across the nation that announced the *Veazie Bank* decision recognized this fact and specifically cited Chase's language, labeling bank notes among "all other objects" as a critical takeaway from the ruling.[53]

Salmon Chase's decision not only acknowledged the materiality of bank notes; it also examined the relationship between the government and the nation's currency supply. The Legal Tender Cases debated the government's ability to control the value and utility of its own bills, but the *Veazie* ruling addressed the much wider issue of the government's control over the nation's entire money supply. Chase and the court's majority argued that Congress had the "undisputed constitutional power, to provide a currency for the whole country" and "to that end may restrain, by suitable enactments, the circulation of any notes not issued under its own authority." Notably, the chief justice did not tie this power solely to constitutional language on taxation, but rather he explicitly grounded his opinion in the nation's lived experience with paper money. Chase explained that it was the federal government's prerogative to "secure a sound and uniform currency for the country," but that antebellum institutions had failed to accomplish this task. So, when the war began, the nation's currency "consisted almost entirely of bank notes issued by numerous independent corporations variously organized under state legislation, of various degrees of credit, and very unequal resources, administered often with great and not unfrequently with little skill, prudence, and integrity." This history mattered because, when hoarded specie and the collapse of state bank note redemption threatened the currency system, it was left to the federal government to step in and respond to the public demand for a solution. The decision next contained a detailed time line of steps taken by the government to create a circulating paper medium—from the creation of Treasury demand notes and greenbacks to national bank notes.[54]

The Veazie Bank ruling ended the state bank note system and empowered Congress to ensure stable and uniform paper circulation. Monetary regulation was no longer a local or even a state matter; it was the unquestioned prerogative of the federal government. Even casual observers understood that the decision had the "good effect to rid the country of the nuisance of State Bank notes" and lauded Chase's decision for being "as comprehensive as it is masterly and direct." Coupled with the legal tender decisions, the postwar court secured the nations' paper money supply of national bank notes and greenbacks and created a new currency paradigm that endured until the passage of the Federal Reserve Act in 1913.[55]

Monetary debates still flourished in the post-Veazie era, but they focused on a very different set of problems than those of the antebellum period. Rather than navigate thousands of different bills in circulation, Americans narrowed their concerns to the benefits of greenbacks versus national bank notes and how to set the proper amount of each type of paper in circulation. A new political party, the Greenback-Labor Party, even rose to defend unbacked legal tender bills and oppose notes solely tied to specie. These were important questions, but they required a different kind of material, personal, and political engagement from paper money holders who had previously had to decipher which money was good and which was uncurrent using their lived experience and detective skills. Bank note tables and counterfeit detectors were no longer needed on a daily basis. Over time, the public's monetary knowledge slipped away as it was no longer a necessity to obtain and wield detailed information about individual banks and their notes in order to participate in common market transactions. Americans gained equity and peace of mind with a stable and uniform paper currency, but they lost some of the tools they needed to understand and shape vital financial decisions.[56]

Not everything about the way Americans engaged their paper money changed with uniform notes. The busy design of national bank notes and greenbacks limited opportunities to write on the bills, but there was no way of getting around physical interactions with paper money. The notion that contaminated notes contributed to cases of smallpox, scarlet fever, and anthrax in the late nineteenth and early twentieth centuries brought physicians and government officials together to create a cleaner money supply. The president of the New York Academy of Sciences, A. Cressy "Clean Money" Morrison, and a series of 1904 articles in the *Journal of the American Medical Association* warned about the danger of "Dirty Money" and the "inevitable effect of spreading all manner of contagious diseases." They suggested a faster process to remove soiled bills from circulation and replace them with crisp, new notes. The *Journal of the American Bankers' Association* likewise called for a governmental war on germs. By 1909, the director of the Bureau of Engraving and Printing, Joseph Ralph, responded

FIGURE 25. Proof sheet for five-dollar note from the First National Bank of Monroe. Courtesy, National Numismatic Collection, National Museum of American History, Smithsonian Institution.

with a plan to wash soiled notes in a chemical bath to prolong their life and offer the public peace of mind about the spread of disease. That plan did not go far enough. After an eleven-year-old Massachusetts girl supposedly contracted smallpox from paper money in 1912, the Treasury Department began to pick up the postage costs for banks to turn in soiled bills. The following year, explicit language in the Federal Reserve Act of 1913 outlined how and when to destroy notes that became "unfit for circulation."[57]

The creation of uniform currency and the nature of monetary debates in the late nineteenth century did not mean that activists were any less passionate than the Loco Focos fifty years earlier. They just operated in a different context and brought different concerns. The Greenbacker partisan Jacob Coxey, who led unemployed men in marches on Washington, showed his commitment when he named one of his children Legal Tender Coxey. Paper money was ever present in the life of young Legal Tender, but being born in the 1890s meant that he did not need to obtain the encyclopedic knowledge of banking institutions necessary to determine whether the notes in his hand were worth their face value. For all their problems, the creation of uniform greenbacks and national bank notes fundamentally changed the relationship between Americans and their paper money and relieved them of having to accumulate significant amounts of financial information just to stay current in the marketplace. The Veazie Bank and Legal Tender Cases ensured that the federal government would protect the new uniform currency and broadcast to Americans that they could use paper money without the need to negotiate its value with each exchange. A dollar was actually a dollar even in Monroe, Michigan.[58]

EPILOGUE

We Don't Need No Monetary Education

In 1850s Montgomery, brokers Emanuel, Henry, and Mayer Lehman bought and sold cotton, dry goods, and enslaved human beings as well as paper securities and paper currency that they moved between Alabama and New York City. The brokerage grew after the Civil War and became one of the nation's largest investment banks and financial traders, a status it kept for over a hundred years. This long history came to a sudden halt in September 2008, when the collapse of Lehman Brothers sent shock waves through the economy and signified a critical moment in what has become known as the Great Recession. The events of the subprime mortgage and banking crisis of 2007–2009 might appear far removed from the early republic bank note system, but the public's response to the financial emergency highlights a modern monetary culture grounded in the experience of legal tender paper currency. When Americans became confident that their money would be accepted at face value, they no longer needed to maintain constant vigilance of banking institutions or acquire and utilize complex financial information just to participate in daily market activities. Over time, they failed to monitor currency markets or check the actions of the professional bankers and government regulators who organized the nation's financial system using ever more specialized information. Without this accumulated monetary knowledge, the public struggled to understand or respond to the Great Recession.[1]

This short epilogue is not the place for a comprehensive dive into the subprime mortgage fiasco and related banking crisis or the government's response to these events. Other scholars have offered rich and nuanced analyses of what happened and why, but it is useful to quickly examine the disconnect between actual monetary policies and how the media presented those policies to an audience that was not expected to fully understand them. Take the case of quantitative easing (QE). In response to early signs of a banking crisis, the Federal Open Market Committee (FOMC) reduced the overnight rates with which deposit institutions loan money to each other. The committee hoped this first step would increase liquidity in the system and shore up capital reserves for troubled institutions. The situation further deteriorated and the FOMC continued to lower rates from 5.25 percent in September 2007 to practically zero by the end of 2008, but this did little to blunt the downturn. With decreasing policy options, the Federal Reserve turned to an aggressive expansion of its balance sheet, called QE, whereby they purchased assets such as debt from housing agencies like Fannie Mae and Freddie Mac as well as mortgage-backed securities (MBS). Through successive rounds of QE, the Fed added upward of $1.75 trillion in balance sheet assets by November 2009; these purchases raised the price of MBS and provided liquidity for commercial banks. Even in this overly simplified version of events, a vast distance existed between the inscrutable actions of government agencies identified by acronyms and the lives of people who experienced the Great Recession through layoffs and underwater mortgages.[2]

It was not always like this. During the early republic, the necessity to navigate the bank note system meant that each individual accumulated monetary information and wielded it during financial transactions or maintained it as part of a database to make sense of wider economic episodes. The Panic of 1837 or Bank War did not require considerable explanation for most Americans whose daily lived experience instructed them about the details of the financial system. Similarly, government actions such as the removal of deposits from the Bank of the United States or the Specie Clause were quickly understood by a cross section of the public. There might not have been equal mastery of all the finer points of these policies, but there could be informed public debate about what was best for the country and its people. The Americans who confronted the Great Recession, however, did not possess a clear understanding of either the nature of the problem or how proposed government solutions would address them. The Federal Reserve's policy of quantitative easing, for example, would have to be thoroughly explained because nothing in most people's 2008 lived experience prepared them for it.

Attempts to educate the public about quantitative easing came in many forms, from TV newscasts and blogs to newspaper columns and journal articles. *Liber8*, a newsletter for students and librarians released by the research library of the Federal Reserve Bank of St. Louis, even dedicated an issue to explaining QE in April 2011. The accompanying teacher's guide provided a list of questions including "Why did the Federal Reserve turn to nontraditional policies, such as quantitative easing?" The answer key explained, "The Federal Open Market Committee had pushed the nominal federal funds rate target close to zero. Because it cannot push short-term rates below zero, it decided to use quantitative easing to provide support for a weakened economy." Simple enough for even a student reading the newsletter to understand? Not really. The difficulty for experts trying to explain QE, and monetary policy in general, was the gulf between Americans' financial knowledge leading up to the Great Recession and the activities of financial institutions. Participation in the modern market did not require the accumulation of specific information about banks and banking regulations, so even belated explanations did little to make a clear connection for the public.[3]

Perhaps the most pointed cultural example of this difficulty came in *The Big Short*, a 2015 film based on Michael Lewis's book about the subprime lending debacle. The movie follows several real-life characters who bet against conventional wisdom and the banks to short the mortgage industry in the run-up to 2008. Confronted with the tension between the production of a profitable Hollywood movie and an accurate portrayal of the inner workings of high finance and banking, the filmmakers employed a number of gimmicks to make the story more accessible to their audience (not to mention starring roles for Brad Pitt, Christian Bale, Steve Carell, and Ryan Gosling). At several moments in the film, the actors break the fourth wall to either provide helpful exposition or offer simplified definitions of complicated financial terms, such as when Margot Robbie, in a bubble bath, explains subprime loans. The most memorable of these asides features Selena Gomez and economist Richard Thaler, on a casino floor, explaining how a synthetic Collateralized Debt Obligation operates like a collection of side bets on side bets.[4]

Without the platform of a major motion picture, journalists attempted to educate the public about monetary policies, terms, and government actions through common-sense sounding metaphors. News reports and editorials routinely described quantitative easing as a "modern day method of printing money" where the government "prints an IOU and 'creates cash' that is injected into the economy," rather than giving a more accurate explanation that the Federal Reserve purchased hundreds of billions of dollars in government bonds, housing–finance firm debt, and mortgage-backed securities from highly leveraged banks which created electronic credits in the accounts that the banks kept with the Fed. The banks got more liquidity and removed the toxic assets from their balance sheets. Some accounts skipped the nuance altogether with the claim that the Fed had "printed more than $1 trillion in new money." This was not just a shortcut for impatient newscasters. Even seasoned economics reporters like Neil Irwin of the *Washington Post* opted for the explanation that "the central bank, effectively, will print more money to pay for the purchases." However, the reality was that there was no increase in the printing of U.S. paper currency; it was just the opposite. According to the Department of the Treasury, the Bureau of Engraving and Printing delivered $6.2 trillion in federal reserve notes in fiscal year 2009, down from $7.7 trillion in 2008, and further down from $9.1 trillion in 2007.[5]

If the amount of paper money issued went down during the Great Recession, why did commentators, pundits, and reporters repeatedly claim that the government was printing more money? The lack of linguistic precision to describe quantitative easing was not always accidental. It made for a convenient story for those who wanted to reassure the public that something was being done while they sidestepped the fact that the Fed bailout targeted the same large entities that helped create the housing market and banking problems in the first place without any real relief for most Americans. In this context the concept of "printing money" was a handy and universal shorthand for goosing the economy that promised to help the country as a whole. Such misdirection was only possible because most of the public was not well enough versed in the details of the program to push back.

For most writers who discussed quantitative easing, the euphemism "printing money" was not employed in the furtherance of a scheme, but because of the strong physical relationship that Americans had with their cash. The phrase provided a useful shorthand to explain an opaque monetary policy and simultaneously provide the public with a material image of currency with which to identify. In an earlier era, it was easier to make the connection between monetary policy and personal finances because an increase in liquidity did mean directly printing more paper money. At a time when they could rip bills in half or write on their backs, antebellum Americans would not have questioned their material connection to the money market. This was not the case during the Great Recession. For people stung by the reality that inscrutable electronic transactions had the power to undermine the economy in general and their lives in particular, the ability to picture the printing of physical currency reassured them that something more concrete than credit cards and wire transfers undergirded the system. The result was that these word games persisted until the Federal Reserve policy reached its conclusion six years later. In the fall of 2014, a National Public Radio segment entitled "What Is Quantitative Easing and Why Is It Likely to End?" told its audience that the government's "printing money" through QE was just about over.[6]

Not everyone supported the bailout program or sought to connect to an older paper money regime. Just months after the collapse of Lehman Brothers and in the midst of international efforts to stabilize the economy and banking sector, a mysterious character supposedly named Satoshi Nakamoto launched Bitcoin, an encrypted digital currency created by users outside of governmental purview. Nakamoto claimed he "wanted to create a currency that was impervious to unpredictable monetary policies as well as the predations of bankers and politicians." The timing was purposeful. The date stamp on the initial group of digital coins included a textual mention of an impending government bailout of British banks. Cryptocurrency was not a new concept in 2008, but Bitcoin solved the long-standing problem of how to log and authenticate the movement of digital files while keeping the transactions anonymous. It was the deployment of blockchain technology shared by users around the globe that provided a solution as well as a potential problem. An anonymous electronic currency that could not be easily tracked by law enforcement appealed to those who sought to use Bitcoin for black market and dark web transactions, so the nongovernmental currency immediately drew red flags from observers who questioned its legality.[7]

Shortly after its launch, lawyers and economists began to debate how Bitcoin should be regulated and specifically whether it ran afoul of the Stamp Payments Act of 1862, the Civil War law that authorized postage currency and curtailed the use of shinplasters. Legal scholars explained that a series of judicial rulings since the Civil War codified certain exceptions to the legislation's shinplaster prohibition based on whether nongovernmental tokens or paper notes were meant to circulate in a limited area, how and whether they were redeemable, and if they tangibly resembled federal currency. On the last issue specifically, supporters of Bitcoin argued that since the crypto coins did not physically resemble either United States coins or federal reserve notes, their electronic form provided a strong case for why the 1862 law did not apply. In the context of *Veazie Bank v. Fenno*, this argument about materiality and regulation was questionable. Under *Veazie*, the court ruled that Congress had the power to decide what was and what was not money and that state bank notes could be federally taxed and regulated because they were not mere representations of wealth, but physical objects like carriages. It is difficult to make the case that Bitcoin is a currency and therefore not merely a representation of wealth, but simultaneously that it should not be regulated as a shinplaster because it is not a similar type of physical object. It would appear to have to be one or the other.[8]

For all the ways this legal scholarship attempts to reconcile Bitcoin with a 150-year-old law passed to curtail shinplasters, it provides little historical context about the state of the Civil War money market that inspired the legislation in the first place. Maybe it is too much to expect Bitcoin boosters to understand how state bank notes and shinplasters operated, but this historical amnesia could explain a rush to introduce a decentralized form of money without a grasp of how Americans fared the last time they had to utilize highly variable currency. State bank notes were notoriously unreliable as they traveled away from their home institutions and they suffered even greater depreciation after the outbreak of the Civil War, while shinplasters' value was not backed by anything but the public's confidence. This left them dangerously vulnerable to market whims and even conscious manipulation. Bitcoin operates in a similar way. Unlike federal reserve legal tender notes backed by the government in specific denominations, Bitcoin is a variable currency without a predetermined face value. It is created in increments whose purchasing power rises and falls according to activity on a variety of online exchanges. The total limit of Bitcoins in circulation is set at 21 million and public confidence or a lack thereof may drive the price up or down, but there is no stable set value that it is supposed to maintain.

It is this unpredictability that presents the biggest challenge for Bitcoin supporters and illuminates how it functions more as a commodity than a currency. The number of individuals who use it for transactions and purchases is staggeringly low, especially compared with those who simply buy and sell the coins like stocks or bonds. The value of a single Bitcoin has fluctuated wildly since its introduction. In May 2010, in what was probably its first formal transaction, a Florida programmer named Laszlo Hanyecz paid 10,000 Bitcoins for a delivery of two Papa John's pizzas (about a $40 value). The price yo-yoed as the infrastructure stabilized and, five years later, one Bitcoin was valued at $500. The price trend was generally higher after 2015, but at any given time rapid price oscillations bounced its value around dramatically. In late 2017, a brief spike in the market brought it to over $19,500. However, competition from other cryptocurrencies complicates the market's confidence in Bitcoin. Any market share seized by a new challenger represents potential value lost. By the spring of 2018, more than 1,600 different cryptocurrencies—including Ripple, Tron, and PotCoin (a digital currency for the marijuana industry)—aimed to supplant Bitcoin. After reaching new highs in late 2017, a yearlong fall left the value of each Bitcoin at less than $3,500.[9]

Such capriciousness offers a chance for big profits for the few who know how to manipulate cryptocurrency markets, but it makes Bitcoin's purchasing value as unreliable as the bank notes and shinplasters of an earlier age. More importantly, it is a reminder that such a complicated and unjust system in the early republic repeatedly led to calls for a sound and uniform currency. It took the immediacy of the Civil War and a slew of judicial rulings to finally end the chaotic state bank note system. Legal tender paper money emerged, even if it did not lead to a static 150 years of circulation. National bank notes gave way to legal tender federal reserve notes during the 1930s, and production of United States notes (greenbacks) ceased in the 1960s, but it has been generations since the public had daily concerns about the stability of their paper money. Whatever problems existed with the new bills, few individuals who experienced early republic bank notes pined for their return.

Americans now take it for granted that their paper money is legal tender and worth its printed face value. Their lived experience has allowed them to become comfortable and contented when it comes to monetary affairs, but it has left them unprepared to understand how banks work or how to deal with variable currency unbacked by the government. Even though there are no significant calls to make Bitcoin a legal tender in the United States, such complacency has been vital to cryptocurrency gaining a foothold in the first place. Removed from the necessity of navigating the market with poor-quality bank notes of dubious spending power, the public views any new currency through the prism of their sound and uniform legal tender paper money. It is hard to imagine any group of Americans clamoring for a new, highly variable form of money when it comes to their daily transactions. In this context, Bitcoin is not really a challenge to federal reserve currency. It is a tradable market commodity made possible because the public does not need to use it as a currency unless they choose to.[10]

Modern episodes like quantitative easing and the rise of Bitcoin might seem remote from the rest of this study, but they highlight how far the public has come from the lived experience of early republic Americans whose chaotic currency regime forced them to accumulate and employ monetary knowledge in their market transactions and political efforts. A lifetime of bank note negotiations ensured that the public encountered the Bank War or Panic of 1837 with concrete notions about monetary policy based on financial information that they had personally amassed. This did not mean universal agreement on whether a larger or smaller circulation of bank notes would fix the economy or whether shinplasters could provide temporary relief for a broken money market. Loco Focos and Whigs disagreed on the path forward. Likewise, the notion that bankers like Nicholas Biddle or political economists like Harvard College professor Francis Bowen had a monopoly on policy prescriptions would have been ridiculous. Eventually, this system's failure to provide for a sound and uniform currency led to its breakdown. During the Civil War, the creation of legal tender paper money and national bank notes accepted at face value began to erode the public's need for currency education.

Over time, the requirement to constantly obtain new monetary knowledge became as dated as a bank note with a vignette of an enslaved fieldworker or a shinplaster from a railroad corporation. Those who confronted the 2008 banking collapse had experienced a lifetime of transactions that did not force them to familiarize themselves with banking policies and an encyclopedia of paper money just to make daily purchases. No shortage of newspaper columns or cable news shows sought to educate the blindsided public about what was happening and how the Federal Reserve planned to confront the crisis through quantitative easing, but to little avail. In the wake of the Great Recession, some people even embraced new cryptocurrencies like Bitcoin even though they came with none of the security or protections provided by legal tender paper. The accumulation of widespread monetary information and subsequent deployment of that knowledge through political engagement was a distant memory.

NOTES

Introduction

1. James K. Paulding, *The History of a Little Frenchman and His Bank Notes: "Rags! Rags! Rags!"* (Philadelphia: published for the author by Edward Earle, 1815), 4. The story was reprinted several times; see "The History of a Little Frenchman," *Journal of Banking* (February 16, 1842): 259–262. For a recent analysis of the story, see Jonathan Senchyne, "Rags Make Paper, Paper Makes Money: Material Texts and Metaphors of Capital," *Technology and Culture* 58, no. 2 (April 2017): 545–555. On banking and currency in 1815, see Bray Hammond, *Banks and Politics in America: From the Revolution to the Civil War* (Princeton, NJ: Princeton University Press, 1957), 227–250; and Michael D. Bordo and Eugene N. White, "A Tale of Two Currencies: British and French Finance During the Napoleonic Wars," *Journal of Economic History* 51, no. 2 (June 1991): 303–316.

2. Paulding, *History of a Little Frenchman*, 4–8.

3. Paulding, *History of a Little Frenchman*, 5–10. For a contemporary translation of the French proverb, see Jerome N. Vlieland, *A Complete Course of Study, for Englishmen to Obtain the French Language at Home* (London: Longman, Rees, Orme, Brown, and Green, 1827), 144.

4. United States Demand notes, Legal Tender notes, and Federal Reserve notes have all been called greenbacks.

5. Eric Newman, *The Early Paper Money of America* (Racine, WI: Whitman, 1967); Dror Goldberg, "The Massachusetts Paper Money of 1690," *Journal of Economic History* 69, no. 4 (December 2009): 1092–1106; and Farley Grubb, "The US Constitution and Monetary Powers: An Analysis of the 1787 Constitutional Convention and the Constitutional Transformation of the US Monetary System," *Financial History Review* 13, no. 1 (April 2006): 43–71. For the best examination of how the English government created money in the colonial era, see Christine Desan, *Making Money: Coin, Currency, and the Coming of Capitalism* (New York: Oxford University Press, 2014).

6. Stephen Mihm, "Funding the Revolution: Monetary and Fiscal Policy in Eighteenth-Century America," in *The Oxford Handbook of the American Revolution*, ed. Edward Gray and Jane Kamensky (New York: Oxford University Press, 2013), 331–338.

7. Susan Juster, *Disorderly Women: Sexual Politics and Evangelicalism in Revolutionary New England* (Ithaca, NY: Cornell University Press, 1994), 172; Patrick T. Conley, "Rhode Island's Paper Money Issue and *Trevett v. Weeden*," *Rhode Island History* 30, no. 3 (August 1970): 95–109; and John D. Lawson, ed., *American State Trials* (St. Louis, MO: F. H. Thomas Law Book, 1915), 4:548–599.

8. Roger H. Brown, *Redeeming the Republic: Federalists, Taxation, and the Origins of the Constitution* (Baltimore: Johns Hopkins University Press, 1993), 81–121; and Robert A. Gross, "A Yankee Rebellion?: The Regulators, New England, and the New Nation," *New England Quarterly* 82, no. 1 (March 2009): 112–135.

9. Edmund Randolph, quoted in Grubb, "US Constitution and Monetary Powers," 50; [Noah Webster], *An Examination Into the Leading Principles of the Federal Constitution Proposed By the Late Convention Held at Philadelphia* (Philadelphia: Prichard & Hall, 1787), 11; James Madison, " 'The Same Subject Continued': The Union as a Safeguard Against Domestic Faction and Insurrection," *New York Packet*, November 23, 1787; Robert G. Natelson, "Paper Money and the Original Understanding of the Coinage Clause," *Harvard Journal of Law and Public Policy* 31, no. 3 (Summer 2008): 1053–1059; Woody Holton, " 'Divide et Impera': 'Federalist 10' in a Wider Sphere," *William and Mary Quarterly* 62, no. 2 (April 2005): 175–212; and Woody Holton, *Unruly Americans and the Constitution* (New York: Hill and Wang, 2007).

10. Walter Buckingham Smith, *Economic Aspects of the Second Bank of the United States* (Cambridge, MA: Harvard University Press, 1953), 56; and Warren E. Weber, "Early State Banks in the United States: How Many Were There and When Did They Exist?," *Federal Reserve Bank of Minneapolis Quarterly Review* 30, no. 1 (September 2006): 28–40.

11. Margaret G. Myers, *The New York Money Market* (New York: Columbia University Press, 1931); Gary Gorton, "Reputation Formation in Early Bank Note Markets," *Journal of Political Economy* 104, no. 2 (April 1996): 346–397; and Viviana A. Zelizer, "Making Multiple Monies," in *Explorations in Economic Sociology*, ed. Richard Swedberg (New York: Russell Sage Foundation, 1993), 193–212.

12. Arthur J. Rolnick and Warren E. Weber, "Gresham's Law or Gresham's Fallacy," *Journal of Political Economy* 94, no. 1 (February 1986): 185–199.

13. George A. Akerlof, "The Market for 'Lemons': Quality Uncertainty and the Market Mechanism," *Quarterly Journal of Economics* 84, no. 3 (August 1970): 489–495; Jae-Cheol Kim, "The Market for 'Lemons' Reconsidered: A Model of the Used Car Market with Asymmetric Information," *American Economic Review* 75, no. 4 (September 1985): 836–843; and Ian Mohlo, *The Economics of Information: Lying and Cheating in Markets and Organizations* (Malden, MA: Blackwell, 1997).

14. "The Bank Note Circulation," *Banker's Magazine* 12, no. 10 (April 1863): 745–748; and Kenneth E. Lewis, *West to Far Michigan: Settling the Lower Peninsula, 1815–1860* (East Lansing: Michigan State University Press, 2001), 176–178.

15. Howard Bodenhorn, *State Banking in Early America* (New York: Oxford University Press, 2003), 95–122; and Stephan L. Kalb, "Currency Competition and Endogenous Money: Experiences from the Suffolk System, 1819–1858," in *Foundations of European Central Bank Policy*, ed. Wolfgang Gebauer (Heidelberg: Physica-Verlag, 1993), 61–75.

16. *Biographical and Historical Record of the Class of 1835 in Yale College* (New Haven, CT: Tuttle, Morehouse & Taylor, 1881), 93; and Nathaniel Saltonstall to Richard S. Varnum, Salem, October 11, 1838, in *The Papers of Leverett Saltonstall, 1816–1845*, ed. Robert E. Moody, vol. 2 (Boston: Massachusetts Historical Society, 1981), 108.

17. One other chartered corporation, the River Raisin & Lake Erie Rail Road Company, issued questionable paper that passed as bank notes. In the second half of 1835 alone, the combined circulation of Monroe banks reached over $150,000. James A. Haxby, *Standard*

Catalog of United States Obsolete Bank Notes, 1782–1866, vol. 2 (Iola, WI: Krause, 1988), 1066–1072; Carter H. Golembe, *State Banks and the Economic Development of the West, 1830–1844* (New York: Arno Press, 1978), 440; and John A. Muscalus, *An Index of State Bank Notes That Illustrate Presidents* (Bridgeport, PA: John A. Muscalus, 1939), 14.

18. Golembe, *State Banks and the Economic Development of the West*, 324–335; "Bank Note Table," *New York Spectator*, November 18, 1839; and "A Table Showing the Highest and Lowest Prices of Bank Notes in Philadelphia, in Each Year, from October 31st, 1814, to December 31st, 1841," *Journal of Banking*, May 11, 1842.

19. Haxby, *Standard Catalog of United States Obsolete Bank Notes*, 2:1067; "Bank Note Table," *Geneva (NY) Courier*, February 2, 1831; and "Bank Note Price Current," *National Gazette* (Philadelphia, PA), February 18, 1834.

20. "The Bank of Monroe," *New York Herald*, September 13, 1836; "Country Banks—Bank of Monroe, Michigan," *New York Herald*, September 14, 1836; "Bank of Monroe," *Monroe (MI) Times*, September 1, 1836; "The Bank of Monroe," *Monroe (MI) Times*, August 18, 1836; and "Bank of Monroe," *Monroe (MI) Times*, February 2, 1837. On Michigan wildcats, see John A. Dove, Gary M. Pecquet, and Clifford F. Thies, "The Michigan Free Bank Experience: Wild Cat Banking or Interference with Contract?," *Essays in Economic and Business History* 32 (May 2014): 1–33; Arthur J. Rolnick and Warren E. Weber, "Free Banking, Wildcat Banking, and Shinplasters," *Federal Reserve Bank of Minneapolis Quarterly Review* 6, no. 3 (Fall 1982): 10–19; and Gerald P. Dwyer Jr., "Wildcat Banking, Banking Panics, and Free Banking in the United States," *Economic Review* 81, no. 1 (December 1996): 1–20.

21. "Mormonism Exposed," *Ohio Repository* (Canton, OH), February 5, 1838; Sheridan L. McGarry, *Mormon Money* (Chicago: American Numismatic Association, 1951), 3–4; Mark L. Staker, "Raising Money in Righteousness: Oliver Cowdery as Banker," in *Days Never to Be Forgotten: Oliver Cowdery*, by Alexander L. Baugh (Provo, UT: Religious Studies Center, Brigham Young University, 2009), 143–254; Alvin E. Rust, *Mormon and Utah Coin and Currency* (Salt Lake City, UT: Rust Rare Coin, 1984), 15–19; and Doug A. Nyholm, "The Mormons and the 'Bank of Monroe' Michigan," *Paper Money* 47, no. 2 (March–April 2008): 84.

22. Linda King Newell and Valeen Tippetts Avery, *Mormon Enigma: Emma Hale Smith* (Champaign: University of Illinois Press, 1994), 62; "Not Bad," *Connecticut Farmer's Gazette and Horticultural Repository* (New Haven, CT), May 15, 1844, italics in the original; and "The Bank of Monroe," *Monroe (MI) Times*, March 16, 1837. For more on Mormon banking, see Dean A. Dudley, "Bank Born of Revelation: The Kirtland Safety Society Anti-Banking Company," *Journal of Economic History* 30, no. 4 (December 1970): 848–853; Scott H. Partridge, "The Failure of the Kirtland Safety Society," *BYU Studies* 12, no. 4 (Summer 1972): 437–454; Dale W. Adams, "Chartering the Kirtland Bank," *BYU Studies* 23, no. 4 (Summer 1983): 467–482; and Marvin S. Hill, Keith C. Rooker, and Larry T. Wimmer, "The Kirtland Economy Revisited: A Market Critique of Sectarian Economics," *BYU Studies* 17, no. 4 (Summer 1977): 389–471.

23. *Journal of the House of Representatives of the State of Michigan, 1837* (Detroit, MI: John S. Bagg, State Printer, 1837), 53, 105, and 516; "For the Telegraph," *Painesville (OH) Telegraph*, March 31, 1837; and "Bills of the Bank of Monroe," *Monroe (MI) Times*, March 16, 1837. Bond also accepted bills from the Kirtland Safety Society Bank.

24. Leverett Saltonstall to Richard S. Varnum, H. Reps, March 27, 1840 and Fisher Howe to Richard S. Varnum, New York, April 9, 1839, in Moody, *Papers of Leverett Saltonstall*, 2:288 and 234.

25. U.S. Congress, Senate, *Report from the Secretary of the Treasury, with Annual Report from the Commissioner of the General Land Office*, 24th Cong., 1st Sess., 1835, S. Rpt. 3; Kenneth E. Lewis, *West to Far Michigan: Settling the Lower Peninsula, 1815–1860* (East Lansing: Michigan State University Press, 2001), 110–121; Roger H. Durand, *Interesting Notes About Territories* (Rehoboth, MA: R. H. Durand, 1992), 89; and David McNeely Stauffer, *American Engravers upon Copper and Steel* (New York: Grolier Club of New York, 1907), 41 and 153. The Northwest included Michigan, Ohio, Indiana, Illinois, and Missouri. On Monroe land development, see Talcott E. Wing, ed., *History of Monroe County Michigan* (New York: Munsell, 1890), 131–141.

26. "Collection of the Public Revenue," *Financial Register of the United States*, November 7, 1838. See also Benjamin Horace Hibbard, *A History of the Public Land Policies* (New York: Peter Smith, 1939), 116–135; U.S. Congress, House, *Affairs of General Land Office, Letter from the Secretary of the Treasury Transmitting a Report of the Commissioner of the General Land Office, on Subjects Connected with the Land Office*, 25th Cong., 2nd Sess., 1837, H. Doc. 23; and U.S. Congress, Senate, *Report from the Secretary of the Treasury, in Compliance with a Resolution of the Senate, of the 20th September, 1837, in Relation to Sales of Public Lands*, 25th Cong., 2nd Sess., 1838, S. Rpt. 85. Land offices in Michigan received more than $45,000 in military land scrip in these years. "Report from the General Land Office," in *Reports of the Secretary of the Treasury of the United States, Prepared in Obedience to the Act of May 10, 1800* (Washington, DC: Blair & Rives, 1837), 3:545.

27. Jane Knodell, "Rethinking the Jacksonian Economy: The Impact of the 1832 Bank Veto on Commercial Banking," *Journal of Economic History* 66, no. 3 (September 2006): 569; Richard H. Timberlake Jr., "The Specie Circular and Sales of Public Lands: A Comment," *Journal of Economic History* 25, no. 3 (September 1965): 414–416; Harry N. Scheiber, "The Pet Banks in Jacksonian Politics and Finance, 1833–1841," *Journal of Economic History* 23, no. 2 (June 1963): 206; and U.S. Congress, Senate, *Report from the Secretary of the Treasury, with Annual Report from the Commissioner of the General Land Office*, 24th Cong., 1st Sess., 1835, S. Rpt. 3. On the Specie Circular's overall effect on the nation's economy, see Richard H. Timberlake Jr., "The Specie Circular and Distribution of the Surplus," *Journal of Political Economy* 68, no. 2 (April 1960): 111; and Peter L. Rousseau, "Jacksonian Monetary Policy, Specie Flows, and the Panic of 1837," *Journal of Economic History* 62, no. 2 (June 2002): 457–488. For a defense of the policy, see "Collection of the Public Revenue," *Financial Register of the United States* 2, no. 19 (November 7, 1838): 289–297.

28. "On the Currency of the Government," *Extra Globe* (Washington, DC), May 31, 1838.

29. Paul W. Gates, "Charts of Public Land Sales and Entries," *Journal of Economic History* 24, no. 1 (March 1964): 23; Jerry A. O'Callaghan, "The War Veteran and the Public Lands," *Agricultural History* 28, no. 4 (October 1954): 163–168; Robert Henry Nelson, *Public Lands and Private Rights: The Failure of Scientific Management* (Lanham, MD: Rowman & Littlefield, 1995), 13–14; "A Grave Stop!," *New Yorker*, April 13, 1839; and I. P. Christiancy, "Recollections of the Early History of the City and County of Monroe," *Pioneer Collections: Report of the Pioneer Society of the State of Michigan* (Lansing, MI: W. S. George, 1884), 6:368.

30. *Laws in Relation to Banking Associations in the State of Michigan* (Detroit, MI: John S. Bagg, 1837); H. M. Utley, "The Wild Cat Banking System of Michigan," *Report of the Pioneer Society of the State of Michigan* (Lansing, MI: W. S. George, 1904), 209–222; "Free

Banking," *Extra Globe* (Washington, DC), June 7, 1838; Charles H. Ravell, *Sixty Years of Banking in Michigan* (Battle Creek, MI: Old National Bank, 1910), 161; and Alpheus Felch, "Early Banks and Banking in Michigan," *Report of the Pioneer Society of the State of Michigan* (Detroit, MI: William Graham's Presses, 1880), 111–124. On free banking in Michigan, see Dwyer, "Wildcat Banking, Banking Panics, and Free Banking in the United States," 6–7; Carter Golembe, "Origins of Deposit Insurance in the Middle West, 1834–1866," *Indiana Magazine of History* 51, no. 2 (June 1955): 115; Hugh Rockoff, "The Free Banking Era: A Reexamination," *Journal of Money, Credit, and Banking* 6, no. 2 (May 1974): 141–167; John A. Dove, Gary M. Pecquet, and Clifford F. Thies, "The Michigan Free Bank Experience: Wild Cat Banking or Interference with Contract?," *Essays in Economic and Business History* 32 (May 2014): 11; Arthur J. Rolnick and Warren E. Weber, "Free Banking, Wildcat Banking, and Shinplasters," *Federal Reserve Bank of Minneapolis Quarterly Review* 6, no. 3 (Fall 1982): 10–19; and Arthur J. Rolnick and Warren E. Weber, "New Evidence on the Free Banking Era," *American Economic Review* 73, no. 5 (December 1983): 1080–1091. After the collapse of the Mechanics & Merchants Bank, lawsuits targeted the bank president Judge Daniel Bacon, the father of Elizabeth Bacon, whose husband George Armstrong Custer spent much of his youth in Monroe. See Shirley A. Leckie, *Elizabeth Bacon Custer and the Making of a Myth* (Norman: University of Oklahoma Press, 1993), 5–6 and 319.

31. William Wells Brown, *Three Years in Europe; or, Places I Have Seen and People I Have Met* (London: Charles Gilpin, 1852), 97–104. Part of this anecdote was reprinted in William Wells Brown, *Clotel; or The President's Daughter: A Narrative of Slave Life in the United States* (London: Partridge & Oakey, 1853), 30–34. The later version leaves out the important context of the visit to the Bank of England. Another reprinting of this anecdote appeared as "The Establishment of a Bank in America," in the *Working Man's Friend and Family Instructor* (January 15, 1853): 247. On shinplaster fiction and race, see Hildegard Hoeller, *From Gift to Commodity: Capitalism and Sacrifice in Nineteenth-Century American Fiction* (Durham: University of New Hampshire Press, 2012), 116 and 125–126; Michael O'Malley, *Face Value: The Entwined Histories of Money and Race in America* (Chicago: University of Chicago Press, 2012), 62–63; Michael Germana, *Standards of Value: Money, Race, and Literature in America* (Iowa City: University Press of Iowa, 2009), 11; and J. P. Conway, "Dog Gone Money: The Passing of Strange Currencies and Strange People in American Democratic Culture" (PhD diss., Washington University, 2008), 247–264. Few of these works provide a full context for the narrative of banking and race relations in 1835 Monroe. Instead, their authors place Monroe in a generic location, and the town and its inhabitants are not fully described. Such approaches nationalize the shinplaster story with no consideration for how local monetary conditions might properly situate William Wells Brown's narrative in Monroe's specific financial reality. Rather than a fantastical tale that unfolds in a hazy time and place, the story includes numerous legal and financial details that fix its events.

32. Brown, *Three Years in Europe*, 100 and 104.

33. *Journal of the House of Representatives of the State of Michigan, 1837*, 421 and 515–516; Golembe, *State Banks and the Economic Development of the West*, 170; and "From Our Correspondent," *Constantine (MI) Republican*, January 18, 1837. On state scrip, see Henry M. Utley and Byron M. Cutcheon, *Michigan as a Province, Territory and State: The Twenty-Sixth Member of the Federal Union* (New York: Americana Press for the Publishing Society of Michigan, 1906), 3:167–168.

Chapter 1

1. B. Y. Martin, *Reports of Cases in Law and Equity Argued and Determined in the Supreme Court of the State of Georgia* (Columbus, GA: Columbus Times Steam Press, 1859), 61–65.

2. The term "paper money men" comes from British poet Thomas Love Peacock's 1837 satire of bankers and political economists. See Thomas Love Peacock, *Paper Money Lyrics, and Other Poems [1837]*, in *The Poems of Thomas Love Peacock*, ed. Reginald Brimley Johnson (New York: George Routledge & Sons, 1906), 300–303; Heinz Tschachler, *The Monetary Imagination of Edgar Allan Poe: Banking, Currency and Politics in the Writings* (Jefferson, NC: McFarland, 2013), 66–67; and David Anthony, *Paper Money Men: Commerce, Manhood, and the Sensational Public Sphere in Antebellum America* (Columbus: Ohio State University Press, 2009).

3. F. Cyril James, *The Growth of Chicago Banks*, vol. 1, *The Formative Years, 1816–1896* (New York: Harper, 1938), 200; Ellen Hartigan-O'Connor, *The Ties That Buy: Women and Commerce in Revolutionary America* (Philadelphia: University of Pennsylvania Press, 2009), 101–128; and Jennifer J. Baker, *Securing the Commonwealth: Debt, Speculation, and Writing in the Making of Early America* (Baltimore: Johns Hopkins University Press, 2005).

4. Juliet E. K. Walker, *The History of Black Business in America: Capitalism, Race, Entrepreneurship*, vol. 1, *To 1865*, 2nd ed. (Chapel Hill: University of North Carolina Press, 2009), 115–116 and 171. Some enslaved men hired at the Buffalo Forge iron works in Virginia received cash payments and even held their earnings in savings banks. See Charles B. Dew, *Bond of Iron: Master and Slave at Buffalo Forge* (New York: W. W. Norton, 1994), 183–185. See also Julie Winch, "'A Person of Good Character and Considerable Property': James Forten and the Issue of Race in Philadelphia's Antebellum Business Community," *Business History Review* 75, no. 2 (Summer 2001): 28.

5. *Remarks on Money, and the Bank Paper of the United States* (Philadelphia: n.p., 1814), 21. For one attempt at state monitoring of bank note production, see "Bank-Note Engraving in America," *Illustrated Magazine of Art* 3, no. 17 (1854): 310.

6. James A. Henretta, "The 'Market' in the Early Republic," *Journal of the Early Republic* 18, no. 2 (Summer 1998): 304; and Roxanna Stowell to Dexter Whittemore, June 1835, quoted in Thomas Dublin, "Women and Outwork in a Nineteenth-Century New England Town: Fitzwilliam, New Hampshire, 1830–1850," in *The Countryside in the Age of Capitalist Transformation*, ed. Steven Hahn and Jonathan Prude (Chapel Hill: University of North Carolina Press, 1985), 64.

7. Nathaniel Ames, *The Diary of Dr. Nathaniel Ames of Dedham, Massachusetts*, ed. Robert Brand Hanson (Camden, ME: Picton Press, 1998), 801; and *Exposition of the Effects of Paper Credit, on the Prosperity of the Town of Bubbleton* (Petersburg, VA: printed at the Office of the Farmers' Register, 1838), 8.

8. Amasa Walker, *The Nature and Uses of Money and Mixed Currency* (Boston: Crosby, Nichols, 1857), 25.

9. Sharon Ann Murphy, *Other People's Money: How Banking Worked in the Early American Republic* (Baltimore: Johns Hopkins University, 2017), 43–49; Robert Eric Wright, *Origins of Commercial Banking in America, 1750–1800* (Lanham, MD: Rowman & Littlefield, 2001), 8–10 and 15; *Shinning It: A Tale of a Tape-Cutter; Or The Mechanic Turned Merchant, by One Who Knows* (New York: M. Y. Beach, 1844); and *Wall-Street; or, Ten Minutes to Three:. A Farce in Three Acts* (New York: n.p., 1819).

10. "Extracts from the Private Diary of a Certain Bank Director No. III," *Journal of Banking* 1, no. 7 (September 29, 1841): 99; Naomi Lamoreaux, *Insider Lending: Banks, Personal Connections, and Economic Development in Industrial New England* (New York: Cambridge University Press, 1994), 37; Robert E. Wright, "Bank Ownership and Lending Patterns in New York and Pennsylvania, 1781–1831," *Business History Review* 73, no. 1 (Spring 1999): 40–60; and Sean Wilentz, *Chants Democratic: New York City and the Rise of the American Working Class, 1788–1850* (New York: Oxford University Press, 1984), 29–30.

11. John Frost, *The Young Merchant*, 2nd ed. (Boston: George W. Light, 1840), 215.

12. Carter H. Golembe, *State Banks and the Economic Development of the West, 1830–44* (New York: Arno Press, 1978), 68–71; "On the Currency of the Government," *Extra Globe* (Washington, DC), May 31, 1838; and "Digest of Recent Decisions," *American Jurist and Law Magazine* 23 (October 1834): 453.

13. Norman Walker Smith, "A History of Commercial Banking in New Hampshire, 1792–1843" (PhD diss., University of Wisconsin, 1967), 74; and Golembe, *State Banks and the Economic Development of the West*, 68–69.

14. "Caution," *Providence [RI] Patriot, Columbian Phenix*, May 13, 1815, italics in the original.

15. A. Walker, *Nature and Uses of Money and Mixed Currency*, 28; and John Stilwell Jenkins, *The New Clerk's Assistant* (New York: Miller, Orton & Mulligan, 1856), 106–107.

16. Steven H. Jaffe and Jessica Lautin, *Capital of Capital: Money, Banking and Power in New York City, 1784–2012* (New York: Columbia University Press, 2014), 39.

17. Howard Bodenhorn, *State Banking in Early America* (New York: Oxford University Press, 2003), 95–122; and Stephan L. Kalb, "Currency Competition and Endogenous Money: Experiences from the Suffolk System, 1819–1858," in *Foundations of European Central Bank Policy*, ed. Wolfgang Gebauer (Heidelberg: Physica-Verlag, 1993), 61–75. Other cities eventually organized sorting systems to provide for easy citywide redemption, but these operations were smaller in scope. See *Assorting House for State Currency, Albany, March 8th, 1858: Sir a Circular* (Albany, NY: n.p., 1858). On fraud in early New England banks, see Jane Kamensky, *The Exchange Artist: A Tale of High-Flying Speculation and America's First Banking Collapse* (New York: Viking Press, 2008).

18. Bray Hammond, *Banks and Politics in America: From the Revolution to the Civil War* (Princeton, NJ: Princeton University Press, 1957), 552; Arthur J. Rolnick, Bruce D. Smith, and Warren E. Weber, "The Suffolk Bank and Panic of 1837," *Federal Reserve Bank of Minneapolis Quarterly Review* 24, no. 2 (Spring 2000): 4; "Bills Uncurrent in Boston," *Hartford (CT) Current*, December 30, 1837; *Clark's New-England Bank Note List, and Counterfeit Bill Detector*, April 1, 1838, 145; and Frances W. Gregory, "A Tale of Three Cities: The Struggle for Banking Stability in Boston, New York, and Philadelphia, 1839–1841," *New England Quarterly* 56, no. 1 (March 1983): 3–38.

19. Sarah Joseph Hale, *Northwood: Of Life North and South* (New York: H. Long & Brother, 1852), 378; George Thompson, *The Brazen Star: or the Adventures of a New-York M.P.* (New York: George W. Hill, 1853), 18; and George Thompson, *Life and Exploits of the Noted Criminal, Bristol Bill, by Greenhorn* (New York: M. J. Ivers, [1851?]), 46.

20. Alexander Bryan Johnson, "A Treatise on Banking," in *The Banker's Common-Place Book*, by Isaac Smith Homans (New York: Office of Bankers' Magazine, 1857), 38; "Bank Note Table," *New York Spectator*, November 18, 1839; "Bank Note Table," *Brooklyn (NY) Daily*

Eagle, October 28, 1841; Everett Birney Stackpole, "State Banking in Maine," *Sound Currency* 7, no. 5 (May 1900): 82–83; "The Still Water Canal Bank at Orono," *Niles' National Register* (Washington, DC), November 6, 1841; and "Bank Failures," *Journal of Banking*, November 10, 1841.

21. George William Dowrie, *The Development of Banking in Illinois, 1817–1863* (Urbana: University of Illinois Press, 1913), 59–71.

22. David C. Wismer, "Descriptive List of Obsolete Paper Money," *Numismatist* 40, no. 3 (March 1927): 145; James A. Haxby, *Standard Catalog of United States Obsolete Bank Notes, 1782–1866* (Iola, WI: Krause, 1988), 2:1049; *Crary's Directory for the City of Buffalo Directory* (Buffalo, NY: Faxon & Graves, 1841), 20; D. W. Garber, *Wildcat Banks on the Mohican Frontier* (n.p: D. W. Garber, 1975), 24–26; and Joseph Felt, *An Historical Account of Massachusetts Currency* (Boston: Perkins & Marvin, 1839), 222. On American place and space, see Wilbur Zelinsky, *Not Yet a Placeless Land: Tracking an Evolving American Geography* (Amherst: University of Massachusetts Press, 2011).

23. "Farmers' Bank of New Jersey," Mount Holly, NJ, 12½¢, January 20, 1815, Obsolete Bank Note Collection, Massachusetts Historical Society; and Haxby, *Standard Catalog of United States Obsolete Bank Notes*, 3:1402.

24. Robert Neil Mathis, "Gazaway Bugg Lamar: A Southern Businessman and Confidant in New York City," *New York History* 56, no. 3 (July 1975): 298–313; Edwin B. Coddington, "The Activities and Attitudes of a Confederate Business Man: Gazaway B. Lamar," *Journal of Southern History* 9, no. 1 (February 1943): 5; and "Bank of Commerce," Savannah, GA, 50¢, November 1, 1856, Currency Collection, American Antiquarian Society.

25. *New York Packet*, August 7, 1786, as quoted in William H. Dillistin, *Bank Note Reporters and Counterfeit Detectors, 1826–1866* (New York: American Numismatic Society, 1949), 2; and Asa Greene, *The Perils of Pearl Street, Including a Taste of the Dangers of Wall Street* (New York: Betts & Anstice, and Peter Hill, 1834), 191.

26. Quoted in N. W. Smith, "A History of Commercial Banking in New Hampshire," 74–75.

27. Theron Metcalf, *Reports of Cases Argued and Determined in the Supreme Judicial Court of Massachusetts* (Boston: Little, Brown, 1852), 10:572; and Garber, *Wildcat Banks on the Mohican Frontier*, 31. Such manipulative dealings led Maryland to outlaw or heavily regulate broker activities following a banking crisis in 1819. See Alfred Cookman Bryan, "History of State Banking in Maryland," *Johns Hopkins University Studies in History and Politics* 17, nos. 1–3 (January–March 1899): 54 and 68.

28. "Shin-Plasters," *Baltimore (MD) Sun*, July 20, 1837.

29. "The Bank of Tecumseh," *Detroit (MI) Free Press*, April 28, 1860.

30. C. C. Dearborn & Co., *Dearborn and Co.'s Newmarket and Boston Express* (Newmarket, NH; n.p., 1847); and James Cooke Mills, *History of Saginaw County, Michigan* (Saginaw, MI: Seeman & Peters, 1918), 742.

31. "Cashing a Check in Illinois," *Philadelphia Inquirer*, March 11, 1861; and Albion W. Tourgée, *A Fool's Errand, by One of the Fools* (New York: Fords, Howard, & Hulbert, 1879), 158, italics in the original. John Hope Franklin argues that the term "carpetbagger" was used as early as 1846, even though the *Oxford English Dictionary* cites the first usage in 1868; see John Hope Franklin, *Reconstruction After the Civil War*, 2nd ed. (Chicago: University of Chicago Press, 1994), 93–94.

32. George B. Reed, *Sketch of the Early History of Banking in Vermont* (Boston: n.p., 1879), 14–15; and "Bank Notes of Other States," *New York Herald*, October 20, 1844.

33. Alexander Lovett Stimson, *History of the Express Companies* (New York: Baker & Godwin, 1881), 357–360; "Worthless Indiana Banks," *Tennessean* (Nashville, TN), December 23, 1854; "Indiana Stock Notes," *Herald of Freedom* (Wilmington, OH), December 29, 1854; and "Indiana Free Banks," *New York Times*, January 19, 1855.

34. "Heavy Robbery at Norwich, Conn," *Pittsfield (MA) Sun*, March 20, 1851; "Great Robbery—$40,000 Stolen!," *Semi-Weekly Eagle* (Brattleboro, VT), March 17, 1851; and Jonathan Harshman Winters, *A Sketch of the Winters Family* (Dayton, OH: United Brethren, 1889), 162–163.

35. Quoted in Golembe, *State Banks and the Economic Development of the West*, 64–65; and Haxby, *Standard Catalog of United States Obsolete Bank Notes*, 4:2573.

36. Haxby, *Standard Catalog of United States Obsolete Bank Notes*, 1:501–504; and "A Banker Hung in Effigy," *Louisville (KY) Courier*, January 30, 1855.

37. "Black Carpet-Bag Men—Gold Grabbers and Their Trial," *Louisville (KY) Daily Courier*, October 16, 1857.

38. "Banker's Mob at Paducah," *Chicago Daily Tribune*, October 14, 1857. For more on carpet bag men in Kentucky during the Panic of 1857, see "The Only Certain Relief," *Louisville (KY) Daily Courier*, October 24, 1857. For a wider discussion on the term "carpetbagger," race, and Reconstruction, see Ted Tunnell, "Creating 'The Propaganda of History': Southern Editors and the Origins of 'Carpetbagger and Scalawag,'" *Journal of Southern History* 72, no. 4 (November 2006): 789–822; and Michael O'Malley, *Face Value: The Entwined Histories of Money and Race in America* (Chicago: University of Chicago Press, 2012), 84–86.

39. Samuel Hooper, *Currency or Money: Its Nature and Uses, and the Effects of the Circulation of Bank-Notes for Currency* (Boston: Little, Brown, 1855), 20.

40. "Mob in Cincinnati," *Niles' National Register* (Washington, DC), January 22, 1842; "Riots in Cincinnati," *Brother Jonathan* (New York, NY), January 22, 1842; "Riot in Cincinnati," *Brooklyn (NY) Eagle*, January 18, 1842; Heinz Tschachler, *The Monetary Imagination of Edgar Allan Poe: Banking, Currency, and Politics in the Writings* (Jefferson, NC: McFarland, 2013), 57; and "A Leaf from the Past," *New York Times*, July 31, 1870.

41. John R. Hurd, *A National Bank, or No Bank: An Appeal to the Common Sense of the People of the United States, Especially of the Laboring Classes* (New York: W. E. Dean, 1842), 25.

42. R. H. Harding Diary, December 25, 1837, and December 31, 1837, Ohio Historical Society. I would like to thank William Wagner for this source.

43. Quoted in William A. Berkey, *The Money Question: The Wealth and Resources of the United States, and Why the People Do Not Enjoy General Prosperity* (Grand Rapids, MI: W. W. Hart's Arcade Steam Book and Job Printing House, 1876), 152. James Kirke Paulding told a related tale about the towns of Fiddledum and Diddledum. See James K. Paulding, *The New Mirror for Travellers; and Guide to the Springs* (New York: G. & C. Carvell, 1828), 193–194, and Thomas Smith, *An Essay on Currency and Banking, Being an Attempt to Show Their True Nature, and to Explain the Difficulties That Have Occurred in Discussing Them, with an Application to the Currency of This Country* (Philadelphia: J. Harding, printer, 1832), 47.

Chapter 2

1. *Exposition of the Effects of Paper Credit on the Prosperity of the Town of Bubbleton* (Petersburg, VA: printed at the Office of the Farmers' Register, 1838), 9; and Kenneth Cohen,

"'The Entreaties and Perswasions of Our Acquaintance': Gambling and Networks in Early America," *Journal of the Early Republic* 31, no. 4 (Winter 2011): 600 and 618.

2. John Neal, *Wandering Recollections of a Somewhat Busy Life: An Autobiography* (Boston: Roberts Brothers, 1869), 124–125.

3. "On the Currency of the Government," *Extra Globe* (Washington, DC), May 31, 1838; Arthur J. Rolnick and Warren E. Weber, "Explaining the Demand for Free Bank Notes," *Journal of Monetary Economics* 21, no. 1 (January 1988): 48; and David M. Henkin, *City Reading: Written Words and Public Spaces in Antebellum New York* (New York: Columbia University Press, 1998), 138 and 143.

4. James Fenimore Cooper, *The Leatherstocking Tales*, vol. 4, *The Pioneers* (New York: George P. Putnam, 1853), 503; and Richard D. Brown, *Knowledge Is Power: The Diffusion of Information in Early America, 1700–1865* (New York: Oxford University Press, 1989), 287.

5. Patricia Cline Cohen, *A Calculating People: The Spread of Numeracy in Early America* (Chicago: University of Chicago Press, 1982), 134–136; Edward Gray Arithmetic Workbooks, ca. 1830–1836, Massachusetts Historical Society; Charles Bulkeley Arithmetic Notebooks, ca. 1820, Massachusetts Historical Society; Harriet Upham Arithmetic Study Books, ca. 1830, Massachusetts Historical Society; Charles Davies, *Arithmetic Designed for Academies and Schools (with Answers)* (Philadelphia: A. S. Barnes, 1843), 74–88 and 197–203; and Samuel G. Goodrich, *The Child's Arithmetic, Being an Easy and Cheap Introduction* (Hartford, CT: Samuel G. Goodrich, 1818), 28–34.

6. *The Perpetual Laws of the Commonwealth of Massachusetts from the Establishment of Its Constitution in the Year 1780, to February, 1807* (Boston: Thomas & Andrews, 1807), 4:294; and Nathaniel Ames Daybook, April 10, 1805, Dedham Historical Society, Dedham, MA.

7. Abel Brewster, *The Universal Vitriolic Test, for Producing an Uniform, Safe and Intelligible Kind of Bank Bills, with an Explanation of Its Importance and Utility* (Hartford, CT: Lincoln & Gleason, 1807), 4; J. Tyler Hodges, *Hodges' New Bank Note Safe-Guard* (New York: Hodges, 1859), 321; Arthur A. Smith, "Bank Note Detecting in the Era of State Banks," *Mississippi Valley Historical Review* 29, no. 3 (December 1942): 371–386; S. J. Sylvester, *Sylvester's Bank Note and Exchange Manual* (New York: S. J. Sylvester, 1833); and Stephen Mihm, *A Nation of Counterfeiters: Capitalists, Con Men, and the Making of the United States* (Cambridge, MA: Harvard University Press, 2007), 235–259.

8. "Beauties of Banking," *People's Democratic Guide* 1, no. 12 (October 1842): 376; "Bank Note Table," *New York Spectator*, November 18, 1839; and U.S. Congress, Senate, *Report from the Secretary of the Treasury*, 25th Cong., 2nd Sess., 1838, S. Doc. 457.

9. J. Wright, *The American Negotiator, or the Various Currencies of the British Colonies in America; As Well the Islands, as the Continent*, 3rd ed. (London: printed for the proprietors by J. Smith, 1765); Nicholas Marshall, "The Rural Newspaper and the Circulation of Information and Culture in New York and the Antebellum North," *New York History* 88, no. 2 (Spring 2007): 133–151; "Bank Note Table," *Christian Advocate* (New York, NY), September 14, 1827; and "Bank Note Table," *Signal of Liberty* (Ann Arbor, MI), June 20, 1842. The *Christian Advocate*'s table came from the *Commercial Advertiser* (New York, NY).

10. *Bicknell's Counterfeit Detector and Bank Note List*, February 1, 1836; and William H. Dillistin, *Bank Note Reporters and Counterfeit Detectors, 1826–1866* (New York: American Numismatic Society, 1949), 49.

11. "Bank Note Table," *Experiment* (Norwalk, OH), March 6, 1844; "Notes of the Old Bank of Michigan," *Prairie Farmer* (Chicago), April 1, 1844; "Bank Note List," *Portage Sentinel*

(Ravenna, OH), July 30, 1845; and "Counterfeit Detector," *Louisville (KY) Daily Courier*, January 27, 1845.

12. Lucy Ann Ward to her Parents, Capt. & Mrs. Wm. Ward, October 13, 1815, Ms. N-1726, box 5, Thomas Wren Ward Papers, Ward Family Correspondence, 1815, Massachusetts Historical Society. I would like to thank Randi Flaherty for this citation. Frederick W. Seward, *Reminiscences of a War-Time Statesman and Diplomat, 1830–1915* (New York: G. P. Putnam's Sons, 1916), 21–22.

13. Q. K. Philander Doesticks (Mortimer Thomson), *Doesticks, What He Says* (New York: Edward Livermore, 1855), 44 and 88; "Broken Banks," *New York Times*, January 6, 1855; and "News by the Mails," *New York Daily Times*, May 31, 1855.

14. Robert Montgomery Bird, *The Adventures of Robin Day* (Philadelphia: Lea & Blanchard, 1839), 120–122. See also Terence Whalen, "Poe's 'Diddling' and the Depression: Notes in the Sources of Swindling," *Studies in American Fiction* 23, no. 2 (Autumn 1995): 195–202; Corey Goettsch, " 'The World Is But One Vast Mock Auction': Fraud and Capitalism in Nineteenth-Century America," in *Capitalism by Gaslight: Illuminating the Economy of Nineteenth-Century America*, ed. Brian P. Luskey and Wendy A. Woloson (Philadelphia: University of Pennsylvania Press, 2015), 109–126; and Jean Braucher and Barak Orbach, "Scamming: The Misunderstood Confidence Man," *Yale Journal of Law and the Humanities* 27, no. 2 (2015): 249–290.

15. "American Manners in 1833," *Dublin Penny Journal* 3, no. 126 (November 29, 1834): 170; and James K. Paulding, *The New Mirror for Travellers; and Guide to the Springs* (New York: G. & C. Carvell, 1828), 78.

16. James K. Paulding, *The History of a Little Frenchman and His Bank Notes: "Rags! Rags! Rags!"* (Philadelphia: published for the author by Edward Earle, 1815), 5, 8–9, and 13. Washington Irving published a wide-ranging review of the story and the history of American banking and money that was even longer than the original text. See "On Banks and Currency," *Analectic Magazine* 6 (December 1815): 489–518. The author is cited as "W."

17. Nathaniel Saltonstall to Leverett Saltonstall, Haverhill, August 20, 1809; Leverett Saltonstall to William Minot, Salem, May 8, 1809; and Nathaniel Saltonstall to Leverett Saltonstall, Haverhill, September 6, 1809; all in *The Saltonstall Papers, 1607–1815*, ed. Robert E. Moody (Boston: Massachusetts Historical Society, 1974), 465–467 and 479–481.

18. William Minot to Nathaniel Saltonstall, Boston, January 4, 1810 [1811], in Moody, *Saltonstall Papers*, 497.

19. "Run on the Girard Bank," *Spirit of the Times* (Philadelphia), January 27, 1842; "Opening of the Second Seal," *Spirit of the Times* (Philadelphia), January 28, 1842; and "Asmodeus Among the Banks, or Philadelphia in an Uproar," *Spirit of the Times* (Philadelphia), March 19, 1842.

20. "Frauds—Uncurrent Money," *Mechanics Free Press* (Philadelphia), April 24, 1830; "To Trade Societies," *Mechanics Free Press* (Philadelphia), January 17, 1829; and "We Can Do Without Them," *Mechanics Free Press* (Philadelphia), January 24, 1829.

21. "Money Brokers," *Niles' Register* (Washington, DC), November 21, 1829; "Butchers Meeting," *New York Evening Post*, June 26, 1819; and "Notice to the Public," New York *Evening Post*, June 17, 1817.

22. "Depreciated Currency," *Prairie Farmer* (Chicago), August 1, 1842; and "Money Matters," *Prairie Farmer* (Chicago), April 1, 1842, italics in the original.

23. Rosalind Remer, "Preachers, Peddlers, and Publishers: Philadelphia's Backcountry Book Trade, 1800–1830," *Journal of the Early Republic* 14, no. 4 (Winter 1994): 505–508.

24. Quoted in Elva Tooker, "A Kentucky Merchant's Problems in the Early Nineteenth Century," *Bulletin of the Business Historical Society* 8, no. 5 (October 1934): 85–86.

25. "Notice to Subscribers," *Common School Assistant* (Albany, NY), September 1837; and "Look at This," *Evangelical Magazine and Gospel Advocate*, November 8, 1834.

26. The organization's official name was the General Missionary Convention of the Baptist Denomination in the United States of America for Foreign Missions. *American Baptist Magazine* 7 (Boston: Lincoln & Edmands, 1827), 177–179; *American Baptist Magazine* 11 (Boston: Board of Managers of the Baptist General Convention, 1831), 183–185; *American Baptist Magazine* 13 (Boston: Board of Managers of the Baptist General Convention, 1833), 232–237; *American Baptist Magazine* 14 (Boston: Board of Managers of the Baptist General Convention, 1834), 240; and *Minutes of the General Assembly of the Presbyterian Church in the United States of America* (Philadelphia: William Bradford, 1825), 384.

27. "A Gentleman Who," *New Hampshire Statesman and State Journal* (Concord, NH), November 30, 1833.

28. "Correspondence of the Commercial Advertiser," *Commercial Advertiser* (New York, NY), January 25, 1834.

29. "Concerning the Experiment in Currency," *Niles' Weekly Register* (Washington, DC), July 19, 1834; "Hezekiah Niles, ESQ," *Niles' Weekly Register* (Washington, DC), August 16, 1834; U.S. Congress, House, *Independent Treasury, Letter from the Secretary of the Treasury*, 26th Cong., 2nd Sess., 1841, H. Doc. 87, 92; "The Norfolk Herald," *Cleveland (OH) Herald and Gazette*, November 28, 1837; and "The People's Currency," *Connecticut Courant* (Hartford, CT), November 25, 1837.

30. U.S. Congress, House, *Independent Treasury, Letter from the Secretary of the Treasury*, 26th Cong., 2nd Sess., 1841, H. Doc. 87.

31. U.S. Congress, House, *Independent Treasury, Letter from the Secretary of the Treasury*, 26th Cong., 2nd Sess., 1841, H. Doc. 87; and "Bank Note Table," *Boon's Lick Times* (Fayette, MO), December 26, 1840.

32. "Losses from Banks and Bank-Paper," in *Writings of Levi Woodbury, LL.D., Political, Judicial and Literary* (Boston: Little, Brown, 1852), 1:432–458.

33. William G. McLoughlin, *Cherokee Renascence in the New Republic* (Princeton, NJ: Princeton University Press, 1986), 317–319 and 373–375; "General Interest. Summary," *Cherokee Phoenix* (New Echota), February 3, 1830; U.S. Congress, House, *Creek Indian Broke &c. Letter from the Secretary of War, Transmitting the Information in Part*, 20th Cong., 1st Sess., 1828, H. Doc. 219; and "Communications. Concluded," *Cherokee Phoenix* (New Echota), July 2, 1828.

34. Ruth A. Gallaher, "Indian Agents in Iowa," *Iowa Journal of History and Politics* 14, no. 3 (July 1916): 375; U.S. Congress, House, *Memorial of the Chiefs, &c., of the Fox Tribe of Indians*, 23rd Cong., 2nd Sess., 1835, H. Doc. 63; U.S. Congress, House, *Memorial of the Chiefs and Warriors of the Sac and Fox Tribes of Indians*, 23rd Cong., 2nd Sess., 1835, H. Doc. 64, italics in the original; and "House of Representatives," *Congressional Globe*, January 12, 1835.

35. "The Sac and Fox Indians," *Niles' Weekly Register* (Washington, DC), July 15, 1837, italics in the original; Thomas J. Lappas, "'A Perfect Apollo': Keokuk and Sac Leadership During the Removal Era," in *The Boundaries Between Us: Natives and Newcomers Along the*

Frontiers of the Old Northwest Territory, 1750–1850, ed. Daniel P. Barr (Kent, OH: Kent State University Press, 2006), 219–235; U.S. Congress, House, *Memorial of the Chiefs, &c., of the Fox Tribe of Indians*, 23rd Cong., 2nd Sess., 1835, H. Doc. 63; U.S. Congress, House, *Memorial of the Chiefs and Warriors of the Sac and Fox Tribes of Indians*, 23rd Cong., 2nd Sess., 1835, H. Doc. 64; "House of Representatives," *Congressional Globe* (Washington, DC), January 12, 1835; and Daniel H. Usner Jr., *American Indians in the Lower Mississippi Valley: Social and Economic Histories* (Lincoln: University of Nebraska Press, 2003), 95–110.

36. Larry E. Hudson Jr., "'All That Cash': Work and Status in the Slave Quarters," in *Working Toward Freedom: Society and Domestic Economy in the American South* (Rochester, NY: University of Rochester Press, 1994), 77–94; Justene Hill Edwards, "Felonious Transactions: Legal Culture and Business Practices of Slave Economies in South Carolina, 1787–1860," *Enterprise and Society* 18, no. 4 (December 2017): 772–783; and Timothy J. Lockley, "Trading Encounters Between Non-Elite Whites and African Americans in Savannah, 1790–1860," *Journal of Southern History* 66, no. 1 (February 2000): 25–48.

37. Charles Ball, *Life of a Negro Slave*, reedited by Mrs. Alfred Barnard (Norwich, CT: Charles Muskett, 1846), 77; Jeff Forret, "Slaves, Poor Whites, and the Underground Economy of the Rural Carolinas," *Journal of Southern History* 70, no. 4 (November 2004): 783–824; and Fletcher M. Green, ed., *Ferry Hill Plantation Journal, January 4, 1838–January 15, 1839* (Chapel Hill: University of North Carolina Press, 1961), 27.

38. Justene Hill Edwards, "Crimes of Economy: Slave Economies and Legal Culture of Early-Nineteenth-Century South Carolina, 1800–1830" (paper presented at the Brown University Nineteenth-Century U.S. History Workshop, Providence, RI, March 6, 2015), 33–35. On Bank of Cape Fear notes, see "Counterfeit Notes," *Newbern (NC) Sentinel*, September 9, 1820; "More Counterfeiting," *Western Carolinian* (Salisbury, NC), May 1, 1821; and "Altered and Counterfeit Notes," *New York Evening Post*, March 31, 1823. On the role of "cash power" in Denmark Vesey's plans, see Douglas R. Egerton, "Slaves to the Marketplace: Economic Liberty and Black Rebelliousness in the Atlantic World," *Journal of the Early Republic* 26, no. 4 (Winter 2006): 617–618.

39. Edward E. Baptist, *The Half Has Never Been Told: Slavery and the Making of American Capitalism* (New York: Basic Books, 2004), 230; Tomoko Yagyu, "Slave Traders and Planters in the Expanding South: Entrepreneurial Strategies, Business Networks, and Western Migration in the Atlantic World, 1787–1859" (PhD diss., University of North Carolina at Chapel Hill, 2006), 64–65 and 251; and Jonathan D. Martin, *Divided Mastery: Slave Hiring in the American South* (Cambridge, MA: Harvard University Press, 2004), 96.

40. Solomon Bayley, *A Narrative of Some Remarkable Incidents in the Life of Solomon Bayley, Formerly a Slave in the State of Delaware, North America, Written by Himself*, 2nd ed. (London: Harvey and Darton, 1825), 27; and Stuart Seely Sprague, "More African Americans Speak: The New Mother Lode," *Journal of Negro History* 78, no. 4 (Autumn 1993): 263.

41. Henry Bibb, *Narrative of the Life and Adventures of Henry Bibb, an American Slave, Written by Himself* (New York: published by the author, 1849), 54–55; Amani Marshall, "'They Will Endeavor to Pass for Free': Enslaved Runaways' Performances of Freedom in Antebellum South Carolina," *Slavery and Abolition* 31, no. 2 (June 2010): 170; and David Waldstreicher, "Reading the Runaways: Self-Fashioning, Print Culture, and Confidence in Slavery in the Eighteenth-Century Mid-Atlantic," *William and Mary Quarterly* 56, no. 2 (April 1999): 244. Michael O'Malley argues that inextricable connections between the languages of

race and money meant that an inherent tension existed for African Americans attempting self-fashioning in the nineteenth century. See Michael O'Malley, "Specie and Species: Race and the Money Question in Nineteenth-Century America," *American Historical Review* 99, no. 2 (April 1994): 369–395.

42. "Ran-Away," *City Gazette* (Charleston, SC), January 28, 1794, as cited in Thomas Brown and Leah Sims, eds., *Fugitive Slave Advertisements in the City Gazette: Charleston, South Carolina, 1787–1797* (Lanham, MD: Lexington Books, 2015), 151; "100 Dollars Reward," *Alexandria (VA) Gazette and Daily Advertiser*, July 14, 1820; and "Stop the Thief," *Cape Fear (NC) Recorder*, October 16, 1824. See also Antonio T. Bly, "'Pretends He Can Read': Runaways and Literacy in Colonial America, 1730–1776," *Early American Studies* 6, no. 2 (Fall 2008): 261–294; Matthew C. Greer, "Bundles, Passes, and Stolen Watches: Interpreting the Role of Material Culture in Escape," *Southern Studies* 21, no. 1 (Spring/Summer 2014): 88; "50 Dollars Reward," *Edenton (NC) Gazette*, April 13, 1810; and "Thirty Dollars Reward," *Arkansas Gazette* (Little Rock, AR), June 5, 1847.

43. "Gross Villany," *Freedom's Journal* (New York, NY), October 24, 1828.

44. Shane White, "Freedom's First Con: African Americans and Changing Notes in Antebellum New York City," *Journal of the Early Republic* 34, no. 3 (Fall 2014): 395 and 400–401.

45. Mihm, *Nation of Counterfeiters*, 232; White, "Freedom's First Con," 400–409; and *Trials and Confessions of Madison Henderson, Alias Blanchard, Alfred Amos Warrick, James W. Seward, and Charles Brown, Murderers of Jesse Baker and Jacob Weaver, as Given by Themselves; and a Likeness of Each, Taken in Jail Shortly After Their Arrest* (Saint Louis, MO: Chambers & Knapp, 1841), 11.

46. Ellen Hartigan-O'Connor, "The Personal Is Political Economy," *Journal of the Early Republic* 36, no. 3 (Summer 2016): 335–341; Ellen Hartigan-O'Connor, *The Ties That Buy: Women and Commerce in Revolutionary America* (Philadelphia: University of Pennsylvania Press, 2009), 109; and David Jaffee, "Peddlers of Progress and the Transformation of the Rural North, 1760–1860," *Journal of American History* 78, no. 2 (September 1991): 529.

47. Catherine Maria Sedgwick, *A New-England Tale; Or, Sketches of New-England Character and Manners* (New York: E. Bliss & E. White, 1822), 169–170.

48. Caroline Kirkland, *A New Home—Who'll Follow?: Or, Glimpses of Western Life* (New York: C. S. Francis, 1839), 204–212.

49. "Asmodeus Among the Banks, or Philadelphia in an Uproar," *Spirit of the Times* (Philadelphia), March 19, 1842.

50. "A Shinplaster Incident," *Detroit (MI) Free Press*, September 24, 1840; Margaret Lynch-Brennan, *The Irish Bridget: Irish Immigrant Women in Domestic Service in America, 1840–1930* (Syracuse, NY: Syracuse University Press, 2009), 53 and 91; and Hasia Diner, *Erin's Daughters in America: Irish Immigrant Women in the Nineteenth Century* (Baltimore: Johns Hopkins University Press, 1983), 141–142. On savings banks, see Nicholas Osborne, "Little Capitalists: The Social Economy of Saving in the United States, 1816–1914" (PhD diss., Columbia University, 2014); and Ann Fabian, *Card Sharps and Bucket Shops: Gambling in Nineteenth-Century America* (New York: Routledge, 1999), 40–52 and 129–136.

51. "More the Shin-Plaster System," *New Era* (New York, NY), March 31, 1838.

52. Brian Luskey, "Jumping Counters in White Collars: Manliness, Respectability, and Work in the Antebellum City," *Journal of the Early Republic* 26, no. 2 (Summer 2006): 204.

53. "Who Are the Thieves?," *Brooklyn (NY) Daily Eagle*, July 22, 1853.

54. "Commonwealth *v.* George W. Stone," in *Reports of Cases Argued and Determined in the Supreme Judicial Court of Massachusetts*, ed. Theron Metcalf (Boston: Little, Brown, 1864), 4:43–49; and "Police Court—Tuesday," *Boston Post*, October 20, 1841.

Chapter 3

1. James A. Haxby, *Standard Catalog of United States Obsolete Bank Notes, 1782–1866* (Iola, WI: Krause, 1988), 1:542–543; Jessica M. Lepler, *The Many Panics of 1837* (New York: Cambridge University Press, 2013), 16; and *Proceedings of the Board of Currency, During the Year 1853* (New Orleans, LA: Emile La Sere State Printer, 1854), 3–5.

2. "New Bank Note," *Daily Picayune* (New Orleans), November 2, 1854.

3. *Laws of the Commonwealth of Massachusetts in Relation to Banks and Banking* (Boston: Press of the Centinel and Gazette, 1836), 13–14; Robert Noxon Toppan, *A Hundred Years of Bank Note Engraving in the United States* (New York: American Bank Note, 1896), 9; *The Public and General Laws of the Commonwealth of Massachusetts from February 28, 1807, to February 16, 1816* (Boston: Wells and Lilly, 1816), 82–84; *Perkins Bank Bill Test, Consisting of Original Impressions from the Permanent Stereotype Steel Plates of Massachusetts Paper Currency, Executed in Conformity to an Act of the Legislature, Passed March 3, 1809, Together with the Standard Check Plate, Which Will Apply Equally to Every Bank in the United States Which Has Adopted or Which May Adopt This Principle* (Newburyport, MA: published by the proprietor W. & J. Gilman Printers, 1809); and "Lucy Ann Ward to her Parents, Capt. & Mrs. Wm. Ward, October 13, 1815," Ms. N-1726, box 5, Thomas Wren Ward Papers, Ward Family Correspondence, 1815, Massachusetts Historical Society. I would like to thank Randi Flaherty for this citation. See also Frances Robertson, "The Aesthetics of Authenticity: Printed Banknotes as Industrial Currency," *Technology and Culture* 46, no. 1 (January 2005): 31–50; and Stephen Mihm, *A Nation of Counterfeiters: Capitalists, Con Men, and the Making of the United States* (Cambridge, MA: Harvard University Press, 2007), 265–269.

4. Abel Brewster, *A Plan for Producing an Uniformity in the Ornamental Part of Bank or Other Bills Where There Is Danger of Forgery, and for Furnishing the Public with a Convenient and Infallible Test for the Same, with a Brief Explanation of Its Importance, Together with a New Set of Figures Designed Particularly for Bank Bills* (Philadelphia: Thomas Town, 1810), 2–4, italics in the original; and Abel Brewster, *A Brief Memoir of Abel Brewster* (Hartford, CT: Folsom & Hurlbut, 1832).

5. "John W. Casilear," *Art Journal* 2 (1876): 16–17; Linda Ferber, *Kindred Spirits: Asher B. Durand and the American Landscape* (New York: D. Giles, 2007); Alice Newlin, "Asher B. Durand, American Engraver," *Metropolitan Museum of Art Bulletin* 1, no. 5 (January 1943): 168; Asher B. Durand Engravings, 1828–1867, carton 21, folder 72, Wright Family Papers, Massachusetts Historical Society; Wayne Craven, "Asher B. Durand's Career as an Engraver," *American Art Journal* 3, no. 1 (Spring 1971): 39–57; John Durand, *The Life and Times of A. B. Durand* (New York: Charles Scribner's Sons, 1894); and Julian Blanchard, "The Durand Engraving Companies," *Essay Proof Society* 26 (April 1950): 81–89, 27 (July 1950): 147–152, and 29 (January 1951): 11–16.

6. Asher B. Durand, "Letters on Landscape Painting: Letter II," *Crayon* 1, no. 3 (January 17, 1855): 34; Diana Strazdes, "'Wilderness and Its Waters': A Professional Identity for the Hudson River School," *Early American Studies* 7, no. 2 (Fall 2009): 338; and Ferber, *Kindred Spirits*.

7. Jeffrey Sklansky, "'A Bank on Parnassus': Nicholas Biddle and the Beauty of Banking," *Common-place* 6, no. 3 (April 2006), accessed October 1, 2019, http://www.commonplace.online/article/sklansky/; and Jeffrey Sklansky, "The Moneylender as Magistrate: Nicholas Biddle and the Ideological Origins of Central Banking in the United States," *Theoretical Inquiries in Law* 11, no. 1 (January 2010): 319–348.

8. "History and Progress of Bank Note Engraving," *Crayon* 1, no. 8 (February 21, 1855): 116–117; "Bank-Note Engraving in America," *Illustrated Magazine of Art* 3, no. 17 (1854): 308–310; and "Cyrus Durand, the Machinist and Bank-Note Engraver," *Illustrated Magazine of Art* 3, no. 17 (1854): 270.

9. Quoted in Q. David Bowers, *Obsolete Paper Money Issued by Banks in the United States, 1782–1866: A Study and Appreciation for the Numismatist and Historian* (Atlanta, GA: Whitman, 2006), 253; and Haxby, *Standard Catalog of United States Obsolete Bank Notes, 1782–1866*, 2:1057 and 1091.

10. E. and C. Starr, *Distypographic Bank Note Specimen* (New York: n.p., 1824); Fairman, Draper, Underwood, & Co., *Philadelphia, Nov. 8, 1822: Sir, the Co-Partnership Carried on for Many Years* (Philadelphia: n.p., 1822); and Bowers, *Obsolete Paper Money Issued by Banks in the United States*, 160.

11. "Envelope Mania," *Littell's Living Age* 897 (August 10, 1861), 367; "Making Money," *Harper's New Monthly Magazine* 24, no. 141 (February 1862): 306–325; and Bowers, *Obsolete Paper Money Issued by Banks in the United States*, 175. For more on Waterman Ormsby, see Mihm, *Nation of Counterfeiters*, 260–304.

12. Julian Blanchard, "A Stamp Dealer Pictured on a Bank-Note," *Essay Proof Journal* 16, no. 4 (Fall 1959): 159–162; and "Egg Harbor Bank," $1, July 1, 1861, Obsolete Bank Note Collection, Massachusetts Historical Society.

13. S. J. Willis, *Evolution of the Blue Hill National Bank of Milton from April 1, 1832, to April 1, 1916* (Milton, MA: prepared for Milton Historical Society, 1913), 24–25 and 85–94.

14. Richard H. Timberlake Jr., "The Significance of Unaccounted Currencies," *Journal of Economic History* 41, no. 4 (December 1981): 862; and Dudley Atkins Tyng, *Reports of Cases Argued and Determined in the Supreme Judicial Court of the Commonwealth of Massachusetts* (Boston: Little, Brown, 1864), 13:158–159.

15. "The Albany City Bank," $3, 18—, New York, Scrapbook of Paper Currency, Library Company of Philadelphia; and Caroline Kirkland, *A New Home—Who'll Follow?: Or, Glimpses of Western Life* (New York: C. S. Francis, 1839), 307. On the New York Safety Fund, see Robert E. Chaddock, *The Safety Fund Banking System in New York, 1829–1866* (Washington, DC: Government Printing Office, 1910); and Howard Bodenhorn, *State Banking in Early America: A New Economic History* (New York: Oxford University Press, 2003), 155–182.

16. Timothy R. Mahoney, "The Rise and Fall of the Booster Ethos in Dubuque, 1850–1861," *Annals of Iowa* 61 (Fall 2002): 407–408 and 415; "Dubuque Central Improvement Company," $1, December 22, 1857, author's collection; and "The North Western Bank of Georgia," Ringgold, GA, $5, June 1, 1857, Obsolete Bank Note Collection, Massachusetts Historical Society.

17. Wendy Bellion, *Citizen Spectator: Art, Illusion, and Visual Perception in Early National America* (Chapel Hill: University of North Carolina Press, 2011), 153.

18. Bowers, *Obsolete Paper Money Issued by Banks in the United States*, 205; Richard G. Doty, *Pictures from a Distant Country: Images on 19th Century U.S. Currency* (Raleigh, NC:

Boson Books, 2004), 52–71 and 114–132; "The National Bank Note Reporter," *Wheeling (WV) Daily Intelligencer*, October 18, 1858; "Latest Counterfeits," *Buffalo (NY) Daily Republic*, December 3, 1858; and "More of the Humbugs," *Evansville (IL) Daily Journal*, March 19, 1860. Several questionable two-dollar notes utilized Ormsby's suggestive reverse design, including those from the Mousam River Bank of Sanford, Maine, the Northern Indiana Railroad Company of Logansport, and the Indiana Coal Bank of Petersburg.

19. George Peyton, *How to Detect Counterfeit Bank Notes: Or, An Illustrated Treatise on the Detection of Counterfeit, Altered, and Spurious Bank Notes* (New York: published for the author, 1856), vii.

20. Drew Lopenzina, "Compromised Currencies: Why Samson Occom Is Not Pictured on the One Hundred Dollar Bill," in *Sovereignty, Separatism, and Survivance: Ideological Encounters in the Literature of Native North America*, ed. Benjamin Carson (Newcastle: Cambridge Scholars, 2009), 18; and E. J. Wilber and E. P. Eastman, *A Treatise on Counterfeit, Altered, and Spurious Bank Notes, with Unerring Rules for the Detection of Frauds in the Same* (Poughkeepsie, NY: published for the authors, 1865), 50.

21. Doty, *Pictures from a Distant Country*, 83–90; and William Wright, *The Oil Regions of Pennsylvania, Showing Where Petroleum Is Found, How It Is Obtained and at What Cost* (New York: Harper & Brothers, 1865), 47, italics in the original.

22. "Manual Labor Bank," Philadelphia, $5, September 1, 1837, Obsolete Bank Note Collection, Massachusetts Historical Society; Bowers, *Obsolete Paper Money Issued by Banks in the United States*, 236–237; and Francine Tyler, "The Angel in the Factory: Images of Women Workers Engraved on Ante-Bellum Bank Notes," *Imprint: Journal of the American Historical Print Collectors Society* 19, no. 1 (Spring 1994): 2–10.

23. Haxby, *Standard Catalog of United States Obsolete Bank Notes, 1782–1866*, 2:792. On producerism, see Jonathan A. Glickstein, *Concepts of Free Labor in Antebellum America* (New Haven, CT: Yale University Press, 1991); and Joshua R. Greenberg, *Advocating the Man: Organized Labor, Masculinity, and the Household in New York, 1800–1840* (New York: Columbia University Press, 2008), 55–59.

24. Scrapbook of Currency Vignettes, Graphic Arts, bound vol. 27, Alfred Jones Papers, American Antiquarian Society; and William Stevens Powell, *When the Past Refused to Die: A History of Caswell County, North Carolina, 1777–1977* (Durham, NC: Moore, 1977), 345–346.

25. "Bank of Lexington," Lexington, NC, $5, January 3, 1860, and "Mississippi Union Bank, Jackson, MS, $10, May 1, 1839, both in Obsolete Bank Note Collection, Massachusetts Historical Society; Doty, *Pictures from a Distant Country*, 40–41 and 125; Heinz Tschachler, *All Others Pay Cash: Dollar Bills and Their Cultural Work* (Heidelberg: Winter 2008), 252; Michael O'Malley, *Face Value: The Entwined Histories of Money and Race in America* (Chicago: University of Chicago Press, 2012), 74; "Conway Bank," Conway, MA, $5, October 1, 1862, Obsolete Bank Note Collection, Massachusetts Historical Society; Charles B. Rice, *Celebration of the Hundredth Anniversary of the Incorporation of Conway, Massachusetts at Conway, June 19th, 1867* (Northampton, MA: Bridgman & Childs, 1867), 60–61; *Ninth Annual Report of the Board of Managers of the Massachusetts Colonization Society* (Boston: T. R. Marvin, 1850), 18; and Francis DeWitt, *Statistical Information Relating to Certain Branches of Industry in Massachusetts, for the Year Ending June 1, 1855* (Boston: William White, 1856), 179.

26. Martin Brückner, *The Geographic Revolution in Early America: Maps, Literacy, and National Identity* (Chapel Hill: University of North Carolina Press, 2006), 113.

27. "Hadley Falls Bank," Holyoke, MA, $10, November 16, 1858, Obsolete Bank Note Collection, Massachusetts Historical Society; and Wilber and Eastman, *Treatise on Counterfeit, Altered, and Spurious Bank Notes*, 49. The authors of the pamphlet also argued that this worked for important buildings or structures, such as the Bunker Hill Monument being a sign for a bank from Charlestown or Boston.

28. Haxby, *Standard Catalog of United States Obsolete Bank Notes, 1782–1866*, vol. 3, 1965; "A Ten Dollar Bill," *St. Charles City (IA) Intelligencer*, March 17, 1859; and Martin Brückner, "The Ambulatory Map," *Winterthur Portfolio* 45, nos. 2/3 (Summer/Autumn 2011): 160.

29. "Manual Labor Banking House," Philadelphia, $5, September 1, 1837, Obsolete Bank Note Collection, Massachusetts Historical Society; and Henrietta M. Larson, "E. W. Clark & Co., 1837–1857: The Beginning of an American Private Bank," *Journal of Economic and Business History* 4, no. 3 (May 1932): 429–460.

30. Farban Zerbe, "Letters to Editor," *Numismatist* 28, no. 5 (May 1915): 177; and "Louisiana Bank," New Orleans, LA, $5, August 3, 1814, and "Northampton Bank," Northampton, PA, $5, December 16, 1834, both in Obsolete Bank Note Collection, Massachusetts Historical Society.

31. Susan Schulten, "Emma Willard and the Graphic Foundations of American History," *Journal of Historical Geography* 33, no. 3 (July 2007): 550 and 545.

32. Doty, *Pictures from a Distant Country*, 17–20. Banks with Battle of New Orleans vignettes included $10 Aberdeen & Pontotoc Rail Road and Banking Company in Mississippi; $10 Agricultural Bank in Mount Sterling, IN; $5 Central Bank of Middletown, a possibly fraudulent bank in Connecticut; $50 Union Bank of Columbia, a possibly fraudulent bank based in Washington, DC; $6 Middletown Bank, CT; $1 Jefferson Bank of New Salem, OH; $50 Fort Stanwix Bank in Rome, NY; $5 Central Bank of Cherry Valley, NY; $100 Bank of Chattanooga, TN; $50 Central Bank of Virginia, Staunton; $10 Jackson Bank, Providence, RI; $5 Central Bank of Tennessee, Nashville; and $5 Southern Bank of Tennessee, Memphis. See Haxby, *Standard Catalog of United States Obsolete Bank Notes, 1782–1866*, vols. 1–4.

33. Roger H. Durand, *Interesting Notes About History* (Rehoboth, MA: R. H. Durand, 1990), 110–111 and 131–133. An image of Fort Stanwix appeared in Benson J. Lossing, *The Pictorial Field-Book of the Revolution* (New York: Harper & Brothers, 1851), 231, but featured only the building, not the treaty signing.

34. William C. Nell, *The Colored Patriots of the American Revolution, with Sketches of Several Distinguished Colored Persons, to Which Is Added a Brief Survey of the Condition and Prospects of Colored Americans* (Boston: Robert F. Wallcut, 1855), 21. I want to thank Margot Minardi for this reference. Veronika Timpe, "Beyond Face Value: Images of Slaves on Nineteenth-Century American Currency," in *Almighty Dollar: Papers and Lectures from the Velden Conference*, ed. Heinz Tschachler (Berlin: Lit Verlag, 2010), 72.

35. Paul E. Johnson, *Sam Patch, the Famous Jumper* (New York: Hill and Wang, 2003), 163.

36. Carrie Rebora Barratt, "Faces of a New Nation: American Portraits of the 18th and Early 19th Centuries," *Metropolitan Museum of Art Bulletin* 61, no. 1 (Summer 2003): 5; John A. Muscalus, *An Index of State Bank Notes That Illustrate Presidents* (Bridgeport, PA: John A. Muscalus, 1939); Doty, *Pictures from a Distant Country*, 1–21; and John A. Muscalus, *An Index of State Bank Notes That Illustrate Characters and Events* (Bridgeport, PA: John A. Muscalus, 1938).

37. David Haven Blake, *Walt Whitman and the Culture of American Celebrity* (New Haven, CT: Yale University Press, 2006), 23; David Chapin, "'Science Weeps, Humanity Weeps, the World Weeps': America Mourns Elisha Kent Kane," *Pennsylvania Magazine of History and Biography* 123, no. 4 (October 1999): 275–301; Mark Metzler Sawin, *Raising Kane: Elisha Kent Kane and the Culture of Fame in Antebellum America* (Philadelphia: American Philosophical Society, 2008), 163 and 339; and Scrapbook of Currency Vignettes, Graphic Arts, bound vol. 29, Alfred Jones Papers, American Antiquarian Society. The image appeared on the following notes: $5 Bank of Bloomington (IL), $20 Marine Bank of Baltimore, $2 Safety Fund Bank (Boston), $5 Northern Bank in Providence (RI), $10 Bank of Orange County (Chelsea, VT), $2 Portage County Bank (Jordan, WI), $5 Bank of Wisconsin (Madison), $3 Menomonee Bank (WI), $1 Northwestern Bank (Stevens Point, WI), and $5 Bank of Superior (WI); see Haxby, *Standard Catalog of United States Obsolete Bank Notes, 1782–1866*, vols. 1–4.

38. Walter Muir Whitehill, "The Centenary of the Dowse Library," *Proceedings of the Massachusetts Historical Society* 71 (October 1953–May 1957): 167–178; Edward Everett, *Eulogy on Thomas Dowse, of Cambridgeport, Pronounced Before the Massachusetts Historical Society, 9th December, 1858* (Boston: John Wilson and Son, 1859); and Daniel J. Herman, "The Other Daniel Boone: The Nascence of a Middle-Class Hunter Hero, 1784–1860," *Journal of the Early Republic* 18, no. 3 (Autumn 1998): 441.

39. A. H. Saxon, *P. T. Barnum: The Legend and the Man* (New York: Colombia University Press, 1989), 193; Leon Jackson, "Digging for Dirt: Reading Blackmail in the Antebellum Archive," *Common-place* 12, no. 3 (April 2012), accessed October 1, 2019, http://www.commonplace/online/article/reading/; "The Pequonnock Bank," *Bankers' Magazine and Statistical Register* 3, no. 12 (June 1854): 1000; and *Report of the Bank Commissioners of the State of Connecticut to the General Assembly* (Hartford, CT: Thomas M. Day, 1855), 56. Barnum discusses chartering the bank, his presidency, and New England currency regulations in Phineas Taylor Barnum, *The Life of P. T. Barnum, Written by Himself* (London: Sampson Low, Son, 1855), 381–383.

40. "Farmers' Bank of the State of Delaware in Georgetown," 6¼ cents, October 17, 1839, Delaware, Scrapbook of Paper Currency, Library Company of Philadelphia; and "The Money That Was Current Yesterday," *New York Times*, October 15, 1857.

41. Chetwood Evelyn, ed., *Table-Talk on Books, Men, and Manners*, Putnam's Popular Library (New York: George P. Putnam, 1853), 39–40; and John Dixon, "Between Script and Specie: Cadwallader Colden's Printing Method and the Production of Permanent, Correct Knowledge," *Early American Studies* 8, no. 1 (Winter 2010): 75–93.

42. Henry C. Foote, *Universal Counterfeit and Altered Bank Note Detector, at Sight* (New York: Mann, Spear, 1852), 29; and "List of Discredited Banks in New England and New York," *Boston Post*, November 24, 1858. There were several guides to counterfeit detection that dealt with paper quality. See George Peyton, *How to Detect Counterfeit Bank Notes: Or, An Illustrated Treatise on the Detection of Counterfeit, Altered, and Spurious Bank Notes* (New York: published for the author, 1856), 9–10; and Ebenezer Watson, *A Protection Against the Alteration of Bank Notes, Bills of Credit, Circulating Notes, Certificates of Stock and Other Instruments of Writing by Any Change of the Sum Thereof* (Albany, NY: n.p., 1838).

43. "To a Note on St. Clair Bank," *Scientific American*, December 18, 1845, italics in the original.

44. Caroline Kirtland, *Forest Life* (New York: C. S. Francis, 1842), 91–92; James Kirke Paulding, *The History of a Little Frenchman and His Bank Notes: "Rags! Rags! Rags!"* (Philadelphia: published for the author by Edward Earle, 1815), 4; "The Case of Jackalow," *New York Times*, January 22, 1861; and Suellen Hoy, *Chasing Dirt: The American Pursuit of Cleanliness* (New York: Oxford University Press, 1995), 3–27.

45. R. Neil Fulgham, "Hugh Walker and North Carolina's 'Smallpox Currency' of 1779," *Colonial Newsletter* (December 2005): 2903–2904; "Small Pox Communicated by Bank Notes," *Corrector* (Sag Harbor, NY), February 7, 1844; "A Western Editor," *Long Islander* (Huntington, NY), May 28, 1852; "Bank Bills vs. Small Pox," *Monthly Jubilee* (Philadelphia), May 1, 1852; and "Peterson's Detector," *Long Islander* (Huntington, NY), May 13, 1859.

46. Thomas H. Buckler, *A History of Epidemic Cholera, as It Appeared at the Baltimore City and County Alms-House, in the Summer of 1849, with Some Remarks on the Medical Topography and Diseases of This Region* (Baltimore: James Lucas, 1851), 4; "Disease Propagated by Bank Notes," *Scientific American*, March 27, 1852; "Disease Propagated by Bank Notes," *Odd Fellow*, March 10, 1852; and Ralph Waldo Emerson, *The Conduct of Life* (Boston: Ticknor and Fields, 1860), 108.

47. "Falling in Love with a Picture on a Bank-Note," *Red, White and Blue* (Philadelphia), September 17, 1859.

48. Robert E. Wright, "The First Phase of the Empire State's 'Triple Transition': Banks' Influence on the Market, Democracy, and Federalism in New York, 1776–1838," *Social Science History* 21, no. 4 (Winter 1997): 528.

Chapter 4

1. Jerry W. Markham, *A Financial History of the United States* (New York: M. E. Sharpe, 2002), 1:123; and David McNeely Stauffer and Mantle Fielding, *American Engravers upon Copper and Steel* (New York: Burt Franklin, 1907), 219–220. Harrison also engraved pastoral scenes for the short-lived Farmers' Bank of New Salem, the only other bank in town from 1815 to 1816. See James A. Haxby, *Standard Catalog of United States Obsolete Bank Notes, 1782–1866* (Iola, WI: Krause, 1988), 3:1983.

2. Waldo C. Moore, "New Salem, Ohio, in Numismatics," *Numismatist* 26, no. 9 (September 1913): 459; and W. H. Hunter, "The Pathfinders of Jefferson County, Ohio," supplement, *Ohio Archaeological and Historical Quarterly* 6, no. 1 (July 1899): 189–190. Another lawsuit developed from the bank bills in the desk, but the jury ruled for Duffield. John C. Wright, *Reports of Cases at Law and in Chancery Decided by the Supreme Court of Ohio, During the Years 1831, 1832, 1833, 1834* (Columbus, OH: Isaac N. Whiting, 1835), 455–457.

3. David Jaffee, "The Village Enlightenment in New England, 1760–1820," *William and Mary Quarterly* 47, no. 3 (July 1990): 327; and David Jaffee, *A New Nation of Goods: The Material Culture of Early America* (Philadelphia: University of Pennsylvania Press, 2010), 48.

4. John Lauritz Larson, *The Market Revolution in America: Liberty, Ambition, and the Eclipse of the Common Good* (New York: Cambridge University Press, 2010), 59. In his study of politics, the public sphere, and Jacksonian paperwork, Jordan Stein claims that "circulation provides impersonal texts with the opportunity to become personal—to be read or misread, appropriated and repurposed." Jordan Alexander Stein, "The Whig Interpretation of Media: Sheppard Lee and Jacksonian Paperwork," *History of the Present* 3, no. 1 (Spring 2013): 39.

5. *Worcester Magazine* 2, no. 25 (third week in September 1786): 294; *A Mournful Lamentation on the Untimely Death of Paper Money* ([Boston?]: printed by Sam. Adams, 1781);

Jennifer J. Baker, "Paper Money Gets Personal: Reading Credit and Character in Early America," *Common-place* 6, no. 3 (April 2006), accessed October 1, 2019, http://www.common place/online/article/baker/; Viviana A. Zelizer, "Making Multiple Monies," in *Explorations in Economic Sociology*, ed. Richard Swedberg (New York: Russell Sage Foundation, 1993), 197; Jennifer J. Baker, *Securing the Commonwealth: Debt, Speculation, and Writing in the Making of Early America* (Baltimore: Johns Hopkins University Press, 2005); and Mark Blackwell, ed., *The Secret Life of Things: Animals, Objects, and It-Narratives in Eighteenth-Century England* (Lewisburg, PA: Bucknell University Press, 2007).

6. "Autobiography of a Fip Shin-Plaster," *Sun* (New York, NY), March 2, 1838. The term "fip" derived from the five-penny bit, but it was used to describe any small denomination.

7. "Meditations over a Bank-Note," *Literary Harvester* (April 1, 1843): 180.

8. "Secreting a Bank Note in a Quid of Tobacco," *Brother Jonathan* (New York, NY), March 10, 1855; and "Epigram for Wall Street," *Evening Mirror* (New York, NY), January 23, 1845. Some scholars attribute the piece to Edgar Allen Poe, who was associated with the *Evening Mirror* at the time, but it probably came from an English publication. See Enrico Brandoli, "'Epigram for Wall Street': Who Did It? Who?," *Edgar Allan Poe Review* 12, no. 2 (Fall 2011): 58–63.

9. Francis Wayland, *The Elements of Political Economy* (New York: Leavitt, Lord, 1837), 294.

10. Quoted in H. Earl Cook, "Iowa's First Banking System," *Annals of Iowa* 32 (1955): 607; Thomas Horton James, *Rambles in the United States and Canada During the Year 1845, with an Account of Oregon* (London: John Ollivier, 1846), 60; and Erling A. Erickson, "Money and Banking in a 'Bankless' State: Iowa, 1846–1857," *Business History Review* 43, no. 2 (Summer 1969): 171–191. The expression "raising the wind" described an economic scam or fraud. See Edgar Allen Poe, "Raising the Wind; or, Diddling Considered as one of the Exact Sciences," *Philadelphia (PA) Saturday Courier*, October 14, 1843.

11. Henry Bradshaw Fearon, *Sketches of America: A Narrative of a Journey of Five Thousand Miles Through the Eastern and Western States of America* (London: Longman, Hurst, Rees, Orme, and Brown, 1818), 290–291; and "Wild Cat Money," *Clark's New-England Bank Note List, and Counterfeit Bill Detector*, May 1, 1838.

12. Quoted in Emily Foster, ed., *American Grit: A Woman's Letters from the Ohio Frontier* (Lexington: University of Kentucky Press, 2009), 49; "On Saturday Last, a Young Man," *National Intelligencer and Washington Advertiser* (Washington, DC), August 19, 1808; James Holbrook, *Ten Years Among the Mail Bags: Or, Notes from the Diary of a Special Agent* (Philadelphia: H. Cowperthwait, 1855); "Remission of Bank Notes Cut in Twain—A Dead Loss to the Receiver," *Ohio Statesman* (Columbus, OH), January 21, 1842; and David M. Henkin, *The Postal Age: The Emergence of Modern Communications in Nineteenth-Century America* (Chicago: University of Chicago Press, 2006), 53.

13. "Facts for the People," *Botanico-Medical Recorder*, June 5, 1847.

14. "Farmers' Bank of Virginia *v.* Reynolds," in Peyton Randolph, *Reports of Cases Argued and Determined in the Court of Appeals of Virginia* (Richmond, VA: Peter Cottom, 1827), 186–188; "Northern Bank *v.* Farmers Bank," in Ben Monroe, *Reports of Cases at Common Law and in Equity* (Frankfort, KY: A. G. Hodges, 1858), 506–511; and "William F. Murdock and others *v.* The Union Bank of Louisiana," in Merritt M. Robinson, *Cases Argued and Determined in the Supreme Court of Louisiana, in the Eastern District, at New Orleans, Commencing April, 1842* (New Orleans: published for the Reporter, 1843), 112–117.

15. "Shenck *v.* Hutcheson," *Carolina Law Repository*, March 1, 1816; Ira B. Cross, "Californians and Hard Money," *California Folklore Quarterly* 4, no. 3 (July 1945): 270–277; and Woodbury & Co., *National Bank Bill and Currency Adhesive Paper!* (Boston: n.p., [1863–1900?]).

16. "Mutilated Bank Bills," *Quincy (IL) Whig*, June 14, 1852; *Bankers' Magazine and Statistical Register*, June 1, 1850; "Shenck *v.* Hutcheson," *Carolina Law Repository*, March 1, 1816; and Waterman L. Ormsby, *New York, 1853: The Rapid Increase of the Crime of Counterfeiting Bank Notes* (New York: n.p., 1853).

17. Dudley Atkins Tyng, *Reports of Cases Argued and Determined in the Supreme Judicial Court of the Commonwealth of Massachusetts* (Boston: Little, Brown, 1864), 10:34–35; and *Proceedings of the Essex Institute*, vol. 4, *1864–65* (Salem, MA: published by the Institute, 1866), 61.

18. "Burning Bank Notes," *Odd Fellow*, July 2, 1851; and James K. Paulding, *Letters from the South by a Northern Man* (New York: Harper & Brothers, 1835), 2:94.

19. Ronald J. Zboray and Mary Saracino Zboray, " 'Have You Read?': Real Readers and Their Responses in Antebellum Boston and Its Region," *Nineteenth-Century Literature* 52, no. 2 (September 1997): 168.

20. *The Autographical Counterfeit Detector: Companion to the Bank Note Reporter, Given Free of Charge, to All Weekly and Semi-Monthly Subscribers to the Reporter, Containing Fac-Simile Signatures of the President and Cashier of Every Bank in the United States* (New York: Wm. W. Lee, 1852); and Stephen Mihm, *A Nation of Counterfeiters: Capitalists, Con Men, and the Making of the United States* (Cambridge, MA: Harvard University Press, 2007), 256–257. Signatures were more important for shinplasters; see "Mr. Beverley Lee; Or, The Days of the Shin-Plasters," in *The Little Frenchman and His Water Lots, with Other Sketches of the Times*, by George P. Morris (Philadelphia: Lea & Blanchard, 1839), 136–137.

21. Tamara Thornton, *Handwriting in America: A Cultural History* (New Haven, CT: Yale University Press, 1998), 78 and 84.

22. "The Warren Bank," Danvers, MA, $5, August 1, 1860; "The Hampden Bank," Westfield, MA, $3, September 10, 1860; "Exchange Bank," Brunswick, GA, $5, January 1, 1842; "Hadley Falls," Holyoke, MA, $10, November 16, 1858; "Blue Hill Bank," Dorchester, MA, $1, March 1, 1852; and "Mississippi Union Bank," Jackson, MS, $50, April 1, 1839; all in Obsolete Bank Note Collection, Massachusetts Historical Society.

23. "The Warren Bank," Danvers, MA, $5, August 1, 1860; and "State Bank," Boston, $2, July 15, 1837; both in Obsolete Bank Note Collection, Massachusetts Historical Society. On counterfeit notes and the Suffolk Bank, see Mihm, *Nation of Counterfeiters*, 7, 134–136, 149, and 154.

24. Caitlin Rosenthal, "Storybook-Keepers: Narratives and Numbers in Nineteenth-Century America," *Common-place* 12, no. 3 (April 2012), accessed October 1, 2019, http://www.commonplace/online/article/rosenthal/; Robin Bernstein, "Dances with Things: Material Culture and the Performance of Race," *Social Text 101* 27, no. 4 (Winter 2009): 69–70; Michael Twyman, "The Long-Term Significance of Printed Ephemera," *RBM: A Journal of Rare Books, Manuscripts, and Cultural Heritage* 9, no. 1 (2008): 19–57; and Michael Zakim, *Accounting for Capitalism: The World the Clerk Made* (Chicago: University of Chicago Press, 2018).

25. "Burrillville Bank," Providence, RI, $2, May 1828, Obsolete Bank Note Collection, Massachusetts Historical Society; Frederic James Wood, *The Turnpikes of New England and*

Evolution of the Same England, Virginia, and Maryland (Boston: Marshall Jones, 1909), 140; "New York Exchange Bank," $3, January 15, 1840, Currency Collection, American Antiquarian Society; "Bank Note Literature," *Numismatist* 18, no. 4 (April 1905): 104; "Vermont State Bank," Woodstock, VT, $10, 1807, accessed April 5, 2018, http://currency.ha.com/c/item.zx?saleNo = 34121&lotNo = 21167; and Kenneth A. Degree, "Malfeasance or Theft?: What Really Happened at the Middlebury Branch of the Vermont State Bank," *Vermont History* 68, no. 1 (Winter/Spring 2000): 5–34.

26. Richard J. Wolfe, *Tarnished Idol: William T. G. Morton and the Introduction of Surgical Anesthesia* (San Anselmo, CA: Norman, 2001), 33–35; and "Farmers' Bank of Seneca County," Romulus, NY, $100, October 1, 1839, Obsolete Bank Note Collection, Massachusetts Historical Society.

27. "Adventures of a Bank Note," *Farmer's Monthly Visitor* (Concord, NH), January 31, 1849.

28. "Bond's Hat Warehouse," *New York Evangelist*, May 28, 1846; "Bond's Hat Warehouse," *American* (New York, NY), July 1, 1834; "Bond's Hat Warehouse," *New York Evening Post*, June 5, 1833; "Bond's Hat Warehouse," *New York Mirror*, November 25, 1826; "Bond's Hat Warehouse," *Commercial Advertiser* (New York, NY), June 11, 1832; "Bond's Hat Warehouse," *Subterranean, United with the Working Man's Advocate* (New York, NY), November 30, 1844; "Another Paper-Money Manufactory," *Niles' Weekly Register* (Washington, DC), March 21, 1829; and "New Jersey Manufacturing and Banking Company," $3, July 4, 1828, author's collection.

29. "Newport Bank," $2, September 1, 1854, Don Kelly Paper Money for Collectors, Rhode Island Obsoletes, Newport, 1854, accessed April 5, 2018, http://www.donckelly.com/obsolete/ri170_g24a.html; and Thomas Allston Brown, *A History of the New York Stage from the Performance in 1732 to 1901* (New York: Dodd, Mead, 1903), 2:1–8.

30. Konstantin Dierks, "Letter Writing, Stationery Supplies, and Consumer Modernity in the Eighteenth-Century Atlantic World," *Early American Literature* 41, no. 3 (Fall 2006): 473–494; and "Rhode Island Agricultural Bank," Johnston, RI, $10, February 4, 1837, Obsolete Bank Note Collection, Massachusetts Historical Society.

31. Lara Langer Cohen, *The Fabrication of American Literature: Fraudulence and Antebellum Print Culture* (Philadelphia: University of Pennsylvania Press, 2012), 99; and H. J. Jackson, *Marginalia: Readers Writing in Books* (New Haven, CT: Yale University Press, 2001), 249.

32. Victoria Carrington, "I Write, Therefore I Am: Texts in the City," *Visual Communication* 8, no. 4 (November 2009): 419; Michael Harris, "Urban Totems: The Communal Spirit of Black Murals," in *Walls of Heritage, Walls of Pride: African American Murals*, ed. R. Prigoff and J. Dunitz (Petaluma, CA: Pomegranate Communication, 2000), 40; and Katherine Reed, "'Charcoal Scribblings of the Most Rascally Character': Conflict, Identity, and Testimony in American Civil War Graffiti," *American Nineteenth Century History* 16, no. 2 (September 2015): 111–127.

33. "Exchange Bank of Tennessee," Murfreesboro, TN, November 1, 1854, accessed April 5, 2018, http://currency.ha.com/c/item.zx?saleNo = 33092&lotNo = 22468; and Haxby, *Standard Catalog of United States Obsolete Bank Notes, 1782–1866*, 4:2379.

34. "Thomas Morrison," Dayton, OH, 6¼¢, February 2, 1838, Heritage Auctions, accessed April 5, 2018, http://currency.ha.com/c/item.zx?saleNo = 329&lotIdNo = 63010; Charlotte Reeve Conover, *The Story of Dayton* (Dayton, OH: Greater Dayton Association,

1917), 133–134; and Robert W. Steele and Mary Davis Steele, *Early Dayton, with Important Facts and Incidents from the Founding of the City of Dayton, Ohio to the Hundredth Anniversary, 1796–1896* (Dayton, OH: U. B. Publishing House, 1896), 167.

35. "Thomas Morrison," Dayton, OH, 12½¢, January 31, 1838, Heritage Auctions, accessed April 5, 2018, http://currency.ha.com/c/item.zx?saleNo=329&lotIdNo=63011.

36. "Urbana Bank," *Daily Ohio Statesman* (Columbus, OH), September 16, 1837; and David C. Wismer, "Descriptive List of Obsolete Paper Money," *Numismatist* 40, no. 5 (May 1927): 271.

37. "Now That Real Money," *New York Evening Post*, August 6, 1834.

38. David Henkin, *City Reading: Written Words and Public Spaces in Antebellum New York* (New York: Columbia University Press, 1998), 137; and "The New Method of 'Endorsing,' &c.," *Man* (New York, NY), June 10, 1834.

39. Rev. Walter Elliott, *The Life of Father Hecker* (New York: Columbus Press, 1891), 17.

40. "Bank Note Endorsements," *Journal of Banking* (Philadelphia), October 13, 1841.

41. "Farmers' Exchange Bank," Gloucester, RI, $5, April 27, 1808, Obsolete Bank Note Collection, Massachusetts Historical Society; and Nathaniel Ames, *The Diary of Dr. Nathaniel Ames of Dedham, Massachusetts*, ed. Robert Brand Hanson (Camden, ME: Picton Press, 1998), 887. For other examples of Ames's use of the term "fudderal" or "fudderalism" to describe Federalists, see Nathaniel Ames Diary, Dedham Historic Society, Dedham, MA, January 8, February 20, April 24, and July 31, 1809; and "Elegance and Sublimity," *Dedham (MA) Gazette*, June 9, 1815. For more on Nathaniel Ames's unique phrasing, see Erastus Worthington, *The History of Dedham, from the Beginning of Its Settlement in September, 1635 to May, 1827* (Boston: Dutton and Wentworth, 1827), 93. I compared the handwriting on the bank note with a sample from Nathaniel Ames's diary and daybook in Nathaniel Ames Papers, 1808–1809, Dedham Historical Society, Dedham, MA.

42. Jane Kamensky, *The Exchange Artist: A Tale of High-Flying Speculation and America's First Banking Collapse* (New York: Viking Penguin, 2008).

43. Robert E. Shalhope, *The Baltimore Bank Riot: Political Upheaval in Antebellum Maryland* (Urbana: University of Illinois Press, 2009); and Denwood N. Kelly, "Baltimore's Shinplaster Bankers: The Beginning of the End—September 9, 1840," *Paper Money* 35, no. 2, whole no. 182 (March–April 1996): 75, italics in the original.

44. "From *the Savannah Georgia*," *New York Spectator*, September 1, 1826; "Pathetic Appeal," *Escritoir: Or, Masonic and Miscellaneous Album* (Albany, NY), October 14, 1826; and "Bank Note Literature," *Numismatist* 18, no. 4 (April 1905): 103.

45. "The Gambler's Fate," *Brooklyn (NY) Eagle*, August 11, 1849; "Bank Note Endorsement," *Gazette of the Union, Golden Rule and Odd-Fellows' Family* (New York, NY), September 15, 1849; and Joshua D. Rothman, "The Hazards of the Flush Times: Gambling, Mob Violence, and the Anxieties of America's Market Revolution," *Journal of American History* 95, no. 3 (December 2008): 651–677.

46. "Bank Note Poetry," *Graham's Magazine* 48, no. 2 (February 1856): 143.

47. "Bank Note Literature," *Numismatist* 18, no. 4 (April 1905): 103; "A Queer Indorsement," *Spirit of Democracy* (Woodsfield, OH), August 24, 1859; "A Queer Indorsement," *Plymouth (IN) Democrat*, August 25, 1859; "A One Dollar Bill," *Burlington (VT) Times*, August 3, 1859; and "All Sorts of Paragraphs," *Buffalo (NY) Commercial*, July 22, 1859.

48. Elliott, *Life of Father Hecker*, 17; and "Defacing Bank Notes," *Detroit (MI) Daily Free Press*, September 14, 1856.

49. "Nearly One Third of the Shinplasters," *Baltimore Sun*, January 10, 1848, italics in the original. I would like to thank Katie Hemphill for this reference.

50. "Bank of the United States," Office of Discount and Deposit in Providence, RI, $5, August 1, 1833, Obsolete Bank Note Collection, Massachusetts Historical Society.

Chapter 5

1. *General Harrison's Speech at the Dayton Convention, September 10, 1840* (Boston: Whig Republican Association, 1840), 5; Jeffrey Bourdon, "Symbolism, Economic Depression, and the Specter of Slavery: William Henry Harrison's Speaking Tour for the Presidency," *Ohio History* 118, no. 1 (August 2011): 5–23; Ronald P. Formisano, "The New Political History and the Election of 1840," *Journal of Interdisciplinary History* 23, no. 4 (Spring 1993): 661–682; and David C. Wismer, "Descriptive List of Obsolete Paper Money," *Numismatist* 40, no. 5 (May 1927): 271.

2. "A Uniform Currency," *New Yorker*, August 11, 1838; Jacob P. Meerman, "The Climax of the Bank War: Biddle's Contraction, 1833–34," *Journal of Political Economy* 71, no. 4 (August 1963): 378–388; Mary Grace Madeleine, *Monetary and Banking Theories of Jacksonian Democracy* (Port Washington, NY: Kennikat Press, 1970); Robert V. Remini, *Andrew Jackson and the Bank War* (New York: W. W. Norton, 1967); Peter Temin, *The Jacksonian Economy* (New York: W. W. Norton, 1969), 28–112; Bray Hammond, *Banks and Politics in America from the Revolution to the Civil War* (Princeton, NJ: Princeton University Press, 1957), 326–450; Sean Wilentz, *The Rise of American Democracy: Jefferson to Lincoln* (New York: W. W. Norton, 2005), 359–424; and Frank Otto Gatell, "Spoils of the Bank War: Political Bias in the Selection of Pet Banks," *American Historical Review* 70, no. 1 (October 1964): 35–58. Stephen Mihm's discussion of the Bank War and counterfeiting is a useful exception to this historiography: Stephen Mihm, *A Nation of Counterfeiters: Capitalists, Con Men, and the Making of the United States* (Cambridge, MA: Harvard University Press, 2007), 103–156.

3. A Friend of the People (John Ronaldson), *Banks and a Paper Currency: Their Effects upon Society* (Philadelphia: n.p., 1832), 3, italics in the original.

4. Jean Alexander Wilburn, *Biddle's Bank: The Crucial Years* (New York: Columbia University Press, 1967); and Daniel Carpenter and Benjamin Scheer, "Party Formation Through Petitions: The Whigs and the Bank War of 1832–1834," *Studies in American Political Development* 29, no. 2 (October 2015): 213–234.

5. "Leonard Bond," *New York Evening Post*, March 28, 1823; *Longworth's American Almanac: New York Register City Directory* (New York: Thomas Longworth, 1823), 85; "Rutgers' Cap," *New York Mirror*, November 25, 1826; "Improved Oval Shaped Clinton Hats," *New York Evening Post*, May 25, 1824; "Leonard Bond," *Statesman* (New York, NY), May 18, 1824; Alexander Jackson Davis, *Leonard Bond's Hat Ware-House*, 1828, Museum of the City of New York; "Insolvent Debtors," *Commercial Advertiser* (New York, NY), September 21, 1829; and "United States District Court," *Commercial Advertiser* (New York, NY), June 22, 1842. Queens' College was renamed after Colonel Henry Rutgers in 1825.

6. "Leonard Bond's Wholesale and Retail," *New York Evening Post*, August 17, 1824; "Twenty-Five Dollars Reward," *National Advocate* (New York, NY), October 7, 1823; "Vassalborough Bank Notes," *New York Evening Post*, September 18, 1826; "Vassalborough Bank," *New York Evening Post*, August 23, 1826; and Walter W. Chadbourne, *A History of Banking in Maine, 1799–1930* (Orono: University of Maine Press, 1936), 70.

7. "Bank Note Table," *New York Spectator*, September 19, 1826; "In Bankruptcy," *New York Evening Post*, February 7, 1845; Henry Bond, *Genealogies of the Families and Descendants of the Early Settlers of Watertown, Massachusetts, Including Waltham and Weston* (Boston: N. E. Historic-Genealogical Society, 1860), 67–71; and "Mr. Leonard Bond," *Hallowell (ME) Gazette*, May 26, 1834.

8. "Tenth Ward," *New York Evening Post*, November 6, 1833; "Charter Election," *American* (New York, NY), March 8, 1834; *Standing Rules and By-Laws of the General Committee of Independent Republican Young Men of the City and County of New York* (New York: W. Applegate, 1834); and "Board of Alderman," *New York Spectator*, May 28, 1835.

9. "Gentlemen," *New York Evening Post*, December 19, 1833; U.S. Congress, House, *Currency: Memorial of Merchants and Dealers in the City of New York, upon the Subject of the Present Deranged State of the Money Market, Internal Exchanges, and All the Commercial Transactions of the Country, February 3, 1834*, 23rd Cong., 1st Sess., 1834, H. Doc. 76; and U.S. Congress, Senate, *Memorial of Merchants, Traders, and Others, of New York, Complaining of the Distresses of the Community, and Suggesting the Propriety of Rechartering the Bank of the United States &c., February 4, 1834*, 23rd Cong., 1st Sess., 1834, S. Doc. 70.

10. U.S. Congress, House, *New York—Currency: Memorial of Mechanics and Artisans in the City of New York, on the Subject of the Present Deranged State of the Money Market, &c., February 10, 1834*, 23rd Cong., 1st Sess., 1834, H. Doc. 88; U.S. Congress, House, *Memorial of Merchants, Mechanics, &c. of the City of New York, Against the Renewal of the Charter of the Bank of the United States, February 10, 1834*, 23rd Cong., 1st Sess., 1834, H. Doc. 89; and U.S. Congress, House, *Maine: Proceedings and Memorial Adopted at a Meeting of Inhabitants of Hallowell, in Relation to the Currency, May 26, 1834*, 23rd Cong., 1st Sess., 1834, H. Doc. 475. Clohesey was a leader of the Journeymen's Hatters' Union; see Joshua R. Greenberg, *Advocating the Man: Masculinity, Organized Labor, and the Household in New York, 1800–1840* (New York: Columbia University Press, 2008), 104.

11. Thomas R. Dew, "Delaware's First Labor Party: A History of the Association of Working People of Newcastle County, 1829–1832" (MA thesis, University of Delaware 1959), 2; Alden Whitman, *Labor Parties, 1827–1834* (New York: International, 1943), 44; "Address," *Free Enquirer* (New York, NY), October 7, 1829, italics in the original; Carol E. Hoffecker, *Brandywine Village: The Story of a Milling Community* (Wilmington, DE: Old Brandywine Village, 1974), 37–46; and J. Thomas Scharf, *History of Delaware, 1609–1888* (Philadelphia: L. J. Richards, 1888), 639–640.

12. U.S. Congress, House, *Memorial of the Farmers, Manufacturers, Mechanics, Traders, and Citizens of New-Castle County, in the State of Delaware, Asking a Restoration of the Public Deposites to the Bank of the United States*, 23rd Cong., 1st Sess., 1834, H. Doc. 140; and "Twenty-Third Congress—First Session," *Niles' Weekly Register* (Washington, DC), March 3, 1834. For a partisan analysis of the public meetings during Biddle's contraction, see David Crouse, *Mr. Crouse's Address, Proving a Secret Conspiracy of the Officers of the Bank of Chillicothe, Against the Democratic Party in This Vicinity* (Chillicothe, OH: John Hough, 1835).

13. "New Castle County Meeting, Del.," *Commercial Advertiser* (New York, NY), April 5, 1834; "Delaware," *National Gazette* (Philadelphia), March 25, 1834; and Richard R. Demirjian Jr., " 'To All the Great Interests': Political Economy in the Early Urban Republic" (PhD diss., University of Delaware, 2013), 324–333.

14. "New Castle County Meeting, Del.," *Commercial Advertiser* (New York, NY), April 5, 1834, italics in the original; and "Delaware," *National Gazette* (Philadelphia), March 25, 1834.

15. "Working Men," *Southern Patriot* (Charleston, SC), January 2, 1834; "Monetary System," *Richmond (VA) Enquirer*, January 4, 1834; "Great Meeting of the People," *Baltimore Patriot and Mercantile Advertiser*, February 26, 1834; and "Great Meeting at Philadelphia," *New Hampshire Sentinel* (Keene, NH), March 6, 1834.

16. U.S. Congress, House, *Memorial of Merchants, Mechanics, Manufacturers, Traders, and Others, Residing in the City and County of Philadelphia, in Relation to the Public Deposits*, 23rd Cong., 1st Sess., 1834, H. Doc. 86; and U.S. Congress, House, *Memorial, &c. of Ten Thousand Two Hundred and Fifty-Nine Citizens of Philadelphia*, 23rd Cong., 1st Sess., 1834, H. Doc. 276.

17. U.S. Congress, House, *Memorial of Merchants, Mechanics, Manufacturers, Traders, and Others*, H. Doc. 86.

18. On the Loco Foco Party, see William Trimble, "Diverging Tendencies in New York Democracy in the Period of the Locofocos," *American Historical Review* 24, no. 3 (April 1919): 396–421; Carl N. Degler, "The Locofocos: Urban 'Agrarians,'" *Journal of Economic History* 16, no. 3 (September 1956): 322–333; Leo Hershkowitz, "The Loco-Foco Party of New York: Its Origins and Career, 1835–1837," *New-York Historical Society Quarterly* 46, no. 3 (July 1962): 305–329; Walter Hugins, *Jacksonian Democracy and the Working Class: A Study of the New York Workingmen's Movement, 1829–1837* (Stanford, CA: Stanford University Press, 1960); Sean Wilentz, *Chants Democratic: New York City and the Rise of the American Working Class, 1788–1850* (New York: Oxford University Press, 1984); Amy Bridges, *A City in the Republic: Antebellum New York and the Origins of Machine Politics* (Ithaca, NY: Cornell University Press, 1987); Jonathan H. Earle, *Jacksonian Antislavery and the Politics of Free Soil, 1824–1854* (Chapel Hill: University of North Carolina Press, 2004), 17–48; and Greenberg, *Advocating the Man*, 191–206.

19. Gustavus Myers, *The History of Tammany Hall* (New York: published by the author, 1901), 127; Fitzwilliam Byrdsall, *The History of the Loco-Foco or Equal Rights Party* (New York: Clement & Packard, 1842), 27; and Ann Daly, "'Men of High Honor and Intrinsic Worth': Silver Coins, Personal Reputations and Monetary Values at the New Orleans Mint, 1835–1840," in "Making an American Coin: Money, Value, and the Federal State, 1792–1857" (PhD diss., Brown University, forthcoming).

20. "To William L. Marcy," *New York Evening Post*, December 24, 1834; "Now That Real Money," *New York Evening Post*, August 6, 1834; and "The 'Good Currency'—Where Is It?," *Scioto Gazette* (Chillicothe, OH), June 9, 1842, italics in the original.

21. *Specie Humbug: Or, The Autobiography of Ferret Snapp Newcraft, Esq.; Being a Full Exposition and Exemplification of 'The Credit System'* ([Philadelphia?]: n.p., [1838?]), 8; "Extracts from the Private Diary of a Certain Bank Director, Number III," *Journal of Banking* 1, no. 7 (September 29, 1841): 100; and "Extracts from the Private Diary of a Certain Bank Director, Number IV," *Journal of Banking* 1, no. 8 (October 13, 1841): 115. On Loco Foco self-righteousness and religion, see Greenberg, *Advocating the Man*, 191–206.

22. "We Wish Some Publick Spirited Man," *New York Evening Post*, March 10, 1835, italics in the original. For more on Leggett, see Hugins, *Jacksonian Democracy and the Working Class*, 33–41 and 159–161; Lester Harvey Rifkin, "William Leggett: Journalist-Philosopher of Agrarian Democracy in New York," *New York History* 32, no. 1 (January 1951): 45–60; and Richard Hofstadter, "William Leggett, Spokesman of Jacksonian Democracy," *Political Science Quarterly* 58, no. 4 (December 1943): 581–594.

23. "A Retail Grocer," *New York Evening Post*, March 11, 1835; and "Mr. Bennett," *New York Herald*, October 4, 1837.

24. "We Have Heard," *Loco Foco* (Swanton, VT), August 22, 1839. For traditional views of Loco Foco political economy, see David A. Martin, "Metallism, Small Notes, and Jackson's War with the B.U.S.," *Explorations in Economic History* 11, no. 3 (Spring 1974): 227–247; Howard Bodenhorn, "Small-Denomination Banknotes in Antebellum America," *Journal of Money, Credit, and Banking* 25, no. 4 (November 1993): 812–827; and Lawrence White, "William Leggett: Jacksonian Editorialist as Classical Liberal Political Economist," *History of Political Economy* 18, no. 2 (1986): 307–325. See also J, *Short Essays on Gold Note Currency* (New York: published for the author by R. Brinkerhoof, 1858), 5–6.

25. "What Two-Penny Paper?," *New York Herald*, September 30, 1837; and "Who Can Deny?," *Loco Foco* (Buffalo, NY), October 11, 1836.

26. "The Working Men of New-York," *Little Rock (AR) Gazette*, May 23, 1837. See also Peter L. Rousseau, "Jacksonian Monetary Policy, Specie Flows, and the Panic of 1837," *Journal of Economic History* 62, no. 2 (June 2002): 457–488; Richard H. Timberlake Jr., "The Specie Circular and Sales of Public Lands: A Comment," *Journal of Economic History* 25, no. 3 (September 1965): 414–416; Ted R. Worley, "Arkansas and the Money Crisis of 1836–1837," *Journal of Southern History* 15, no. 2 (May 1949): 178–191; and Temin, *Jacksonian Economy*, 120–128.

27. Henry Dacre and Henry R. Robinson, *Specie Claws* (New York: Henry Robinson, [1838?]); and Leverett Saltonstall to Richard S. Varnum, H. Reps., March 27, 1840, in *The Papers of Leverett Saltonstall, 1816–1845*, ed. Robert E. Moody (Boston: Massachusetts Historical Society, 1981), 2:288.

28. "Mr. Robert Dale Owen," *New Yorker* 7, no. 1 (March 23, 1839): 15.

29. Joseph B. Felt, *An Historical Account of Massachusetts Currency* (Boston: Perkins & Marvin, 1839), 212–222; and H. A. Gray, "Early Boston Shinplasters," *Numismatist* 28, no. 7 (July 1915): 260–261.

30. *Laws of the Commonwealth of Massachusetts in Relation to Banks and Banking* (Boston: Press of the Centinel and Gazette, 1836), 14; and Davis R. Dewey, *State Banking Before the Civil War* (Washington, DC: Government Printing Office, 1910), 71.

31. Messrs Casy & Co. to Samuel Hooper, March 10, 1836, Samuel Hooper Papers, Massachusetts Historical Society; and Samuel Hooper, *A Brief Notice of a Pamphlet 'by a Practical Banker,' on the Suppression of Small Bills: From 'The Bee'* (Boston: n.p., 1856), 6.

32. Samuel Hooper, *Small Bills: An Appeal to the Legislature for an Ounce of Prevention* (Boston: J. S. Potter, 1855), 2–4; Bruce D. Smith and Warren E. Weber, "Private Money Creation and the Suffolk Banking System," Working Paper 9821 (Federal Reserve Bank of Cleveland, December 1998), 5–6; and Gary Gorton, "Comment on Private Money Creation and the Suffolk Banking System," *Journal of Money, Credit and Banking* 31, no. 3, pt. 2 (August 1999): 663–667. What eventually ended the Suffolk Bank system was a brash challenge from the upstart Bank of Mutual Redemption. See *Springfield, Mass., Sept. 29, 1858: A Meeting of the Representatives of the Following Named Banks Was Held This Day* (Springfield, MA: n.p., 1858); Boston Clearing House Association, *Remarks upon the Bank of Mutual Redemption to Become a Member of the Boston Clearing House* (Boston: John Wilson and Son, 1858); and Wilfred S. Lake, "The End of the Suffolk System," *Journal of Economic History* 7, no. 2 (November 1947): 183–207.

33. Hooper, *Small Bills*, 4; William A. Richardson, *Banking Laws of Massachusetts* (Boston: Sanborn, Carter & Bazin, 1855), 18 and 64; and *The General Statutes of the Commonwealth of Massachusetts* (Boston: Wright and Potter, 1860), 306–307 and 807–811. For New Bedford banker James Bunker Congdon's support of the Suffolk Bank system regarding small notes, see A Practical Banker, *A Defence of the Currency of Massachusetts in a Letter to His Excellency, Henry J. Gardner, Governor of the Commonwealth* (Boston: C. C. P. Moody, 1856).

34. Hooper, *Small Bills*, 11.

35. Hooper, *Small Bills*, 11–12.

36. "Money," *Boston Courier*, May 7, 1855; Samuel Hooper, *Specie Currency: The True Interests of the People* (Boston: Bee Office, 1855), 5; Samuel Hooper, *Currency or Money: Its Nature and Uses, and the Effects of the Circulation of Bank-Notes for Currency, by a Merchant of Boston* (Boston: Little, Brown, 1855), 81 and 99; and Hooper, *Small Bills*, 3. An earlier use of "Robin's alive" to describe bank note movement is found in "Specie Payments," *Daily Herald and Gazette* (Cleveland, OH), November 11, 1837. For a description of "Robin's alive," see Eliza Leslie, *American Girl's Book: Or, Occupation for Play Hours* (Boston: Munroe and Francis, 1831), 4–6. For bank notes compared to the game "pass the button," see "Death of a Kansas Wild Cat," *Chicago Daily Tribune*, April 15, 1858.

37. Samuel A. Eliot to Samuel Hooper, Boston, May 7, 1855; Abbot Lawrence to Samuel Hooper, Cambridge, May 7, 1855; and Horace Mann to Samuel Hooper, Antioch College, May 23, 1855; all in Samuel Hooper Papers, Massachusetts Historical Society.

38. Francis Bowen to Samuel Hooper, Cambridge, March 19, 1855, Samuel Hooper Papers, Massachusetts Historical Society, italics in the original.

39. Edward Everett to Samuel Hooper, Boston, May 31, 1855; and Nathan Appleton to Samuel Hooper, Boston, May 5, 1855; both in Samuel Hooper Papers, Massachusetts Historical Society.

40. "Small Notes," *Scioto Gazette* (Chillicothe, OH), January 3, 1839.

41. Lawrence H. White, "William Leggett: Jacksonian Editorialist as Classical Liberal Political Economist," *History of Political Economy* 18, no. 2 (Summer 1986): 307–324.

42. "Progress of the Rag Money Cheat," *Radical, in Continuation of Working Man's Advocate* 1, no. 1 (January 1841): 13.

Chapter 6

1. Thomas Mendenhall, *An Entire New Plan for a National Currency* (Philadelphia: J. Rakestraw, 1834), 5; and "Jackson's First Annual Message, December 8, 1829," in *The American's Own Book* (New York: Leavitt & Allen, 1853), 274.

2. "The National Currency," *Pittsburgh (PA) Weekly Gazette*, April 20, 1830; and "National Currency," *Hazard's Register of Pennsylvania* (Philadelphia), April 17, 1830.

3. A Citizen of Washington (Thomas Mendenhall), *National Money, or a Simple System of Finance; Which Will Fully Answer the Demands of Trade, Equalize the Value of Money, and Keep the Government out of the Hands of Stock-Jobbers* (Georgetown, DC: W. A. Rind, 1816), 14–15, italics in the original.

4. Mendenhall, *Entire New Plan for a National Currency*, 7–8.

5. Mendenhall, *Entire New Plan for a National Currency*, 16 and 25.

6. U. S. Congress, House, *Memorial of Littleton Dennis Teackle, of Maryland Presenting a Plan of National Currency and State Banks*, 25th Cong., 2nd Sess., 1837, H. Doc. 30; *The Remedy, in a National Bank of the People, Versus a Treasury Bank and National Bank of a*

Party: An Appeal to the People of the United States (New York: Wiley and Putnam, 1838); George Sullivan, *Popular Explanation of the System of Circulating Medium Recently Published in the Form of an Act of Congress, Shewing the Destructive Action of the Bank of England upon the Welfare of the United States, and the Means of Self Protection Against It* (New York: Samuel Colman, 1839), 3; John Russell Hurd, *A National Bank, or No Bank: An Appeal to the Common Sense of the People of the United States, Especially of the Laboring Classes* (New York: W. E. Dean, 1842); and Elias Levy, *The Republican Bank: Being an Essay of the Present System of Banking, Showing Its Evil Tendency and Developing an Entirely New Method of Establishing a Currency, Which Will Not Be At All Subject to the Various Ill Effects of Our Present Paper Money, by a Citizen of Indiana* (Madison, IN: W. H. Webb, 1839).

7. Jane Flaherty, "'The Exhausted Condition of the Treasury' on the Eve of the Civil War," *Civil War History* 55, no. 2 (June 2009): 244–277; Bray Hammond, *Sovereignty and an Empty Purse: Banks and Politics in the Civil War* (Princeton, NJ: Princeton University Press, 1970), 59–70; David M. Gische, "The New York City Banks and the Development of the National Banking System, 1860–1870," *American Journal of Legal History* 23, no. 1 (January 1979): 21–33; and Frederick J. Blue, *Salmon P. Chase: A Life in Politics* (Kent, OH: Kent State University Press, 1987), 303–304.

8. "Suspension of Specie Payments," *Baltimore Sun*, August 7, 1861; "Rebel Currency," *Buffalo (NY) Commercial*, November 19, 1861; "The Demand Treasury Notes," *New York Times*, December 4, 1861; "The Demand Treasury Notes," *New York Times*, December 6, 1861; and Department of the Treasury, Comptroller of the Currency, *Annual Report of the Comptroller of the Currency*, vol. 2, Doc. 2789 (Washington, DC: Government Printing Office, 1917), 45.

9. "Balance of Trade," *Chicago Tribune*, September 5, 1861; "Suspension of Specie Payments by the Banks," *New York Times*, December 30, 1861; and "Suspension of Specie Payments," *New York Times*, December 31, 1861. New York banks' outstanding notes shrank from $8.6 million to $5.4 million in the first two months of 1862. See Wesley C. Mitchell, "The Circulating Medium During the Civil War," *Journal of Political Economy* 10, no. 4 (September 1902): 541–543.

10. "New National Currency," *Chicago Tribune*, October 12, 1861; George Herbert Blake, *United States Paper Money: A Reference List of Paper Money* (New York: Wynkoop, Hallenbeck, Crawford, 1908), 8; and Hammond, *Sovereignty and an Empty Purse*, 252.

11. "The Danger of Shinplasters," *New York Times*, July 13, 1862; and Henry Russell Drowne, "U.S. Postage Stamps as Necessity War Money," *American Journal of Numismatics* 52, no. 1 (1918): 64 and 69.

12. George P. Sanger, ed., *The Statutes at Large, Treaties, and Proclamations, of the United States of America, from December 5, 1859, to March 3, 1863* (Boston: Little, Brown, 1863), 12:592; Fred L. Reed III, "Collectors Note Postage Currency," *Bank Note Reporter* 61, no. 7 (July 2012): 106–118; and "Small Change a New Legal Tender," *New York Times*, July 18, 1862.

13. "Small Change," *Brooklyn (NY) Eagle*, July 29, 1862; "Small Change Panic in Cincinnati," *Cincinnati (OH) Enquirer*, November 5, 1862; and Fred L. Reed III, "Postage Currency Riot of 1862," *E-Sylum* 15, no. 46 (November 4, 2012): 27.

14. "The Postage Stamp Currency," *New York Times*, October 11, 1862, italics in the original.

15. Observer, *"Greenbacks"; or, The Evils and the Remedy of Using "Promise to Pay to the Bearer on Demand"* (New York: Dion Thomas, 1864); Abraham Lincoln, "Second Annual Message," as reprinted in *A Compilation of the Messages and Papers of the Presidents, 1789–1897*, ed. James D. Richardson (Washington, DC: Government Printing Office, 1897), 6:129–130; Gabor S. Boritt, *Lincoln and the Economics of the American Dream* (1978; repr., Urbana: University of Illinois Press, 1994), 199–201; Hammond, *Sovereignty and an Empty Purse*, 290–291; and Stephen Mihm, *A Nation of Counterfeiters: Capitalists, Con Men, and the Making of the United States* (Cambridge, MA: Harvard University Press, 2007), 330–331.

16. Mihm, *Nation of Counterfeiters*, 332–334; "Congressional," *Evansville (IL) Daily Journal*, January 20, 1863; and Samuel Hooper, *Speech of Hon. Samuel Hooper of Massachusetts on the Necessity of Regulating the Currency of the Country* (Washington, DC: L. Towers, 1864).

17. John Wilson Million, "The Debate on the National Bank Act of 1863," *Journal of Political Economy* 2, no. 2 (March 1894): 251–280; George P. Sanger, ed., *The Statutes at Large, Treaties, and Proclamations of the United States of America, from December 5, 1859, to March 3, 1863* (Boston: Little, Brown, 1863), 12:665–682; and Hammond, *Sovereignty and an Empty Purse*, 321–351.

18. Heather Cox Richardson, *The Greatest Nation of the Earth: Republican Economic Policies During the Civil War* (Cambridge, MA: Harvard University Press, 1997), 91–92.

19. *The National Bank Act* (New York: Office of the Banker's Magazine and Statistical Register, 1870), 1–28; and John M. Gould, *The National Bank Act* (Boston: Little, Brown, 1904), 68.

20. John Sherman, *Recollections of Forty Years in the House, Senate and Cabinet* (Chicago: Werner Company, 1895), 244; and Arthur L. Friedberg and Ira S. Friedberg, *Paper Money of the United States* (Clifton, NJ: Coin & Currency Institute, 2006), 18:76.

21. Marc D. Weidenmier, "Turning Points in the U.S. Civil War: Views from the Grayback Market," *Southern Economic Journal* 68, no. 4 (April 2002): 875–890; Gary Pecquet, George Davis, and Bryce Kanago, "The Emancipation Proclamation, Confederate Expectations, and the Price of Southern Bank Notes," *Southern Economic Journal* 70, no. 3 (January 2004): 616–630; and "Interesting Letter from a Tuscarawas Soldier Now in Prison in Richmond," *Ohio Democrat* (Dover, OH), December 4, 1863. For an alternative reading on graybacks, see Christian M. Lengyel, "Pictures Frozen in Time: Determining Whether or Not Confederate Currency Vignettes Functioned as Proslavery Propaganda," *Past Tense* 4, no. 1 (2016): 1–21.

22. "Refugees from Norfolk," *New York Times*, October 28, 1861; and "News from the South," *Hartford (CT) Courant*, September 25, 1861.

23. "The Indians Issuing Shinplasters," *New York Times*, August 3, 1862; "From the Lower Potomac," *New York Times*, November 19, 1861; "Trophies of the War," *Brooklyn (NY) Daily Eagle*, April 10, 1862; Charles Y. Alison, *A Brief History of Fayetteville, Arkansas* (Charleston, SC: History Press, 2017), 50; "Shinplasters," *New York Times*, May 21, 1861; and Joshua R. Greenberg, "The Era of Shinplasters: Making Sense of Unregulated Paper Money," in *Capitalism by Gaslight: Illuminating the Economy of Nineteenth-Century America*, ed. Brian P. Luskey and Wendy A. Woloson (Philadelphia: University of Pennsylvania Press, 2015), 53–75.

24. "Southern Financiering," *New York Times*, May 24, 1861; "Paper Is King," *New York Times*, June 22, 1861; W. H. Merrell, *Five Months in Rebeldom; Or Notes from the Diary of a*

Bull Run Prisoner, at Richmond (Rochester, NY: Adams & Dabney, 1862), 56–57; and Mihm, *Nation of Counterfeiters*, 328–329.

25. "Rebel 'Small-Change,'" *Scioto Gazette* (Chillicothe, OH), December 24, 1861; "Scarcity of Money in the Southwest," *New York Times*, December 31, 1861; "The Feeling of the People in Tennessee," *New York Times*, March 9, 1862; and "The Thirty-First Ohio," *Newark (NJ) Advocate*, March 21, 1862.

26. Mark E. Neely Jr., *The Boundaries of American Political Culture in the Civil War Era* (Chapel Hill: University of North Carolina Press, 2005), 91; *The Old Continental and the New Greenback Dollar* (Philadelphia: n.p., 1864), 1, italics in the original; and Montgomery Wilson, *The Copperhead Catechism* (New York: Sinclair Tousey, 1864), 22.

27. Alexander Delmar, *The National Banking System: An Essay from the New York Social Science Review, for April, 1865* (New York: New York Social Science Review, 1865), 6–7, italics in the original.

28. William Watson Davis, *The Civil War and Reconstruction in Florida* (New York: Longmans, Green, 1913), 177–183.

29. "Writing on Obsolete Paper Money," *Numismatist* 32, no. 4 (April 1919): 151; and Margaret Mitchell, *Gone with the Wind* (New York: Penguin Books, 1947), 503. The Florida note was signed "Baldwin, Florida, May, 1865."

30. Green-back, *Green-back to His Country Friends* (New York: n.p., 1862), 16; and *Money by Steam: John Law, His Body Moulders in the Ground, but His Soul Is Marching On* (New York: n.p., 1864), 18.

31. "Postage Stamp Currency," *Western Reserve Chronicle* (Warren, OH), August 6, 1862; "General News," *Smoky Hill and Republican Union* (Junction City, KS), August 30, 1862; and "Postage Stamp Currency," *Cleveland (OH) Morning Leader*, October 13, 1862.

32. "United States Treasury Notes—How They Are Made," *Baltimore Sun*, September 4, 1861; and "The New Treasury Notes," *Baltimore Sun*, August 10, 1861.

33. Charles E. Allen to Nathaniel Paine, Quincy, IL, August 23, 1864, Records of the Western Illinois Sanitary Fair, italics in the original. One argument in favor of national bank notes came in an article that highlighted their benefits in contrast with earlier shinplasters and depreciated bank notes. It included a shortened version of James Kirke Paulding's *The History of a Little Frenchman and His Bank Notes: "Rags! Rags! Rags!"* See "Origin of the National Banking System," *Historical Magazine* 10, no. 8 (August 1865): 252–256.

34. Mihm, *Nation of Counterfeiters*, 335. State bank notes varied wildly in size, and even notes from the same bank were not necessarily uniform.

35. George P. Sanger, ed., *The Statutes at Large, Treaties, and Proclamations of the United States of America, from December 5, 1859, to March 3, 1863* (Boston: Little, Brown, 1863), 12:675 and 680.

36. Jacob Abbott, *John Gay; Or, Work for Boys* (New York: Hurd & Houghton, 1864), 10–15.

37. Abbott, *John Gay*, 39–41, 46–52, and 96–98.

38. "Bank Monster; or, Specie vs. Shin-Plasters," *Dramatic Mirror* (New York, NY), September 18, 1841, italics in the original; "A New Play at the Arch Street Theatre," *Public Ledger* (Philadelphia), September 20, 1841; "Arch Street Theatre," *Dramatic Mirror* (New York, NY), September 25, 1841; "Epigram on Chase and His Shinplasters," *Old Guard*, 2, no. 4 (April 1864): 90; M. F., "The United States Bank Waltz or A Squabble Between the Bank and the

Government" (Philadelphia: G. E. Blake, [183?]); "Song—The Conservative to His Bank Note," *United States Magazine and Democratic Review* 3, no. 9 (September 1838): 93–94; Sep. Winner, "The Greenback Quick Step" (Philadelphia: Lee & Walker, 1863); E. Mack, "Secretary Chase's Grand March" (Philadelphia: Lee & Walker, 1863); Jo Benson, "Shin-Plaster Jig" (Nashville, TN: C. D. Benson, 1864); and F. Chase, "Legal Tender Polka" (St. Louis, MO: Balmer & Weber, 1863).

39. Dan D. Emmett, "Greenbacks!: New Song for the Times" (New York: William Pond, 1863); E. Bowers and G. W. H. Griffin, "Dan Bryant's 'How Are You Green-backs!'" (New York: William Pond, 1863); Hans Nathan, "Two Inflation Songs of the Civil War," *Musical Quarterly* 29, no. 2 (April 1943): 242–253; and Steven Cornelius, *Music of the Civil War Era* (Westport, CT: Greenwood Press, 2004), 51–52. Some versions of "We Are Coming, Father Abraham" are attributed to William Cullen Bryant. See also "Song of Greenbacks," in *Songs and Ballads of Freedom: A Choice Collection; Inspired by the Incidents and Scenes of the Present War* (New York: J. F. Feeks, 1864), 44.

40. Bowers and Griffin, "Dan Bryant's 'How Are You Green-backs!'"; Alexander Saxton, "Blackface Minstrelsy and Jacksonian Ideology," *American Quarterly* 27, no. 1 (March 1975): 21–22; Robert C. Nowatki, "'Our Only Truly National Poets': Blackface Minstrelsy and Cultural Nationalism," *American Transcendental Quarterly* 20, no. 1 (March 2006): 366; and "Abraham the First (Repudiator)," in *Songs and Ballads of Freedom: A Choice Collection; Inspired by the Incidents and Scenes of the Present War* (New York: J. F. Feeks, 1864), 29.

41. "The Temple of Music: California Minstrels!," *San Francisco (CA) Chronicle*, March 4, 1868; "Laura Keene's Theatre," *New York Times*, March 12, 1863; and "Amusements," *National Republican* (Washington, DC), April 8, 1863.

42. "How Are You Greenbacks?," *Brooklyn (NY) Daily Eagle*, February 24, 1864; "How Are You, Greenbacks?," *Portsmouth (OH) Daily Times*, January 23, 1864; and "Money," *Luzerne Union* (Wilkes-Barre, PA), July 20, 1864.

43. "How Are You Greenbacks?," *Pittsburgh (PA) Daily Commercial*, October 19, 1863; *A Record of the Metropolitan Fair in Aid of the United States Sanitary Commission* (New York: Hurd and Houghton, 1867); Neely, *Boundaries of American Political Culture*, 71–73; and "How Are You Greenbacks?," *Buffalo (NY) Evening Post*, April 28, 1864.

44. Gordon M. Bakken, "Law and Legal Tender in California and the West," *Southern California Quarterly* 62, no. 3 (Fall 1980): 239–259; Richard H. Timberlake, *Constitutional Money: A Review of the Supreme Court's Monetary Decisions* (New York: Cambridge University Press, 2013), 87; and *Opinions Delivered by the Judges of the Court of Appeals, on the Constitutionality of the Act of Congress, Declaring Treasury Notes a Legal Tender for the Payment of Debts* (Albany, NY: Weed, Parsons, 1863).

45. Kenneth W. Dam, "The Legal Tender Cases," *Supreme Court Review* 1981 (1981): 367–412; and Timberlake, *Constitutional Money*, 86–155.

46. Charles Fairman, "Mr. Justice Bradley's Appointment to the Supreme Court and the Legal Tender Cases," *Harvard Law Review* 54, no. 6 (April 1941): 977–1034.

47. "Digest of Recent Decisions," *American Jurist and Law Magazine* 23 (October 1834): 453; "Robert Weatherhead *vs.* Robert M. Boyers," in George S. Yerger, *Reports of Cases Argued and Determined in the Supreme Court of Tennessee During the Years 1834–5* (Nashville, TN: S. Nye, 1836), 7:545–564; Dam, "Legal Tender Cases," 367–412; Gerard N. Magliocca, "A New Approach to Congressional Power: Revisiting the *Legal Tender Cases*," *Georgetown Law Journal*

95, no. 1 (November 2006): 119–170; Robert G. Natelson, "Paper Money and the Original Understanding of the Coinage Clause," *Harvard Journal of Law and Public Policy* 31, no. 3 (Summer 2008): 1017–1081; Leon Sachs, "Stare Decisis and the Legal Tender Cases," *Virginia Law Review* 20, no. 8 (June 1934): 856–885; Robert Bruce Murray, *Legal Cases of the Civil War* (Mechanicsburg, PA: Stackpole Books, 2003); and John J. Chung, "Money as Simulacrum: The Legal Nature and Reality of Money," *Hastings Business Law Journal* 5, no. 1 (Winter 2009): 109–168.

48. "Ladies' Relief Association," *Courier-Journal* (Louisville, KY), June 19, 1867; "Ladies Southern Relief Association," *Louisville (KY) Daily Courier*, July 19, 1867; and "Masonic," *Louisville (KY) Daily Courier*, October 20, 1868. Hepburn was no stranger to economic lawsuits; see "Real Estate Transfers," *Louisville (KY) Daily Courier*, February 12, 1861; "The Tax-Lien Question," *Courier-Journal* (Louisville, KY), October 4, 1881; and "Louisville," *Cincinnati (OH) Enquirer*, March 13, 1884.

49. Timberlake, *Constitutional Money*, 89–90.

50. Murray, *Legal Cases of the Civil War*, 110–126; Kevin Walsh, "The Legal Tender Cases and the Post-Civil War Origins of Modern Constitutional Interpretation" (PhD diss., Southern Illinois University, 1999), 98–131; and *The Legal Tender Cases of 1871* (New York: Office of the Banker's Magazine and Statistical Register, 1872).

51. *Veazie Bank v. Fenno*, 75 U.S. (8 Wallace) 548 (1869); *National Bank Act*, 29–30; and "The National Currency—Vicious Attempts to Create Distrust," *New York Times*, August 17, 1865.

52. "The Case of the Veazie Bank," *Pittsburgh (PA) Daily Commercial*, October 18, 1867; "New York," *Courier-Journal* (Louisville, KY), March 14, 1868; Robert E. Shalhope, *The Baltimore Bank Riot* (Urbana: University of Illinois Press, 2009), 32–69; "The American Difficulty," *Bankers Magazine* 29 (May 1869): 518–519; and Bernard C. Steiner, *Life of Reverdy Johnson* (Baltimore: Norman, Remington, 1914).

53. *Veazie Bank v. Fenno*, 75 U.S. (8 Wallace) 546 (1869); "Associate Justices Nelson and Davis," *Boston Daily Advertiser*, December 17, 1869; "Chief Justice Chase's Opinion," *Ashtabula (OH) Weekly Telegraph*, December 18, 1869; "Important Bank Decision," *Tiffin (OH) Tribune*, December 17, 1869; and "The Supreme Court," *Burlington (VT) Free Press*, December 14, 1869. Libertarian scholars cite the dissent in *Veazie Bank v. Fenno* to argue that the federal government's power to tax state bank notes out of circulation overstepped Congress's taxing authority. See Timberlake, *Constitutional Money*, 79–85.

54. *Veazie Bank v. Fenno*, 75 U.S. (8 Wallace) 533, 536, and 549 (1869). Chase also looked to Congress's actions on counterfeiting and the Secret Service to demonstrate their currency authority. See Mihm, *Nation of Counterfeiters*, 358–359.

55. "Taxing State Banks," *Reading (PA) Times*, December 18, 1869; and "Chief Justice Chase's Opinion," *Ashtabula (OH) Weekly Telegraph*, December 18, 1869.

56. Matthew Hild, *Greenbackers, Knights of Labor, and Populists: Farmer-Labor Insurgency in the Late-Nineteenth-Century South* (Athens: University of Georgia Press, 2007); and Gretchen Ritter, *Goldbugs and Greenbacks: The Antimonopoly Tradition and the Politics of Finance in America, 1865–1896* (New York: Cambridge University Press, 1997).

57. *Hearings Before the Committee on Banking and Currency, Fifty-Third Congress, First and Second Sessions* (Washington, DC: Government Printing Office, 1894), 514; "Danger in Soiled Money," *New York Medical Journal and Philadelphia Medical Journal* 79, no. 12 (March

19, 1904): 556; "Dirty Money," *JAMA* 43, no. 10 (July 2, 1904): 35; "One Instance of Dirty Money," *JAMA* 43, no. 17 (July 7, 1904): 210; "The Circulation of Dirty Bank Notes," *Medical Times* 33, no. 12 (December 1905): 384; "Tainted Money," *JAMA* 50, no. 16 (April 1908): 1269; "Clean Paper Money New Treasury Plan," *Journal of the American Bankers' Association* 2, no. 3 (September 1909): 103–104; "Does Money Carry Disease?," *Literary Digest* 40, no. 10 (March 5, 1910): 433; "Smallpox in Paper Money," *Evening Star* (Washington, DC), December 31, 1912; and V. Gilmore Iden, *The Federal Reserve Act of 1913* (Philadelphia: National Bank News, 1914), 71.

58. "Coxey Has Bonus Project," *New York Times*, March 13, 1922.

Epilogue

1. Edward E. Baptist, *The Half Has Never Been Told: Slavery and the Making of American Capitalism* (New York: Basic Books, 2014), 352–353; and Michael R. Cohen, "Cotton, Capital, and Ethnic Networks: Jewish Economic Growth in the Postbellum Gulf South," *American Jewish Archives Journal* 64, nos. 1 and 2 (2012): 116–118.

2. Alan S. Blinder, "Quantitative Easing: Entrance and Exit Strategies," *Federal Reserve Bank of St. Louis Review* 92, no. 6 (November/December 2010): 465–479; and Joseph Gagnon, Matthew Raskin, Julie Remache, and Brian Sack, "The Financial Market Effects of the Federal Reserve's Large-Scale Asset Purchases," *International Journal of Central Banking* 47, no. 1 (March 2011): 3–43. On the Great Recession, see Andrew Ross Sorkin, *Too Big to Fail: The Inside Story of How Wall Street and Washington Fought to Save the Financial System—and Themselves* (New York: Viking Press, 2009); Alan S. Blinder, *After the Music Stopped: The Financial Crisis, the Response, and the Work Ahead* (New York: Penguin Press, 2013); and Michael Lewis, *The Big Short: Inside the Doomsday Machine* (New York: W. W. Norton, 2010).

3. Lowell R. Ricketts, "Quantitative Easing Explained," *Liber8: Classroom Edition* (April 2011): 5.

4. *The Big Short*, directed by Adam McKay (Hollywood: Paramount Pictures, 2015); and Patrick Durkin, "Why *The Big Short* Works: Margot Robbie in a Bubble Bath Talking Finance," *Sydney Morning Herald*, January 14, 2016.

5. "Fed Takes the Easy Way Out," *Telegraph* (Nashua, NH), May 24, 2009; "Fed to Inject Additional $1.2 Trillion into Economy," *Los Angeles Times*, March 18, 2009; Edmund L. Andrews, "As Rates Near Zero, the Fed Turns to Unproven Methods," *New York Times*, December 14, 2008; Neil Irwin, "Fed to Pump $1.2 Trillion into Economy," *Washington Post*, March 19, 2009; Jacob Leibenluft, "Start the Presses?," *Slate*, November 26, 2008; and United States Department of the Treasury, Bureau of Engraving and Printing, *Chief Financial Officer Performance and Accountability Report 2009*, 26–27.

6. "What Is Quantitative Easing and Why Is It Likely to End?," NPR's *Morning Edition*, October 28, 2014.

7. Joshua Davis, "The Crypto-Currency: Bitcoin and Its Mysterious Inventor," *New Yorker*, October 10, 2011, 62; and Benjamin Wallace, "The Rise and Fall of Bitcoin," *Wired*, November 23, 2012.

8. Reuben Grinberg, "Bitcoin: An Innovative Alternative Digital Currency," *Hastings Science and Technology Law Journal* 4, no. 1 (Winter 2012): 182–191; Daniel Smith, "More Money, More Problems: The Bitcoin Virtual Currency and the Legal Problems That Face It," *Journal of Law, Technology and the Internet* 3, no. 2 (2012): 427–442; Robert McMillan, "Could a Civil War–Era Law Stamp Out Bitcoin?," *Wired*, January 8, 2014; Matthew Kien-Meng Ly,

"Coining Bitcoin's 'Legal-Bits': Examining the Regulatory Framework for Bitcoin and Virtual Currencies," *Harvard Journal of Law and Technology* 27, no. 2 (Spring 2014): 598–599; Ethan D. Jeans, "Funny Money or the Fall of Fiat: Bitcoin and Forward-Facing Virtual Currency Regulation," *Colorado Technology Law Journal* 13, no. 1 (2015): 99–128; Nikolei M. Kaplanov, "Nerdy Money: Bitcoin, the Private Digital Currency, and the Case Against Its Regulation," *Loyola Consumer Law Review* 25, no. 1 (January 2012): 111–174; and Kevin V. Tu and Michael W. Meredith, "Rethinking Virtual Currency Regulation in the Bitcoin Age," *Washington Law Review* 90, no. 1 (March 2015): 271–347.

9. Wallace, "Rise and Fall of Bitcoin"; David Z. Morris, "Bitcoin Hits a New Record High, but Stops Short of $20,000," *Fortune*, December 17, 2017; and Matthew Frankel, "How Many Cryptocurrencies Are There?," *Motley Fool*, March 16, 2018.

10. In 2013 FinCen (Financial Crimes Enforcement Network) clarified that while virtual currencies like Bitcoin might operate as a medium of exchange and can have values equal to real currency, they have no "legal tender status in any jurisdiction." Trevor I. Kiviat, "Beyond Bitcoin: Issues in Regulating Blockchain Transactions," *Duke Law Journal* 65, no. 3 (December 2015): 590.

INDEX

ACKNOWLEDGMENTS

MY FIRST FORAY into describing the chaotic world of early republic paper money was at SHEAR a dozen years ago. The presentation included an anecdote about someone who ripped a note in half to make change and another about someone who stitched together two demi-notes to create a new bill. I did not know how the material would be received, so I was eager to hear the audience's reaction. In what was the most theatrical conference comment I have ever witnessed, Tim Gilfoyle proceeded to rip a one-dollar and a five-dollar note in half and tape the mismatched pieces together. He then handed me the newly created bill and remarked how easy it was to make new money in this way. The enthusiastic response pushed me to think more about how early republic Americans actually understood and materially used their paper money and I began to work on this book in earnest. I still have that "three-dollar bill" in my office and it serves as a constant reminder of the debt I owe the people who have inspired me along the way.

The early republic financial world was endlessly complicated. The further my research delved into it, the more I leaned on friends and colleagues more knowledgeable than I. This book would not have made sense or cents without the aid of Paul Erickson, Jessica Lepler, Brian Luskey, Stephen Mihm, Sharon Murphy, Seth Rockman, and Wendy Woloson. They have been overly generous with their time, and this book is better because of their years of support. This project has taken a long time, and the list of people who have helped is likewise lengthy. I would like to thank the following, whether as a panelist, a collaborator, or a partner at a late-night conference meal: Sean Adams, Zara Anishanslin, Lara Cohen, Seth Cotler, Alec Dun, Hannah Farber, Katie Hemphill, Hunt Howell, Cathy Kelly, Will Mackintosh, Justine Murison, Brian Murphy, Julia Ott, Emily Pawley, Kyle Roberts, Jonathan Senchyne, Katherine Smoak, Rachel Van, William Wagner, and Karin Wulf for their gracious help and guidance.

I have been lucky that so many people believed in this project and chose to support it over the years. No one deserves more of my gratitude than Bob Lockhart at the University of Pennsylvania Press for his thoughtful advice and always insightful vision of where this book should go. I received invaluable feedback from the anonymous readers and board members at Penn Press and especially Andrew Cohen on behalf of the American Business, Politics, and Society series. Bridgewater State University's Center for the Advancement of Research and Scholarship provided me with a Faculty/Librarian Research Grant and aided my research travel for many years. My former Bridgewater State University colleagues Andrew Holman, Michael Ierardi, Keith Lewinstein, and Brian Payne likewise supported this project from its inception and I thank them for their thoughtful contributions. I would also like to thank Peter and Anne Weller for their generous contribution to my personal collection of paper money. In less academic ways, my last years of writing have been made possible by the underappreciated staff at Noah's Bagels in Lafayette, California.

These days it feels like a lot of history research is done on electronic databases in the middle of the night, but so much of the most important detective work can be accomplished only in the archives and with the direction of knowledgeable archivists and librarians. I wish that I had made it to the Smithsonian's National Numismatic Collection earlier in my research, but the behind-the-scenes tour made possible by Jennifer Gloede and Ken Cohen was illuminating. When I lived in Massachusetts, I frequented the amazing collections at the American Antiquarian Society often. Those trips and the direction of Jaclyn Penny and other librarians on staff helped flesh out this book in remarkable ways. My greatest archival/institutional debt belongs to the Massachusetts Historical Society, where I held a long-term National Endowment for the Humanities Fellowship from 2011 to 2012. The core of this book and my understanding of early republic paper money came together during that year thanks to the tireless assistance and wisdom of Sabina Beauchard, Anne Bentley, Anna Clutterbuck-Cook, Kate Viens, and Conrad Wright. My time at the Massachusetts Historical Society would not have been remotely as fruitful without my fellow fellows, Joanne Melish and Margot Minardi, whom I pestered with questions and document show-and-tell on a daily basis. Thank you for teaching me so much.

Whether they are nearby or far away, my family's unwavering support is a constant source of strength. Thank you, Mom, Ben, Dad, Cindy, Julie, Robert, Sasha, Scarlett, Alan, Betty, Micky, Paige, Charlotte, Olivia, David,

Alli, and Zachary for always being there. I started working on this book before I met Rachel and Molly, but I could never have finished it without them. Their daily encouragement and love kept me focused and enabled me to push through whenever I had doubts about my ability to finish this project. They are the inspiration for everything I do and I dedicate this book to them with all of my heart.